EVERYDAY LIFE IN NEW TESTAMENT TIMES

The EVERYDAY LIFE series is one of the
best known and most respected of all
historical works, giving detailed insight
into the background life of a particular
period. This edition provides an invaluable
and vivid picture of the everyday life in
New Testament times—the Jews, the Gentiles
and the Romans, and how they were affected
by the teaching of the Gospel.

4cde

Other EVERYDAY LIFE BOOKS

EVERYDAY LIFE IN PREHISTORIC TIMES: THE OLD STONE AGE
EVERYDAY LIFE IN PREHISTORIC TIMES: THE NEW STONE AGE
EVERYDAY LIFE IN THE VIKING AGE
EVERYDAY LIFE IN ROMAN TIMES
EVERYDAY LIFE IN ANGLO-SAXON TIMES
EVERYDAY LIFE OF THE PAGAN CELTS
EVERYDAY LIFE IN MEDIEVAL TIMES
EVERYDAY LIFE IN EARLY IMPERIAL CHINA
EVERYDAY LIFE IN RENAISSANCE TIMES
EVERYDAY LIFE IN OLD TESTAMENT TIMES

and published by CAROUSEL BOOKS

Everyday Life in New Testament Times

A. C. Bouquet

Illustrated from Drawings
by
Marjorie Quennell

CAROUSEL EDITOR: ANNE WOOD

CAROUSEL BOOKS
A DIVISION OF TRANSWORLD PUBLISHERS LTD

EVERYDAY LIFE IN NEW TESTAMENT
TIMES

A CAROUSEL BOOK 0 552 54060 9

Originally published in Great Britain
by B. T. Batsford Ltd.

PRINTING HISTORY
Batsford edition published 1953
Batsford seventh impression published 1970
Carousel edition published 1974

Carousel Books are published by Transworld Publishers Ltd.,
Cavendish House, 57–59 Uxbridge Road, Ealing, London W.5.

Printed in Great Britain by
Richard Clay (The Chaucer Press) Ltd.,
Bungay, Suffolk

PREFACE

THIS book has been composed under a double shadow. It is perhaps not given to many authors to lose in one year both a much-loved wife and also a friendly and enthusiastic publisher, to whose zeal the idea of engaging in this work owes almost everything.

To these two then I dedicate what is here unfolded. My plan and purpose I have set forth in the introduction which follows. In the epilogue I have ventured to write something which will I hope be of service to older readers, though I do not think that it is really beyond the understanding of intelligent boys and girls of the ages of sixteen to eighteen.[1]

To my friends and colleagues in Cambridge I owe much. To Professor Norman Sykes for persuading me to undertake the book. To Professor Winton Thomas for some valuable advice. To Mr. F. H. Sandbach of Trinity College for some helpful talks and letters of counsel regarding the Gentile world of the first century. To Dr. John Bradfield of Trinity College for kindly reading and criticising the draft of the epilogue. To the Master of Selwyn for some valuable information about the Princeton University Expedition to Antioch, and also to the Hort Fund, of which he is the secretary, for kindly helping to finance a visit to

---

[1] Younger readers can, if they like, miss out the footnotes, but older students will, I think, find interesting details in them, sometimes drawn from my own personal experiences. I have tried to aid not only readers of the New Testament, but also those who are studying the classical writers of ancient Rome.

Jerusalem. I have also to thank the authorities of the Jewish Museum in Tavistock Square, London, for some useful information. I owe a great deal to Mr. Samuel Carr and his colleagues at Messrs. Batsford's headquarters. They have been both friendly and helpful, and have shown themselves full of understanding, and always ready to be sympathetic and encouraging.

My indebtedness to friends in the Middle East is a heavy one. First and foremost to all at St. George's Hostel, Jerusalem, from the Bishop and Mrs. Stewart downwards, for much help and comradeship and wise counsel, and herein especially to the Warden, Miss Irvine, to Canon Every, and to Mr. Stewart Perowne, also to The Revd. Ronald Brownrigg for taking me to see Bethlehem. Next, to the various heads of special institutions in and around the Old City, to Mr. Yusuf Sáad, Director of the Rockefeller Institute; to Père de Vaux of the Dominicans, at the Ecole Biblique, to Dr. and Mrs. Tushingham at the American School of Archaeology, and to the Chaplain of the Dom Polsky, for much help and courtesy; to The Great Sheyk of the Haram es Sherif for graciously allowing me to visit its precincts in privacy, and to explore the whole of the Temple area freely, and also for his kind hospitality to a Frankish stranger; to the British chaplain at Amman, The Revd. Donald Blackburne, to Miss Adela Soltau-Symons of Fuhais,[1] and to Mr. G. Lankester Harding, Government Director of Antiquities at Amman, for making my visit to the Decapolis area so fruitful; to the Israel Director of Antiquities, Dr. Yeivin, and his colleagues, Dr. Avi-Yonah and Dr. I. Ben Dor, for giving me the opportunity of such a useful and profitable visit to sites within the area of the Republic, and also for some useful photographs;

[1] By the time this appears, Mrs. Edward Every.

PREFACE

to Dr. Hans Kosmala and all friends at the Swedish
Theological Institute in Israeli Jerusalem for their very
kind and generous hospitality and their friendship, and
for making it possible for me to visit a number of
synagogues at the time of Rosh Hashannah; to the
Revd. Ronald Adeney for enabling me to visit
Nazareth, Tiberias, and the neighbourhood of Capernaum; and finally to the British Consul-General in
Jerusalem, Mr. Monypenny, and his colleague, Mr.
Waddell, for their skilful handling of visa and immi-
gration problems.

Thanks are due to the Secretary of the Orbilian
Society, Mr. G. M. Lyne, for a fine cartoon of Roman
houses in the first century, and to Miss Liversidge of
the Museum of Anthropology and Archaeology at
Cambridge for help with illustrations; to Dr. G. H. S.
Bushnell of the Anthropological Museum at Cambridge for the kind loan of a Palestinian woman's costume from the neighbourhood of Mount Carmel, and
to Mr. Rayner of Emmanuel College, Cambridge, for
the loan of a large tallith; also to my cousin, Diana
Sicely, for help in arranging and indexing the
illustrations.

The late Mr. M. P. Charlesworth's fine book on the
Roman Empire was out of print at the time when I was
composing this work, and has only again become
accessible since I finished the draft. My general indebtedness to its method will be evident to many, and
I have found it possible to draw from it for the
amplification of some of my statements.

Above all, let me thank most warmly Mrs. Marjorie
Quennell for the skill and patience with which she has
sought to illustrate my text, and for all her beautiful
drawings. I would also like to thank Miss Rachel
Engledow for some valuable drawings, and Mr.

John P. Williams, for his skill and care bestowed upon the maps.

I should add that the illustrations are only a selection from the wealth of material available for my purpose. It is no exaggeration to say that, had more space been at our disposal, almost every item mentioned in the text could have been illustrated.

NOTE

In Chapter XI, in the section on medicine and surgery beginning on page 247, I have stated that it is possible that some anaesthetics, local or otherwise, *may* have been used as early as the first century A.D. I have since discovered that they were actually used much earlier. Homer is said to mention the anaesthetic use of *nepenthe*, while other Greek writers refer to *mandragora* as being used by surgeons to keep patients drowsy during operations. In two treatises written about fractures and dislocations as far back as 600 B.C. the observations are almost as good as any made by modern surgeons.

CONTENTS

ACKNOWLEDGMENT

THE Author and Publishers wish to thank the following whose photographs appear in this book:

Department of Antiquities, State of Israel, for figs. 4, 97 and 98; The Trustees of the British Museum, for fig. 23; English Photo Co., for fig. 102; Exclusive News Agency Ltd., for fig. 61; Palestine Archaeological Museum, Hashemite Kingdom of Jordan, for figs. 3, 70, 71, 72 and 73; Picture Post Library, for figs. 59, 60 and 96; Paul Popper Ltd., for figs. 2 and 22.

Figs. 1, 24, 74 and 101 are from books in the University Library, Cambridge.

INTRODUCTION

Not long after the October Revolution in Russia two peasants were overheard talking in a train. The one said to the other: 'Of course, you know, Jesus Christ lived a long time ago, and he was not so well-educated as Lenin and Trotsky.' Perhaps everyone wouldn't put it quite so bluntly, but I fancy that it would not be hard to find young folk in our Youth Clubs and school sixth forms who, if they didn't say something like that, were at times tempted to think it. This book is written very largely to help such people, and to do so not by special pleading, but by giving facts.

Let us begin, however, by getting out of our heads that it was really so very long ago that the Christian movement entered the world. Some of us will remember how Sir James Jeans compared the relation between the length of time since the earth came into being and the age of the human race, up to date, to the ratio between the height of Cleopatra's needle and the thickness of an ordinary penny. But within the history of the human race the story of the Christian movement belongs to the latest lap. Creatures that could be called men appeared on the face of this planet roughly some 600,000 years ago, whereas what has been called the great Axial Age, when all the great religious achievements of humanity appeared, runs only from about 800 B.C. to A.D. 300, a mere 1100 years in all, and about $\frac{1}{545}$th of the whole. We can get at it another way. Suppose that a generation of human beings be taken as averaging 28 years, in order to allow for the short expectation of life in antiquity, and the increased expectation which medical science has given us today. Then the beginning of the Christian movement would be about 70 generations away from us, the beginnings of civilisation about 392 generations away, and the emergence of man about 21,428 generations away. I know that these figures are only very roughly calculated, but they are near enough to show that the life of Christ on earth is, relative to the age of mankind, a very recent event.

Still it may be thought that his world was a very different kind of world from ours, and that his education must have been so different, that anything he said or did, however beautiful it may seem, can hardly apply to folk living in what we call the age of science and machinery. Well, in this book we are going to see what the everyday life and thoughts of ordinary people were really like in Christ's day. That after all is the only way of finding out whether his world was as different from ours as some of us imagine it to have been.

We shall take a sort of tour through it, then, and try to picture to ourselves, from what we are able to discover through the remains of it, and through survivals of the same sort of society in parts of the world like India, what it must have been like to live in. We shall look at the homes of the people, their food, clothes, tools, schools, amusements, and religion. We shall see what happened when children were born, how they were reared, what went on at weddings and funerals, what they did when they fell sick, how they did their shopping, how they paid their bills and wrote their letters. We shall journey along their roads, visit their sea-ports, and see something of their trade and commerce, and see also how order was kept, and whether they had anything like our police force. We may hear some of them talking about life, and, by listening, find out what they thought about it; and when we get to that point, although I do not want to anticipate overmuch, I believe we shall find that there were some important things in which their world was unfortunately a good deal like our own.

Although these people did not have our advantages in speed (if indeed they *are* advantages), although they had no aircraft, no radio, no mechanical transport, and no electrical gadgets, they had plenty of gadgets of their own, they were no more stupid than we are, and in many ways they had a very complete adjustment to life, and perhaps better sanitation than Europe in the Middle Ages. In one respect at least they were ahead of us, in that they had achieved a 'united Europe', and within what we know as the Roman Imperial system, they had a pooling of raw materials.

Yet their age, I fear, was, like ours, not really a happy one. It was only the southern part of Europe that was united. To the North and East lay hordes of savage tribes, ready to swarm in and visit the settled provinces of the Empire with murder and pillage, and it was only a strong, and of course expensive, army that kept things secure, and nobody could be sure how long that security would last. Some people even began running away into the desert in order to avoid paying the heavy taxes, and there was a Greek word for this. The masses in the big cities were kept good-tempered by doles of food and free entertainments, but from top to bottom, the literature that has come down to us shows that people lived without very much hope for the future. One man wrote that the world was perishing and running down and reaching its last end, and it is clear that the Greeks in particular were depressed by the manner in which things decayed and rotted and vanished away. So if they enjoyed life at all it was generally by not thinking too much about it, and by living for the day. It was also, as we shall see, rather a cruel world. The Nazi massacres would not have seemed surprising or out of place to people who lived in it.[1]

Yet it did breed some good and wise men, and their thoughts were not so very far removed from those which we today associate with the more serious pagan thinkers of our own age, such, for example, as Julian Huxley and Lord Russell. Why these wise and good men did not succeed in shaping the world of their time, and why in the end they gave way to the followers of Jesus Christ, is really a story by itself; but this much may be said. They did not hold out any real hope of transforming the world in which they lived into a better place, and only offered people one of two alternatives, either how to school themselves to bear the unhappiness of their existence with stern fortitude, or how to escape out of that existence into another and less perishable one. In this way they were in line with the wise men of India and China who have taught similar precepts up to our own day, and they only got as far as they did and no farther. People came to follow the Christians not only because they seemed to offer a more substantial hope for the future, by making the name of Deity more than an empty phrase, and by insisting that He had a purpose for the world, but also

---

[1] Working-class folk who became embarrassed with unwanted children merely exposed them to die. The letter written by an Egyptian first-century workman to his wife has often been quoted: " . . . if it is a boy, keep it. If it is a girl, throw it out." But it is important to note, as we shall again in chapters VI and X, that the man *could* write.

because they seemed able to transform society by persuasion rather than by force, and to make it gentler, kinder, and juster; and all this on the basis of fact, and not of myth or fantasy. Many of us would say that our world, living as it does under the shadows of atomic warfare and the fearful evils which would be bound to ensue, stands in exactly the same position today, and is faced with the same choice, and the same offer of a sure and certain hope. But that again is a story by itself.

The various items we shall survey will, I think, convince us at any rate that the 'behaviour policy' of material adjustments of life was just as active in A.D. 50 as in A.D. 1950; but such adjustments can only take place within the framework of human life-times. Man can adjust himself to climate, to food shortages, to drought, to storms. He can even adjust his physical make-up by dietetics, selective breeding, gland modification, and operations on the brain, although these may involve some surrender of his freedom, and will not in themselves guarantee him happiness. But man finds it a more difficult matter to adjust himself to death. Hence fictitious adjustments like mummification, or like trying to buy immortality by paying fees to people who initiate you into a mystery. The ultimate frontier is always there for every human being, and for the race.

But now the time has come to begin our tour, and let us start by looking at the landscape, both in town and country.

Chapter I

THE SCENE AND THE PEOPLE

IF we are to study fairly the everyday life of the Mediterranean world, and especially of Palestine, in New Testament times, we must try first to get a picture of what the landscape looked like. Most of us know something in a general way of the geography of that part of the world which lies roughly between Marseilles on the west and the Iraqi frontier on the east. Some may even have seen photographs of part of it taken from the air(2). But we have to remember that it looked a good deal different nineteen hundred and fifty years ago. At that time it was much more heavily timbered, and the cutting down of the trees since then has uncovered a great deal of the soil, which has been dried up by exposure to the hot Mediterranean sun and washed away by the heavy rains, so that some areas are now barren and treeless to a degree which was not the case in the time of Christ.[1] Other districts, for example the surroundings of the sea of Galilee,

[1] Some authorities have recently come to maintain that, in the first century and earlier, the rain-belt extended farther south than it does now, so that the rainfall of the country round Beirut, as it is today, then covered an area approaching the Egyptian border. This would make the present aridity not entirely a matter of denudation. I don't know what the evidence is for this alleged change, but it seems to me that the results of tree-planting in Gilead, and on the large experimental farm near Amman, both of which I have seen, are already showing how quickly the land recovers when it is properly looked after and has a chance to retain its moisture, while the reclaiming of the Negeb demonstrates that even the present rainfall, if it is not wasted, can turn seemingly useless desert into good corn-growing country.

were also much better cultivated in the first century
A.D. than they were in the nineteenth, and indeed the
replanting of these by the Republic of Israel and the
Hashemite Kingdom of Jordan, and the attempts to
restore the soil to its former fertility by irrigation,
terracing, and re-afforestation, are beginning to make
parts of Palestine look once again very much as they
did when Jesus of Nazareth walked and talked in
them.[1] Classical writers like Plutarch said that the
Palestinian fruit of the first century was of a quality
superior to that of any other Mediterranean country;
and indeed the Jews themselves boasted about the
richness of their crops. One man said that he travelled
along a road from Lydda to a neighbouring village
which was ankle-deep in the juice of ripe figs, and
another made the following excuse to his employer for
being an absentee from his job for three days: 'My
father left me a vine and I had to harvest it. The first
day I cut three hundred clusters each yielding a barrel
of juice. The second day I cut another three hundred
clusters, each yielding half a barrel of juice. The third
day I cut another three hundred clusters, each yielding
one-third of a barrel—and I have still left behind half
the crop.'

The climate of the Mediterranean in summer is, of
course, much hotter than that of Northern and Central
Europe. During my visit in September 1952 the ther-
mometer stood at 100 degrees Fahrenheit at breakfast
time, 7.30 a.m., and was said to have risen later on to
120 degrees, and it went on like this for weeks, though
this may have been exceptional. Much of the country
covered by the incidents in the New Testament looks

[1] The Lebanon and Carmel areas seem always to have been
well timbered, and the tall cedars of Lebanon were reserved for
the use of the Roman fleet.

entirely brown by the end of the summer, except in places like Jericho where there is a supply of water. The country in general from Rome to Jerusalem is mountainous, and in places volcanic, with hot springs[1] and eruptions here and there of subterranean fires. The sea, though wonderfully blue in fine weather, is apt at times to break out into very unpleasant storms and, therefore, travel upon it in the first century, in vessels only propelled either by oars or sails, had to be undertaken carefully at certain seasons in the year. The culture of the soil in the Mediterranean has always been one of trees. The vine, the olive, the sweet chestnut, and the fig and date are good examples. The worst crime was to cut down a tree belonging to some-one else; and the worst term of abuse was to call a man a 'qosēs ben qos̄s'—'a cutter and the son of a cutter'. Of course there were always patches of level ground where cereals could be grown, but the great storehouse for corn was Egypt with its adjoining provinces, and we always have to remember that the City of Rome under the Empire could never feed all its people with-out importing this corn. To cut off the corn ships from Alexandria was, in effect, to starve out Rome, and to try to do it was a treasonable and dangerous offence. In many hilly areas it was then, as it still is, only possible to grow cereals and smaller vegetables by the careful practice of terracing, which of course is a very ancient device, perhaps three thousand years old.

Palestine itself has always suffered from great ex-tremes of temperature. Up in the mountains it can be very cold. Down in the swampy country of the Jordan valley it can be positively tropical, and although wild animals are pretty scarce there today, in earlier times

[1] At Tiberias in Christ's day there were hot medicinal springs frequented by invalids, just as there are now.

there would seem to have been the usual jungle beasts in the lower levels, such for example as lions, and on the higher levels such creatures as bears and wild goats. In this particular respect there is a marked difference between the literature of the Old and New Testaments. In the former, the existence of lions, leopards, and so forth is assumed as normal. In the Gospels this disappears. The inference is that by the middle of the first century man had killed off the large fauna, partly perhaps in providing animals for the gladiatorial shows. Today there are still bears up in the mountains and on the lower hills hyaenas occasionally occur, while jackals and foxes are still common. The very peculiar gorge in the earth's surface which results in the formation of the Dead Sea is distinctive; so also is the remarkable mountain situation of the ancient city of Jerusalem, while the coastal plain running from Gaza to Caesarea is the principal level region, the rest being mostly rocky hills. The spring with its celebrated flowers is very beautiful, but rapidly gives way to a hot and dusty summer. To the east of the Jordan valley is the mountainous region which we now call the Arab state of Jordan, extending, since the armistice, so as to take in the eastern zone of the city of Jerusalem itself. To get to its capital, Amman, you have to go down through the mountains, among which is one known as the mount of temptation, to the terribly hot plain by Jericho, which is well below sea level,[1] and then up again the other side into more mountains.

Although periods of intense cold do occur, in the winter, even in the Mediterranean and the Middle East, the preoccupation of the people is much more with heat and its effects, and it is a grave error to sup-

[1] Below, near the Allenby Bridge, more than 600 ft. or, according to one estimate, 1280 ft.

pose that the Christian religion arose in a temperate climate, so that it is unsuited to people dwelling in the tropics, and does not answer their problems. The mid-day sun in Jerusalem, at certain times in the year, can be just as dangerous and exhausting as anywhere in tropical India. Much work has to be done at dawn and in the evenings, and people rest in the middle of the day. Even if you can walk about in the sun, it is perilous to *sit* in the sun. You must get under a tree, or 'the shadow of a rock'. Long periods of drought occur, and the rain is not, as in England, fairly evenly distributed.

The rainfall of the winter is the salvation of such a sun-bitten country, but it can easily be wasted without a proper system of storage. In the first century at any rate this was realised, witness the old tanks and cisterns which exist everywhere, and many of which, alas, have been in later centuries neglected and allowed to get out of repair. The best rain is said to come about the 4th December (St. Barbara's Day) and there is an Arab Christian proverb: 'When the feast of St. Barbara comes, the builder's labourers can play the flute'— because the ground will be too sodden for building-operations. It does not, however, rain every day, even in the wet season. A Jewish proverb says that rain on Wednesdays is well timed, rain on Fridays is a curse (since it upsets preparations for the Sabbath), rain on the Sabbath is beneficial, but the sun on the Sabbath is a blessing to the poor.

One very fertile spot to the east of the Jordan was the well-watered district known to us in the Old Testament as Gilead, and in the New Testament as 'The country of the Gerasenes', with its centre at Gerasa, which in Roman times was known as Antioch on the Chrysorrhoa, or Golden River, to distinguish it from Antioch

5   A group of racial types

a. Jesus of Nazareth, and *b.* St. Paul, from early representations in Roman catacomb paintings

c. a Greek, bearded and wearing a helmet   *d.* a Roman civilian

e. a Gaul (note he wears an "Imperial"—chin beard)

on the Orontes, and which is now known as Jerash, but which in Old Testament times was in all probability the important town of Ramoth-Gilead. Much is now being done to restore the agriculture of this area, but in the first century A.D. it was already a wealthy and luxurious Graeco-Roman city, and one has heard it described as 'The equivalent of a Y.M.C.A. for the Roman Army in Syria', i.e. the place where legionaries

were sent for leave, and to keep them fit and contented. The inhabitants, as we know, were not Jews,
and kept herds of swine—unclean animals but lucrative. It has been suggested that in the tale of the
Prodigal Son the 'riotous living', followed by the career
as a swineherd, may be imagined as having occurred
in the locality of Gerasa. Ruins of the Graeco-Roman
period include a wonderful circular colonnade, a
hippodrome, and two amphitheatres, the acoustics of
one of which are so good that when a distinguished
visitor once tested them by reciting some Greek verses
in the midst of the stage, his voice was heard clearly
all over the auditorium. We have no record of the
plays and spectacles which were provided here for the
troops on leave and for the local inhabitants, but there
is reason for thinking that they were not of a very high
order, in fact just the sort of cheap music-hall entertainment so often provided for the masses today, full of
coarse witticisms. This district is the Decapolis of the
Gospels (literally 'Ten Towns') and it is rather impressive, after one has visited it, to re-read the Gospels
themselves, and to observe how often it was traversed
by Jesus, and how many of the events and speeches
recorded in the narrative occurred there.[1] He may

[1] Since there seems to be some dispute as to whether Christ
really saw very much of Decapolis, perhaps I may be allowed to
give my reasons for supposing that he did. The expressions
'borders of Decapolis' and 'coasts of Decapolis' seem to be capable
of a wider interpretation than we might suppose. Thus, 'the
coasts of Sidon' seem to have extended right across almost to the
banks of the Jordan, so that to 'pass through the borders' might
mean quite an extensive tour. Again, whatever the places Gadara
and Gerasa in the gospel text really were, they imply a visit at any
rate to some of the Decapolis cities, and the Peraean ministry
implies another one. If it be argued that as a Jew Christ was
unlikely to enter one of these Greek cities, the answer is that Jews

even have walked in the streets of the old Amman (the earliest of the Decapolis cities), then called Philadelphia (much as Americans name a city 'Concord')

did enter them, and that they contained considerable Jewish quarters. But in any case the whole attitude of the Galileans was lax in regard to their relations with the Gentiles, and it would have been impossible to avoid sometimes going to Sepphoris for shopping, even if you lived in a village outside. I still incline therefore to think that Christ freely moved about among these Greek cities, and that this had some kind of connection with the development of what Baron has called 'The Great Shism'. Lest anyone should harbour misgivings as to whether these various Greek cities were really in existence at the time of Christ's ministry I would append a few dates.

(1) The Decapolis cities were certainly in existence in 63 B.C., when Pompey renewed their privileges.

(2) Philadelphia (Amman) was re-named and reconditioned much earlier, prior to 246 B.C.

(3) Samaria was rebuilt by Herod and re-named Sebaste about twenty years before the birth of Christ, with an enclosing wall two-and-a-half miles long and a temple to Augustus, and another one to the goddess Korē.

(4) Gerasa's city wall, setting the boundary planning limit for its growth, is actually dated by an inscription on the wall itself as A.D. 75–76, and a complete rebuilding plan preceded it—i.e. mid-first century, although the colonnade round the forum may have been finished after A.D. 100.

(5) Sepphoris was the capital of Galilee right up to the time when just before the beginning of Christ's ministry Herod Antipas transferred the local government to Tiberias, which he rebuilt in magnificent style.

(6) Tarichea, famous for shipbuilding and fisheries, was so populous that Vespasian 'compulsorily directed' labour from it, to the extent of 6000 young men, to provide navvies for the projected Isthmus of Corinth canal (which does not appear to have been finished).

(7) Caesarea Philippi, where Peter made his famous confession, was wonderfully adorned by the Herods with fine buildings, and was visited during the first century by at least two emperors, besides being the centre of the worship of Pan.

and have seen the citadel in all its glory, crowned by a great temple to Herakles, and a forum with colonnades, and provided with an amphitheatre probably capable of accommodating the whole resident population. It is difficult to believe that the mushroom Graeco-Roman culture of these Gentile cities—as modernistic in its day as that of the new Amman of the twentieth century—cannot have made a profound impression on the mind of Our Lord and His immediate disciples, and that the universalism of the Christian movement did not owe something to a blending between it and the austere Hebraism of John the Baptist, within the range of which Jesus clearly opened His ministry.[1] Having seen something of this Decapolis area myself, I feel less disinclined to doubt that he was able to understand and to speak at least some Greek, in addition to his own Aramaic. This means that the conversation between Pilate and Jesus could have been carried on in that language, as one well-known scholar thinks that it was.

Another important Greek city was Sepphoris. This was actually on the west side of the sea of Galilee, and was the capital of the Galilean district and, as we should say, the shopping centre for this rural area. Although it is now no longer an inhabited spot, in the days of Christ it had a large population, and possessed a government arsenal. The modern military garrison installations in the island of Cyprus, in the Canal Zone

---

[1] In case anyone should retort that I am suggesting a purely humanistic origin for the Christian movement, let me put it this way. We now generally accept that God's creative power works through the process of evolution. It is just as fair to say that God also works through what is called dialectic, i.e. the tension between A and B which produces a combination to form something new, C.

and at Tripoli form an exact parallel to those made by the Roman army authorities in Transjordania.

It would take too long to describe in detail all the different types of people living in the Mediterranean world, for they were many(5). First of all, in Palestine itself, besides the Jews, there were the descendants of the various old Canaanite tribes, who are there still, especially in the villages, and who still constitute the bulk of what we know as the Arab population. It is thought that the more primitive of these have altered very little in appearance, dress and habits during two thousand years, although the old ways are now fast disappearing. Then there were the Egyptians in the south-east corner, a bright brown or Venetian-red people, with mixtures coming from the African negro on the one hand and the people of Mesopotamia on the other. Across the sea to the north there were the Greeks, comprising a variety of types, from the small dark Iberians to the tall fair invaders from over the Balkans. In Asia Minor, besides Greeks on the coast, there would be in the interior the descendants of Hittites, Hurrians, Mitanni, Gauls, Assyrians and Persians. Farther west, in Italy, there would be in the south, and in Sicily, the survivors of Greek colonies, but farther up there would be the strange people whom we know as the Etruscans, also reddish-brown in colour, who are believed to have migrated thither from Asia Minor, and who blended with people who have moved southwards over the Alps, both round-headed Alpines and fair Nordics, to produce a sturdy hybrid type whom we know as the Romans. It is a mistake to think of the latter as though they were like many of the modern Italians. The real Roman stock was bred and matured in the colder climate of the uplands of Italy, in the more bracing air of the Apennines, and the result was a hardy race, in temperament perhaps rather like the Lowland Scots. Everywhere in all the principal cities and towns there were at least some Jews, and very often a considerable number. We think of Palestine as the main home of the Jew, but we have to remember that he came there from Mesopotamia, and that although the Hebrew people multiplied and developed in Palestine, many of them got displaced or deported after the fall of Samaria, and still more after the fall of Jerusalem in 586 B.C., so that by the time of Christ there were Jews not only in Mesopotamia but also in Egypt, where there was a big colony in Alexandria, in Asia Minor at such places as Ephesus and Tarsus, and as far west as Rome, where again there was a big colony. If you were a Jew you were expected not to live more than a ninety days' journey, by ordinary traffic routes, from Jerusalem, and also to pay a voluntary tax of half a shekel annually towards the upkeep of your national sanctuary, the Jerusalem Temple.

The Jew, being on principle prolific, with no leanings towards celibacy, multiplied wherever he settled, and we have a few figures available, if they can be trusted, as to the numbers of Jews in various localities.[1] There were said to be 8000 in Rome under Augustus, and Tiberius is reported to have drafted 4000 young Jews into a labour camp in Sardinia. Philo estimates that there were about a million in Egypt at the beginning of the first century, and in Asia Minor there are said to have been at the same period about 180,000 all

---

[1] The population of Palestine in the first century has been estimated at 5 or 6 millions. The British Mandate figures for the same territory in 1928 give it as 865,000. In both cases, however, we have to reckon with the inclusion of a number of non-Jews, and more particularly of a fluid population of Bedouin nomads.

told; but these were not evenly distributed, but were mostly concentrated in such places as Ephesus, Miletus, and so on. It is a mistake to think of all these as dark whites. St. Paul was in the latter category, if we may believe the traditional portraits of him in the Roman catacombs, and one can often see Syrians in Jerusalem old city who resemble these portraits facially. But other Jews, especially in the district of Galilee, were not by any means of pure dark stock, but were actually more like the Celts in colouring, with reddish hair, green-blue eyes and fair skins. These are said to have been the result of intermarriage with the people referred to in the Bible as Amorites. There were also a good many so-called Jews who were the result of proselytism, and had themselves not a drop of genuine Jewish blood in their veins, but had been roped in as the result of Pharisaic zeal in the same way that the aboriginal tribes in India are gradually becoming absorbed into the sphere of Hinduism.

The Galileans were scorned by the Jerusalem aristocracy. They were often of mixed blood, with very slight Jewish education, and of doubtful orthodoxy. Many of them were non-observant Jews, lax in keeping the Law. One famous Rabbi exclaimed: 'Galilee, Galilee, thou hatest the Torah. Before long thou wilt make common cause with the tax-gatherers.' It is said that the Galileans were 'bullied by the political bosses in Jerusalem, exploited by absentee landlords, oppressed by the tax collectors, and made to feel that their Jewishness was under suspicion'. Nevertheless they occupied the richest and most thickly populated area in Palestine.

We shall find, as we go on with our survey, that the story of the New Testament world is one of contact and influence between East and West. It is possible to say of course that a large part of the history of our planet consists in this. We know now that the Greeks were influenced more than we used to think by customs and ideas coming from the direction of India. There has, however, been no Asiatic influence comparable to that which produced the great Christian movement, and it is the influence of the Jew on the everyday life of the Roman Empire which we are now largely to study. We shall understand the rise of Christianity best if we see it in this light, since the everyday life of the country where it began was essentially oriental, in spite of the fact that the age of Alexander the Great and the Roman occupation which followed it, introduced much that was not at all like the traditional life of the Jews. To this day the basic culture of Palestine is Asiatic, though, like the culture of the rest of Asia, it is rapidly being undermined by elements deriving from Europe and America.

Now the whole of the area we have just been surveying, and a good deal more as well, was at this time united under a single authority, that of the Roman Empire. At the time of Christ this Empire comprised thirty provinces, and it is the nearest approach that there has ever been up to the present to a united Europe. Of course this union was not voluntary,[1] but was the result of conquest and occupation, but once it had taken place, its benefits were apparent, since the Romans were good organisers. If Hitler had succeeded, no doubt he would have tried to create a German Empire of somewhat the same sort.

---

[1] Parts of the Eastern Mediterranean, however, were always more or less in a state of nationalistic sedition. In Egypt the priests had periodically to be 'screened' by the Roman administration to make sure that they were not fomenting rebellion, and the Jews, as we know, actually fought two unsuccessful wars of liberation.

6   Palestine and surrounding areas

What kind of advantages did the Romans provide? We need to remember that in New Testament times the actual Empire as founded by Augustus was rather new, and had only been in existence a few decades, but even then it included central Europe up to the Rhine and Danube, France (then called Gaul), Spain, the greater part of North Africa, the Balkan countries, and what are now Belgium and Holland. Although as we shall see the different provinces were not all under the same system of administration, the Emperor's government was supreme everywhere, and it really did govern and keep order, and strove to put down lawlessness on sea and land. This in itself was a good thing. Then it made and maintained an excellent system of roads, some of the finest ever constructed. A good series of public buildings and works was provided, with local offices for the government, markets, town halls, baths, stadiums, and so on. The Romans allowed considerable freedom to the cities and towns in the provinces, and there was a fair amount of municipal government. But for all this people had to pay taxes, and just as in these days it is a matter of concern to everyone as to how to pay one's income-tax, so then it was not always pleasant to have to pay taxes to what many folk no doubt regarded as a foreign power. There were various forms of taxation, just as there are today, and some were direct, like the poll-tax, which in Syria is said to have been one per cent on your assessed income, or the *tributum*, which was also a special sort of property tax, levied in time of emergency, and from which at some periods Roman citizens were exempt. Then there were duties on food, duties payable on the transfer of property, including the sale of slaves, there were land-taxes, taxes on the profits of mining, and so forth, and there were also customs dues to be paid on all exports, purchase-taxes of 1 or $\frac{1}{2}$ per cent on sales, death-duties, etc. The city-dwellers are said to have loathed the purchase-tax.

How were these taxes collected? There was a Roman official called the Censor, and it was the business of his department to see that the revenue was collected in the cheapest manner possible. One common method was to auction the task to the lowest bidder, so that he who tendered the lowest rate of commission got made collector of taxes in a given area. This was no doubt the way that things were done in Palestine, and we know that the tax-gatherers there were unpopular with the citizens, partly because they were collaborators with an alien government, partly because they often extorted more money than they really had a right to do, and pocketed the difference. The contracts with these collectors were for five years at a time. Such a contract of course allowed them in theory a fixed scale of percentage, but they often exceeded this, and cheated the tax-payer and probably the government too, and it is very likely that they took bribes to let off rich citizens from paying their full share of the taxes. Like the unjust steward in the parable, they would say to a wealthy tax-payer: 'and how much owest thou unto the government? Take thy demand-note and sit down quickly and alter it by 50 per cent.' It is not surprising that the *publicani* as they were called, were classed together with 'sinners', which in this case means chiefly people who did not keep the Jewish law of Moses as they should.[1]

The form of government under which one lived

[1] The Jericho tax-collector, Zacchaeus, need not have been an obscure person. From his wealth he would seem to have been quite an important Revenue official. He is described as 'the chief of the *publicani*'.

varied according to the locality. Thus Rome was governed by officials chosen by the Emperor. Italy was nominally ruled by the Roman Senate, but actually most of the work was done by the local municipal authorities, to whom the Senate delegated the power. Outside Italy, Europe was divided into two sorts of provinces. The first of these had their governors, who were called *proconsuls*, appointed by the Senate, just as they had been in republican days, and these proconsuls were changed every year, so that if you got a governor who was disliked, you knew that you did not have him for long. The second class were the provinces which the Emperor ruled through his deputies, who in the larger areas were called *legati*, in the smaller and more difficult ones, *procuratores* or *praefecti*. These officials remained at the same stations for four or five years at a stretch, so that they came, it is said, to take more interest in their work, with the result that the imperial provinces were better administered. Still, if you had an unpleasant procurator,[1] you knew you were saddled with him for some time. The legati and proconsuls were both chosen from men of senatorial rank, but the procurators were of a lower social order, more like our business men or traders. Greece and Asia Minor except Galatia and Cappadocia, which were imperial provinces, were under the Senate. Judaea was under the Emperor, except between A.D. 41 and 44, when it was under a native king holding allegiance to Caesar, so that the administration was then as we say 'indirect'.

It is to be feared that the masses in Palestine lived in considerable poverty and squalor, and the profits of trade went into the hands of a limited number of rich merchants who did not disclose their incomes for tax

[1] Pontius Pilate was a procurator.

purposes. The Romans squeezed these profiteers, but they did not put anything substantial back into social services, only into public buildings, and a man like the procurator Ventidius was jibed at even by his Roman contemporaries, who said: 'He entered rich Syria poor, and left poor Syria rich.' Yet on the other side it may be said that the Roman government was cunning enough to know how much human nature would stand, and even bad Emperors treated severely any officials they found guilty of extortion.

JEWS AND GENTILES

It is important to understand the rather strange relations which existed between Jews and non-Jews. We have perhaps no parallel to it in the world today other than that in India between strict Brahmins and non-Brahmins, and it was more severe in some ways even than this. Of course, there were no doubt lax Jews, especially outside Palestine, but observant Pharisaical Jews seem to have been quite uncompromising. All Jews would certainly avoid contact with pagan religion and any tolerance of its rites, and they would be careful only to eat *kōsher* food, and especially to avoid buying any meat in the butchers' shops which had been sold from a heathen temple. But Pharisaism went a good deal further. Three days before a heathen festival all transactions with Gentiles were forbidden, so as to afford them neither direct nor indirect help towards their rites. This prohibition extended even to private festivities such as a birthday. On heathen festivals strict Jews avoided if possible passing through a heathen city, or buying in shops that were festively decorated. Jewish workmen were forbidden to take part in any construction which might minister either to pagan worship or pagan government, and this included the erection of government buildings. To enter the house of a Gentile made one ceremonially defiled until the evening, so that all familiar intercourse with Gentiles was taboo. This rigidity was so terrible that a strict Jewess felt herself forbidden to help her Gentile neighbour even in a confinement. If a Jew had a shop, he might sell bread and oil prepared by Gentiles, and also milk drawn from a cow by Gentiles, but he might not sell them to Jews. There was an interpretation of the law which allowed meat to be bought which was on its way to a heathen temple, but not that which was being brought away from the temple, for the obvious reason that the former had not been consecrated, but the latter had. If a Gentile were invited to a Jewish house, he might not be left alone in the room, otherwise every article of food or drink on the table would become ceremonially unclean. If a Jew bought cooking utensils from a Gentile they had to be purified either by fire or by water; if he bought knives they would have to be re-ground. Cups used by Gentiles would have either to be purified or broken. (This is on all fours with the breaking by strict Hindus of crockery which has been used by Europeans.) It was considered unlawful to let a house or a field to a Gentile, or to sell cattle to him, presumably because he might erect a temple on the field, put idols in the house, or use the cattle for sacrifice. If a weaving shuttle had been made of wood grown in a grove devoted to some pagan deity, every web of cloth made by it had to be destroyed, and if pieces of the defiled cloth were mixed with undefiled strips or rolls, these also became unclean and had to be destroyed.

The Gentiles, though they often found it convenient to be tolerant, naturally had their own way of retorting. They continually ridiculed such things as circumcision, the strict observance of the Sabbath, and especially Jewish abstinence from swine's flesh. When the Emperor Caligula gave audience to a solemn embassy from some Jews, one of the first things he said to them was: 'Why on earth don't you eat pork?' and he went on to complain: 'You sacrifice to another god, and not to me. Whatever good does that do to me?' To be fair, however, the Jews did make mention of the Emperors in their prayers, just as, later on, the Christians did.

There were continual squabbles between the stiff-necked Israelites and their rulers, and the former did not always have the worst of it. Thus, between A.D. 48 and 52 under the procurator Ventidius Cumanus, a Roman soldier found a scroll of the Torah, or Law of Moses, tore it in bits and threw it on the fire. This caused such an uproar among the Jews that Cumanus only appeased them by having the culprit executed. Tiberius ordered all Jews to leave Italy, and sent 4000 of them to a labour camp, but twelve years later he relented, and rescinded this harsh edict. Later still, however, Claudius found the Jews so tiresome that he lost patience with them, and renewed the edict, and this is referred to in Acts 18².

We may say finally that the Jew, then as now, tended to emphasise his physical separateness from the rest of the human race. ('We be Abraham's seed.') The whole people, so far as they were orthodox, regarded themselves, like the Brahmins, as physically a hereditary sacred body, a 'royal priesthood'. The assumption of such a title by the Christians, who declared themselves to be the true *spiritual* Israel, was to the Jews something difficult to accept, since then as now their religion centred round the nation. It was the Chosen People first, and God rather a long way second. Paul says rightly that their advantage did lie in having entrusted to them 'the oracles of God', a doctrine of his Unity and Moral Holiness and Lordship over History, but this did not content them. Like the Brahmins of India, they saw themselves as the spiritual aristocracy of mankind, a religious Herrenvolk.[1] Whether the modern emancipated Jew, secularised and unorthodox, regards his nation in this light, is a rather debatable matter. A final point to be made is the immense legacy of Greece (Hellas) to the world of the Mediterranean. By the first century A.D. the art and architecture of Greece had spread its influence from Britain to the Punjab (witness the technique of Stonehenge, the coinage of British kings, and the pillar with a Greek inscription at Taxila). Greek ways of thought had influenced both Romans and Jews, and it was not Palestinian Judaism which formed the bulk of the Dispersion, but Hellenised Judaism, talking Greek, and using a Greek version of the Old Testament. In the everyday life of the first century Greek was the language of cultured people, and was more of an international medium of communication from Rome to the borders of Asia, than Latin.

[1] What is today called 'Noachism' is the modern counterpart of this. A number of educated Jews maintain that Israel is destined physically and spiritually to be the religious centre for mankind, maintaining a strict exclusiveness; and that the Goyim or Gentiles may be appendages to it, observing certain moral commandments as enjoined upon them by Yahweh in the days of Noah.

Chapter II

THE ROMAN ARMY

IF you had been a Jewish boy living in Jerusalem at the time of Christ, one of the familiar sights that you would have seen as you went about the streets would have been soldiers of the Roman Army. The principal depot for these troops was down on the coast at Caesarea, which was the headquarters for the Army in this area, but a detachment was always kept as a garrison in Jerusalem, where there were, no doubt, large barracks. It is, therefore, worth while to try to understand what the army was like at this time, what it did, how it was organised, and how the soldiers were equipped. There had been a Roman army for many centuries, and it had been quite successful and efficient in the days of the Republic, but under the early Empire it was reorganised,[1] and by the time of Tiberius it had subdued practically all the countries bordering on the Mediterranean. The first thing that our Jewish boy would have said to himself would be, 'These are foreigners and they are occupying our country.' He would have known also that neither he nor any brother he might have had would be called upon to serve in this army, because the Romans had exempted all young Jews from military service. This had been a concession to public opinion, since the Jewish religious tradition forbade the carrying of weapons on the Sab-

[1] As Mr. Quennell has already written much on this subject in his *Everyday Life in Roman Britain*, it seems hardly necessary to repeat this in detail, and the reader is referred to Chapter IV in the latter work. Certain additional facts, however, especially as relating to Palestine, must be related here.

bath, and so it would have been really impossible for
any Jew to serve in the Roman Army. But more than
this, there were also religious ceremonies which the
soldiers had to attend, corresponding to our church
parades, which involved taking part in heathen worship, and again the Jews were forbidden to do this. So
it happened that the army in Palestine was rather in
the same position as that which the British Army used
to occupy in India, that is to say it was of two sorts,
Italian troops with officers of their own, and native
troops recruited in Syria from the non-Jewish population, sometimes with Roman officers, sometimes
with officers drawn from the same material as the
ranks. There were two reasons for keeping a substantial army in this particular province. One was the
turbulent nature of the population, for the Jews were
touchy, and inclined to riot at intervals. But secondly,
not very far away over the north-eastern border, there
was a great state called Parthia, which occupied more
or less the territory which is today that of the modern
state of Persia, or Iran. This state the Romans never
conquered. They sometimes thought about doing so,
but they never did, and, as a matter of fact, it seems to
have been rather too strong and formidable for even
the Roman Army to tackle successfully. Numerous
engagements were fought from time to time with the
Parthians, but not infrequently they ended in a Roman
reverse, so it seems that the best that could be done was
to keep the Parthians out over the frontier, and to have
a number of small satellite states near by to act as
buffers. About sixty years before the birth of Christ the
Parthians had actually invaded Palestine and occupied
Jerusalem, and had set up Jewish high priests who
were their own nominees. But they were driven out
again, and we saw in the last chapter how the Romans

proceeded to govern Palestine when they took it. You can always tell the Parthians in any contemporary picture by their curious scaly armour, which has pointed pieces of metal overlapping one another sewn on to a leather base. We all have heard the phrase 'a Parthian shot', and this is due to the practice of the Parthians having cavalry armed with bows, so that they were very mobile, and able to shoot rapidly and then ride off out of reach of a return shot.

And now let us look at the Roman Army itself. First as to recruiting. The government had the right to conscript men, and to make levies where it thought it was necessary, but it did not often do so, since the terms of service were so attractive that it was nearly always easy to get volunteers. We have seen above that the Jews were exempt from the conscription law on what we should call grounds of conscientious objection. The legal term of service was twenty years, but regular soldiers were often kept on active service for longer periods, especially in the first century A.D., while the centurions or company officers, as we may call them, were often employed still longer. A soldier's normal pay was probably a denarius a day (? a shilling) and out of this he was supposed to buy his equipment and any ordinary luxuries, and he appears sometimes to have paid his company commander a small sum (which was really a bribe) to let him off some of his duties.[1] If he came from a Roman city he was of course already a Roman citizen, but if he were not, upon his entry into the service he was granted Roman citizenship, with all the legal privileges which

[1] The serious rise in the cost of living towards the end of the New Testament period is reflected in the raising of the soldier's annual pay from 225 to 300 denarii. Since the Roman year had 355 days, does this mean that the soldier's leave was without pay?

went with it, and at the end of his service he received
a gratuity on his discharge consisting of a lump sum of
money, together with what we should call a small
holding, a piece of land which was either in Italy, or
more likely, under the Empire, in one of the frontier
provinces which the Romans wanted to develop and
also to protect, since they knew that if these areas were
peopled by old soldiers they could call up the latter for
the service of defending them.

The reorganisation of the army by Augustus tended
to make the method of recruitment local. The result
was that eastern and western areas became largely
separate for recruiting purposes, so that it would not
be usual for the locally formed regiments in Palestine
to contain non-Syrians.

The regular Army was divided into legions of infantry. Each of these had about 6000 men, divided into
ten cohorts; these in turn were subdivided into three
maniples, each with two centuries. The number of
legions varied from time to time, but it looks as though
at the time of Tiberius there must have been about
twenty-two. Each legion also had attached to it a body
of cavalry numbering about 120 horse. How many
troops were there in Palestine in the time of Pontius
Pilate? There appear to have been at least four regular
legions, the tenth, the third, the sixth and the twelfth,
each of which had its own special name. Three of these
had been in Julius Caesar's army, and possibly the
fourth one as well. In addition to these four regular
legions, a number of others, the fifth, the fifteenth and
the fourth were brought into Syria in the early days of
Nero. Accompanying the legions in each province
were auxiliary troops who were not usually Roman
citizens, but received their citizenship at the end of
their term of service, and these included special types

7   Roman army ambulance service, with camp in background

of soldiers, not only cavalry and infantry but also slingers (8),[1] archers, a camel corps, engineers, and men in charge of siege weapons. Augustus and his successors introduced an army medical service, since they found that often more soldiers died of their wounds than fell in battle. Every legion, therefore, came to have its 'medicus' with some assistant surgeons, perhaps four to each cohort. These doctors had special privileges, which sometimes included double pay. There were garrison hospitals, varying according to

[1] In the Jerusalem Museum may be seen some specimens of the lead bullets used by such slingers. It is said that soldiers sometimes scrawled facetious remarks on them such as 'From the Corinthians —a present', much as a British gunner might have scratched on a shell-case, 'with love to Jerry'.

the local needs, sometimes one for three legions, sometimes one for five or six, and there were male nurses,
corresponding to our R.A.M.C. orderlies(7). There
were also infirmaries for horses and mules, with
veterinary surgeons to attend to them.

Army rations were fixed by regulations. The private
soldier had 60 lb. weight (or 27 kilos) per month. The
cavalryman who had two grooms to feed received
62 lb., plus fodder for three horses.

Roman army camps were so wonderfully organised
that disciplined troops could lay them out very quickly
and have all the necessary departments working in a
few hours' time.[1]

Mr. and Mrs. Quennell have described and illustrated the appearance of the Roman infantry and
cavalry in their volume on Roman Britain, so that
there is no need for it to be done again here.

These then would be the sort of soldiers to be seen
about the streets of Jerusalem, and indeed in any city
of the Roman Empire. Their drill and discipline were
strict, and they were formidable antagonists.

How were such troops used in peace time? Mainly
of course to keep order in the streets when there was
likely to be rioting, but also to guard prisoners who
were being taken about. This is why there were soldiers
at the Crucifixion, for there was always a guard at an
execution to prevent the rescue of the criminal, and it
was the business of the soldiers to see to the details of
the execution itself. Again, we remember that when
there was a disturbance over Paul's visit to the Temple
at Jerusalem, and the mob threatened to lynch him, he

[1] At Masada in Transjordania may be seen the remains of as
many as eight military camps, doubtless built and occupied by
Roman regiments in A.D. 71 just after the siege of Jerusalem. One
of these has been photographed by O.C.R.A.F. Middle East.

was rescued by soldiers, and sent away under a strong guard to the depot at Caesarea, where the case later on was heard.

A word should be said about the officers. There were a great many grades of them, and those who are interested will find the names of some of them in a footnote.[1] The class of officer we read most about in the New Testament is that of the centurion, and from names mentioned, such as Cornelius, and the fact that one of them is said to have been friendly to the Jews, 'He loveth our nation and hath himself built us a synagogue', we may infer that most of them were actually Romans, so that their position would have been much the same as that of British officers in India in the nineteenth century, though the men under their command might have been Syrians. We learn from one Roman writer that they were very carefully appointed by the Consul, with the advice of the Military Tribune, on grounds of merit; and as to qualifications, they were to be, not so much daring fellows of the Commando type, but 'steadfast men with the gift of sober

[1] The centurion was a cross between a ranker officer and a good senior N.C.O. He was in fact chosen from the ranks, and was not necessarily a stylish person. Juvenal says somewhere that centurions were the natural subject for mild jokes, rather, as Morton remarks, as we make jokes about policemen and their large boots. There were over 50 different kinds of centurion, from the *primipilus* to the *cohorte x hastatus posterior*.

Among minor officers were the standard bearer (*signifer, vexillarius*, and *aquilifer*), the trumpeters (*tubicines* and *cornicii*), the *tesserarii* who looked after the rationing, the *curatores fisci* or paymasters, the officers, who looked after the riding-school and the armoury, the drill-sergeants, the *cornicularii* or, as we should say, adjutants, the *medici*, the *questionarii* who appear to have dealt with crimes and orderly-room affairs, and persons who are variously called *candidati, haruspices* and *victimarii*, who conducted religious ceremonies.

leadership, their courage deep rather than superficial, not hasty in battle, but if hard pressed always ready to stand firm and to die in defence of their post'. It is not surprising, therefore, that the centurions we encounter in the pages of the New Testament seem to be men of character and sincerity. As we may guess, a centurion was virtually a company officer nominally in charge of

8   Slinger and weapons

a hundred soldiers, and there were fifty-nine of them to a legion, but the first century had double the usual number of men. There were junior and senior centurions, and below them were a number of petty officers, or as we might say, N.C.O.s, and from these the centurions were usually promoted. As they advanced in service, centurions could be transferred from cohort to cohort, and even from legion to legion, but in most cases the highest promotion was to the rank of camp prefect, an officer who was allowed to take part in councils of war.

Regimental standards are of some interest. There were a great many of them, and they usually had on them some symbol drawn from paganism. The result of this was that the Jews strongly objected to them,[1] and the concession was made by the officer commanding troops in Jerusalem that regiments stationed in the city should leave their standards behind at Caesarea, and not bring them within the precincts of the Temple. With this proviso, the Jews were prepared to take advantage of the Roman soldiery for police purposes, and it would appear that some soldiers were always on duty in the Temple area (though not of course within the inner courts), for the purpose of maintaining order, especially at the time of festivals, very much as soldiers in India during the British occupation might maintain order during Hindu festivals, and also prevent Hindus and Moslems from injuring one another in sectarian riots(10). It is thought therefore by Edersheim that the band of police which arrested Jesus of Nazareth consisted partly at any rate of Roman troops, and that this was why it was not unnatural for them to take Him to the Roman Governor, and also to keep Him for a time in the guard-room. The reddish cloak which was draped round Him at the time of the mocking was the regular soldier's cloak (*sagum*), which we have not hitherto mentioned, but which was the usual overall garment for keeping a man warm, corresponding to our Army overcoat, and was also worn by the mounted troops, where it must have looked very much like the

---

[1] A recently discovered Jewish manuscript, one of the Dead Sea Scrolls, actually accuses the Roman troops of worshipping their standards, but this may have been a faulty inference drawn from a mere salute. We ourselves salute the flag, but we don't *worship* it.

long red cloaks worn by some of
our Household Cavalry. A short cape
called a *lacerna* was also sometimes
worn round the shoulders instead of
the heavier cloak.

The Praetorian guards (9) were a
very old institution, and dated from
the time when the praetor, a Roman
magistrate, commanded them. Latterly they became special regiments
which constituted the emperor's body-
guard, and had standards of their own.
They are mentioned by Paul in his
letter to the Philippian Church as having come under his influence at Rome,
but they would not usually be seen
in the provinces. They were paid at
double the rate of ordinary legionaries,
and served for only sixteen years instead of twenty
before receiving their discharge.

9 A Praetorian
guard

The higher command in the armies was in the hands
of the legate and the military tribunes. There was one
legate to each legion, and he was therefore equivalent
to our general commanding a division. Each legion
had six tribunes, so that these were more or less of the
same status as colonels. The tribunes usually began as
young men in cavalry regiments, or on the staff of a
legate, but as they were also actually magistrates, they
passed for a time into the civil service before coming
back to the army. This meant that when they got out
into the provinces they were well equipped for govern-
ing as well as for military duties. The tribunes were
usually men of high rank, but sometimes they were not.
Thus the tribune Claudius Lysias, who sent Paul to
Caesarea, admitted that he had had to buy his status

10   Roman soldier arresting a Jew

as a Roman citizen for a large sum, whereas Paul was able to say, for some reason which we don't know: 'I was a Roman citizen by birth', i.e. 'my father had been one before me'. The legates from the time of Caesar were men of senatorial rank, usually ex-magistrates, and were appointed by the Emperor himself, who was thus assured of the loyalty of persons entrusted with such a large body of soldiers.

The value of the army in maintaining order in the provinces, and securing the safety of the trade routes was considerable, but the privileged position of the soldier reminds us unhappily of that of the Prussian

troops in the old days of the Hohenzollerns. Juvenal,
though he likes the army, and had actually served in
it, complains that in lawsuits a soldier has an unfair
advantage. If a civilian is assaulted by a soldier, he
dare not prosecute, because no other soldier will give
evidence against a comrade, and no civilian will dare
to give evidence against a serviceman. On the other
hand, a soldier who brings an action can always get his
case heard at once, no matter how many civilian cases
there may be on the list in front of his.

We have in the Jerusalem Museum the memorial
tablet (3) of a soldier of the tenth legion who died on
garrison duty while quite young. It runs:

D M L MAGNIUS FELIX

MIL LEG X FRET

B TRIB MIL ANN XVIII VIX XXXIX

which, freely translated, means:

> Sacred to the memory of L. Magnius Felix
> A soldier of the tenth legion, the Fretensis,
> Who was an orderly to the tribune,
> Served eighteen years, and died aged thirty-nine.

Chapter III

MATERIAL CULTURE

HOUSES

I T is a complete mistake to imagine that the world of city-dwellers into which the Christian movement entered was a world like that of medieval Europe, with narrow insanitary streets. It is considered that Syrian Antioch, where 'the disciples were first called Christians', was, so far as town-planning is concerned, even in the first century as fine as anything we can see today. It was the third largest city in the world of that age, and there is no reason for thinking it exceptional.[1] Excavation and research are said to have revealed that Antioch had at least 2½ miles of streets colonnaded and paved with marble, racecourses, baths, theatres, fountains, temples, and market-places, and a complete system of night-lighting, which, even if not electric, was apparently almost as effective as our own; while the city itself was endowed with one of the finest climates in the world, comparable perhaps with that of Hollywood today, so that it became a paradise for wealthy parvenus seeking pleasure in retirement. Even if the Christian movement began in a village, even if Christ made his original converts by the shore of the Galilean lake, the first considerable conquests of the faith he and his

---

[1] Since one of the ancient cities of Ceylon has been reckoned to have had a diameter of sixteen miles of 'built-up area', and Nineveh is described in the book of Jonah as 'a city of three days journey', i.e. perhaps six miles in diameter.

followers proclaimed were achieved in cities as full of
a complex urbanised culture as any of our own.[1]

What were the houses like which the people mentioned in the New Testament lived in? It is safe to say
that the poorer folk lived in houses of a very perishable
material, so that we have not much trace of them left,
and can only conjecture what they were like. The
well-to-do lived in dwellings of stronger material,
either brick or stone, or plastered mud baked hard, and
even the latter was not as strong as stone or brick.

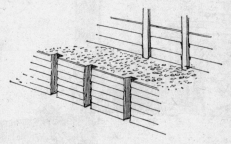

11   How the Romans made concrete

There is every reason to think that anything made of
wood must have perished long ago, and references to
mud huts in the Bible show that they were liable to
quick damage from heavy rain and strong winds, and
that they were none too secure, since thieves could
break through the mud walls and steal the contents.
But even stone-built cottages were often not much
better, since they were put together with inferior
mortar which tended to become like soap after heavy
rain, and in this way whole villages in Palestine are
known to have given way after a single night of storm.
The best sort of houses were those built of good squared

[1] Sepphoris, the capital city of the Galilee area, was after all
only four miles from Nazareth and was completely Hellenistic.

12   Outside of a Palestinian house,

showing staircase and flat roof

stone. Isolated houses were uncommon, since it was safer to live in groups. The houses of the poor in villages were, as they often still are, just one big square box-like apartment, of ground-floor only, and divided into two parts, not by a wall, but by one part being on a higher level than the other (13). The upper part had on it the beds, chests for clothes, and cooking utensils, and was used by the family.[1] The lower part of the dwelling when necessary could house the livestock, but when these were outside, it could be used for other purposes, such as the children's play, or any necessary handicrafts. The roof would be flat, and not made of very thick material, perhaps rough rafters with branches laid across, and the whole plastered with mud, so that to 'take off the roof' and let someone down through it, as was done at Capernaum, would be quite easy. After rain it would be necessary to roll the mud of the roof, and this is still done today with a cylindrical stone roller of precisely the same pattern as of old. There would be a parapet round the edge of the roof and a flight of steps up outside the house to give access to the flat roof (12). It is a mistake to think that such houses are only to be found in Palestine. They are to be seen elsewhere in the Mediterranean to this day, as for example in out-of-the-way districts in Corsica. People could use the house-top for many purposes, such as sleeping, drying vegetables, ripening fruit, and saying one's prayers. Houses of the com-

---

[1] A house which I saw in an old-fashioned Jordan village had a good many of these primitive features. I specially remember the large recesses or pigeon-holes round the walls, with no doors to them, and sometimes quite near the ground. Into these were stuffed all sorts of things which it was desired to store, but the absence of any device for sealing the entrance must have made it doubly easy for moth and rust to get at perishable articles.

13 Palestinian house, interior, showing the two levels of floor

paratively well-to-do might or might not be enlarge-
ments of this pattern, but in towns and cities they
would be, as they are now, tall buildings some forty to
sixty feet high, set in narrow streets, and with very few
windows opening on to them. To such houses there
would be a heavy street-gate or door, opening on to a
passage or courtyard, and the main part of the house
might be built round one or more courtyards, probably planted with trees. In a small house the principal
rooms would be on the ground floor, but in larger
houses the best rooms would be upstairs, and the guest
chamber or upper chamber would be the best fitted
up, and the one given to any visitor whom it was desired to honour. There would be in most well-to-do

establishments a winter and summer room, roughly
corresponding to upstairs and downstairs. The beds in
an eastern peasant's house are not put on bedsteads,
but are simply a mat or mattress to lie on and a coverlet to spread on the top. People do not change into
night-clothes, but sleep in one of their day garments, so
sheets are unnecessary. To carry your bed was under
such conditions quite easy. But in the catacomb paintings the man carrying his bed has a sort of simple
wooden framework (35), so it seems that there were
bedsteads in Rome, and in those parts of the provinces
where eastern customs did not prevail. But even in
Palestine there is evidence that bedsteads were used in
the houses of the well-to-do to raise the bedding off the

14   Palestinian house, interior, showing storage and cave stable

ground. Sometimes at the present day, where there are more beds available than are actually in use, several may be stacked upon one another, and a bedstead made in this way. Or the bedding may be rolled up and piled away in a store-room during the daytime, and all this was doubtless done in some social circles in the first century A.D., but its prevalence today is a sign

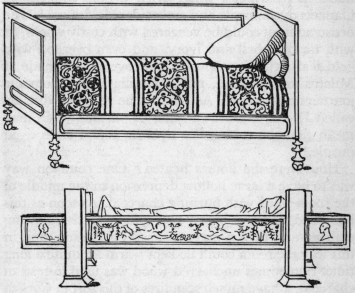

15   Roman bed, and Roman funeral bier

of Arab influence, and in the first century it is not likely to have been common. It seems to have been quite usual for a man and his family all to sleep in one bed, so that the man in Luke who gave this as a reason for not getting up to help his neighbour had a valid excuse, especially if the children were asleep. It would seem that among the citizens of the first-century empire the poorer the individual the nearer to the ground did he sleep. Slaves, soldiers in the field, and poorer citizens had little more than mats or mattresses laid on the floor. It was only the more expensive beds which were like the one illustrated here, and these had bedding of a more elaborate description and much higher quality. Stuffing for pillows and mattresses varied from rushes to wool and feathers. One emperor is said to have had his pillows stuffed with the soft plumage from under a partridge's wing. Rich people could have blankets dyed purple and embroidered with gold. The bedstead itself could be veneered with costly woods, or with tortoise-shell and ivory, and even overlaid with gold leaf (15). Very special bed-covers were made at Miletus and Corinth, places familiar to us from the journeys of St. Paul. At Philippi he gained a disciple called Lydia, who was a seller of purple, which may mean that she sold either dyes or actual cloth dyed purple.[1]

How were the houses heated? One common way was to have a large hollow depression in the middle of the room filled with burning charcoal. As soon as this had died down a board was laid over the glowing embers, and then a carpet spread on the top, and in this way the room could be kept warm for quite a long time. Sometimes uncharred wood was used instead of charcoal. I have myself seen fires of this sort in Corsica today in a hollow in the middle of the floor, so it is evidently a form of heating which was known all over the Mediterranean. But of course sometimes a bronze or pottery brazier was used, and in this case it was raised up and was open, and people could warm themselves, directly at the fire, as they are represented as

[1] There is some doubt as to the exact shade of some of the different colours, as will be seen from the discussion in Dalman's five-volume work on social life in Palestine (Arbeit und Sitte, vol. 5).

doing in the court of the high-priest's house on the night of Christ's arrest. Roman houses, as we shall see, were quite differently built from the ones in Palestine, but rich Jews might have imitated them, and in any case Roman officials would expect home comforts, so that it is more than likely that Pontius Pilate the Roman procurator would have had central heating of some sort in his residence, which was known as the Antonia. This was a great palace built by one of the Herods, and taken over by the Romans, and it must have been, like a good many other public buildings erected by the Herods, in the classical style of architecture. (For details of central heating see *Everyday Life in Roman Britain*.[1])

People sometimes wonder why the houses of the well-to-do in the Mediterranean area and Palestine were built with so few windows outside, and with a central courtyard. Two reasons may be given. First the climate. In hot weather shade is essential, and a house is cooler if it is built in this way, besides affording a shady place in the middle where one can sit out of doors. But another reason was the absence of any proper police force. Thieves when caught might be handed over to the government for trial and sentence, but it was the business of the private individual to look after his own property, so those who could afford it did not offer much scope for burglars to get in from the outside; and those who were able also kept a porter to lock and unlock the front door and to act as watchman. In hot weather people would take their beds up on to the roof, and sleep there; and for shelter make a sort of booth or summer-house over it as they still do in

[1] A hypocaust found in a house in Jerash is of exactly the same pattern as one recently excavated on a Roman site in the north of England.

places. In large country houses it is said that there was often an inner court, which contained the more private apartments. Most rooms opened directly on to the courtyard, but there were also rooms which opened out of other rooms, and these were either treasuries or store-rooms, and are referred to in the gospels as 'the secret chambers'. Eastern rooms are not much cumbered with furniture, and even rich folk will have only a few mats, couches and small movable tables in them, in addition to the heating brazier in winter. The floors would be either of stone, or of earth beaten hard, with mats or rugs spread about.

When we come to deal with houses of Greeks and Romans, we are concerned of course with buildings of a rather different sort. We have, however, two most useful sources of information. *First*, there is the work of the writer Vitruvius, who flourished during the reigns of Julius Caesar and Augustus, and who was therefore probably alive in the time of the childhood of Christ. In the *second* place we have the discoveries which have been made by excavators at: (1) the *famous Italian town of Pompeii*,[1] where large numbers of dwellings have been found preserved intact under a thick bed of volcanic ash, which overwhelmed the whole area in A.D. 70, nine years after the siege of Jerusalem by Titus; (2) *various centres in Palestine*. Here many towns were rebuilt, after the Roman annexation, by Gabinius the governor of Syria. Thus at Samaria (4) we find a rectangular arrangement of streets, each block consisting of four houses. The usual feature of these rebuilt Roman centres was a street

[1] This town can be seen from the air, between Naples and Vesuvius, since the ordinary B.O.A.C. route to Palestine passes almost directly over it. It was damaged by an earthquake in A.D. 63.

with colonnades leading through the middle of the city from a triple gate, and crossed by secondary streets at right angles, with a tetrapylon at each intersection. These streets would be lined with shops, baths, theatres, etc., and must have been almost as modern-looking in their way as Beirut and Cairo today, where one can see bits of Paris transplanted into the East. At Jericho the remains of a great winter-resort for Jerusalemites of the first century has just been excavated by an American team, and it shows that a Roman contractor must have built it exactly on the model of first-century Rome, both in construction and ornament. It comprised a winter-palace for the Herodian kings, with what appears to have been a kind of pergola where one could sit out and have drinks (the equivalent of a cocktail bar). The whole affair was magnificent and luxurious, as we might say 'Tiberside in Transjordania, and no expense spared'. But the same thing is happening in the same country all over again today. At Ramallah, a country-town, only a few miles north of Jerusalem (the Ramathaim-Zophim of Samuel) alongside of camel-trains and simple peasantry, one may see today in the development of a modern Arab city, with a large cinema of American type advertising 'Johnny Belinda', expensive American cars by the dozen, a fine new bank which would not disgrace Lombard or Wall Street, uniformed police directing one-way traffic, and finally a luxury hotel where week-end dances are held.

Vitruvius is concerned mainly, of course, with the houses of the well-to-do, but he is quite clear as to the general principles on which these should be laid out. 'The winter eating rooms and winter baths ought', he says, 'to face westwards, for they are to be used in the afternoon, and need both light and heat at that time of day. Bedchambers and libraries should front the east, as this aspect is better suited for the preservation of books, and for keeping bedding dry, since the southern and westerly winds are laden with moisture and tend to generate damp and moths. The spring and autumn dining-room should also look to the east, but the summer dining-room to the north, in order that it may be as cool as possible. Picture galleries and rooms for painting and embroidery should also look to the north, because the colours used in this work keep their brilliancy longer when exposed only to a regular and constant light. In laying out the house, the relation of the private and public parts is next to be considered. The private parts are those into which strangers do not enter except by invitation, such as the dining-rooms and baths. The public parts such as the vestibule and the court or *atrium*, where the owner receives his crowd of morning visitors are, of course, open to strangers. A small house for men of modest income will not need such a large vestibule or court. Those who sell the produce of their farms or gardens will need shops and stables at the entrance to the house, and communi-cating with its interior; and below these, granaries and store-houses, all of which are more useful than beauti-ful. The houses of bankers and inland revenue offi-cials, besides being handsomer, should also be secured from attack. Lawyers and advocates will require larger and more elegant rooms, and those who hold offices of state will need fine and large halls and spacious courts, with plantations and extensive walks, laid out with every attention to magnificence. They should also have libraries, picture galleries, and audience cham-bers planned on the scale of public buildings, for in their mansions both public business and private suites are often decided.' The floors of these mansions were usually of fine mosaic, albeit of somewhat stereotyped patterns. Examples are abundant in the excavated areas. The main difference between the Greek and the Roman house lay in the absence from the latter of the *atrium* or court. Rich men who had houses of this sort seem to have let out much of the surrounding site in shops (17). A good many of these, from an old ground plan part of Rome which has been found, would seem to have been what we call 'lock-up premises', though others had living-apartments at the back. It is unusual at Pompeii to see a whole house set apart for purposes of trade. The effect of surrounding the houses of the wealthy by shops must have spoilt the appearance of them, but there is no doubt that they brought in a very large income to the lessors. We learn that one rich lady in Pompeii owned as many as nine hundred shops, and Cicero in one of his letters speaks of some of his shops having fallen into disrepair. Curiously enough, he seems to suggest that this is going to mean an advantage for him, either, one supposes, because he expects to receive large sums by way of dilapidations, or because, the leases having fallen in, he can re-let to new tenants, who by the terms of their new leases will have to do all reconditioning. It sounds as though his house-property must have been rather old! From excavations it has been possible to make a conjectural restoration of one shop, which seems to have been kept for selling cooked foods. In front of it is a pavement, with a kerbstone pierced with holes, perhaps for tying up tradesmen's draught animals. The shop is open to the front, and into the broad stone counter are built four jars of pottery, which may have held oil for cooking, or fish-pickle, a relish for which Pompeii was celebrated, and which was called *garum* and was made from a fish rather like a mackerel which came in from the Atlantic through the Straits of Gibraltar. (The sauce must have been rather like our anchovy sauce, and is said to have sold for about £4 a gallon.) These premises, in fact, have the appearance of one of our fish-and-chip shops. Another shop seems to have been a place for the sale of hot drinks. Here the counter is covered with marble, and similar drinking-shops have been found in a good many parts of the town, with stains left upon the counters by wet glasses. We note that the cooked-food shop was opposite a passage lead-ing from behind a small theatre, so it may have been used by the audience for refreshments after per-formances.

There were of course, no wall-papers, but it was the general fashion to paint the walls of houses with pictures, and this was the case not only in the houses of the wealthy, but also in smaller houses, where the subjects are occasionally rather vulgar. The paintings, as often as not, represent scenes from Greek and Roman mythology. There will sometimes be episodes from Homer, or Greek tragedy. Sometimes there will be farmyard scenes, sometimes a frieze with battle pictures, and occasionally scenes which suggest that the premises were used as a wine-shop. Sometimes a sort of tapestry was hung on the walls, and at other times the walls were painted so as to make the room look bigger than it really was. The ground-plan of a small house shows that people of moderate incomes were content with an entrance and passage, a small garden with an outdoor *triclinium* for meals in hot weather, a large room for winter meals, with perhaps a small kitchen attached, to the right of the passage a small room for a domestic slave, and presumably, up the staircase at the end of the passage, sleeping accom-modation for the family, and a small terrace running out over the top of the passage, which might be used for sitting out, or perhaps for sleeping in hot weather. Beyond the kitchen is a little chamber which from its furniture was obviously a prayer room or domestic chapel. This practice of having a small room set apart for domestic worship is characteristic of pre-Christian Gentile religion, and we find it in China even today, and also among Hindus in India. Large houses and castles in medieval Christian Europe also had such chapels. In this case the room has a small altar in the middle, in front of a niche with the painting of a goddess.

Up to the reign of Augustus the method of heating houses was by charcoal braziers, but during the first century the system of central heating by means of hot air or hot water was invented, though it did not become at all universal until the second century, when not only the floors but the walls as well were warmed by means of hot air, generated by a furnace and conveyed by pipes to the different parts of the building. There used to be some dispute as to whether the Romans glazed their windows, but they certainly knew how to make glass, as it was widely used for utensils, and I think it is generally agreed now that they did also make and use window glass. In Rome and probably in other cities of the Empire the lower and middle classes lived not in detached houses but in what was called an *insula* (island) or block-dwelling of several storeys (16) let out either in floors or in separate rooms to different tenants, and therefore greatly resembling our modern blocks of flats. The ground floor of such buildings also was often let out in shops. Rents in Rome were high. A poor tenant might be charged £17 or £18 rent per annum for a single room, while it is known that one well-to-do man paid as much as

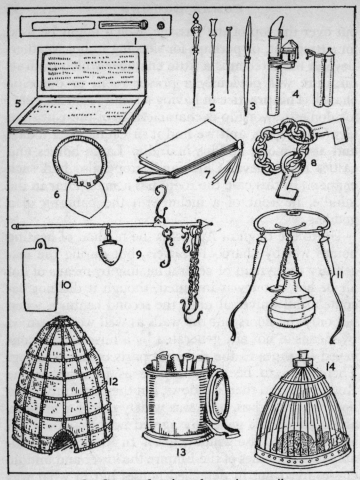

18   Group of various domestic utensils

1. Block for pen and ink
2. Three pins
3. Stylus, for writing on wax
4. Two types of ink-container, the second apparently for two colours of ink
5. Writing-tablet (two faces, hinged together)
6. Slave's collar with identification label

7. Sheaf of small papyrus sheets
8. Keys on chain
9. Steel yard for weighing
10. Dog-collar label for name or owner
11. Pot of oil for use in bath, with two strigils for scraping skin
12. Beehive
13. Box for manuscript rolls
14. Cage for rabbits

£266 per anuum for a third floor flat—three times as much, says Cicero, as it was worth. We do not hear of any rent-restriction edicts, nor of government-controlled block-dwellings, but the provision of these *insulae* seems to have been a matter of private enterprise, and was rather a profitable speculation. There was, however, an old law prohibiting any building to be less than 2½ feet from the one next to it, and in the reign of Augustus a number of further building regulations were introduced. By these the height of any new house was limited to 70 feet, and if it was of several storeys it had to be constructed on stone piers, and to have its walls made of concrete and burnt brick, and no longer of sun-dried clay. Nero revised these regulations, and ordered that fire-proof materials were to be used for the outside walls of all houses. The chief substance employed for this purpose was a hard volcanic stone called today *peperino*. Nero also decreed that all buildings were to be detached, with a space or *ambitus* round them, and that *insulae* were to have colonnades up to the first floor built in front of them to serve as fire-escapes. It is thought by contemporary historians that this Emperor was guilty of deliberate incendiarism, and wilfully caused the notorious fire, the blame for which he put upon the Christians, in order to bring his new building-regulations into immediate operation, and to clear away slum property. If so it was a rather drastic proceeding.

WATER-SUPPLY

Whatever may have been the practice of water-supply in Palestine (20, 21), we have a very clear idea as to how it was arranged by the Romans for any districts directly administered by themselves. To begin with, they looked for a good source, in the shape of springs usually well up in the mountains, so as to be free from contamination. They then built an aqueduct (19), to bring the water from some kind of reservoir to the area or city which they wished to connect with it. The ownership of this water was strictly in the hands of the State, and the Emperor was in theory the owner of it, and delegated its control to the care of an officer of high rank. It was in effect nationalised, and the business of the officer was to let out this public water to private persons. Water-rate was thus a direct source of revenue to the government, and great care was taken to prevent fraud, or the unauthorised tapping of the aqueducts. Each aqueduct was charged with a certain number of supply-pipes, and no new pipe could be inserted without special application to the imperial headquarters for a licence. Permission thus being obtained, the overseer allotted to the applicant a *calix* or stop-cock (19) of assigned dimensions. This *calix* regulated the quantity of water which was passed through to the private consumer, and was of the nature of a brass or earthenware measure. Presumably an industrial consumer would get a larger *calix* than someone who wanted a supply for a private house, and the regulation of the size of the *calix* would be to make sure that the applicant did not get a larger supply than was inscribed on his licence. Beyond the *calix* the pipe was private property, and the cost of laying it naturally fell upon the applicant, but again, to prevent fraud, there was a law that for fifty feet from the *calix* the size of the pipe must be of the same diameter as the orifice of the *calix*, and it was forbidden for any person to obtain a water-supply except direct from one of the reservoirs in which the aqueduct terminated, so that no unauthorised person could legally tap a licensed pipe. The right to a supply of water was personal, like our

WATER PIPE OF CLAY.

19   Aqueduct and calix

telephone-service, and was not attached to houses, so
that at every change of ownership the State engineers
cut off the supply at the *calix*; but here came in a
difference from our own State services, since the
licence to a water-supply, once granted, could be sold,
as it fell in, to the highest bidder, so that if you were
taking a house, it was necessary to make sure whether
anybody was bidding against you in respect of the
water-supply, and there was no fixed charge for instal-
lation, as in the case of our telephone-service. This may
seem to us to be a serious defect, and it meant that in
the matter of the tenancy of houses the scales were
weighted in favour of rich persons. Those who could
not afford such a private water-supply, had to make
arrangements to fetch their water from the public
fountain. We possess the figures as to the amount of
water available at Antioch during the first century.
One reservoir there is reckoned to have been able to

supply 1500 litres per second to the aqueducts of the
city. This may be compared with the water-supply of
Rome, which is calculated to have been at the rate of
15,000 litres per second. It is likely, therefore, that
more than one source was available for feeding water
to Antioch, since in the first century it was about
one-third the size of Rome, with rather under half-a-
million inhabitants. It must, therefore, have needed
5000 litres' supply per second and not merely 1500.
Most of the water-mains at Antioch are believed to
date from the time of Julius Caesar and that of
Caligula, the latter apparently repairing them after
damage caused through a severe earthquake.[1]

It is worth noting that the Jewish official who was in
charge of the supply of water to the Temple at the time
of Christ was called Nakdimon ben Gurion. This man
may actually have been the Nicodemus ('a ruler of the
Jews') who is mentioned in the fourth gospel, and it is
noticeable that the first President of Israel adopted the
name of ben Gurion.

BATHS

The question of bodily cleanliness is one about
which there is often much misapprehension. The
present-day provision of at least one bathroom in every
house, and the existence of public baths in every large
town, tend to make us think that in this sort of thing
we are much advanced. This is mainly because such
provision was almost unheard of 150 years ago. Our
ancestors, as Dr. Inge once said, were grimy in their
habits. Dr. Johnson said that he did not approve of

[1] Martial complains that lead water-mains were not always
very well made, and were apt to crack and burst. Syphons were
less used than aqueducts with mains, because it was harder to
keep them free from fur in the pipes.

'frequent immersion', and I believe that nuns in the past have been exhorted to wash 'once a month'. To this day the Indian tends to think of the Englishman as dirty, and the Moslem is rather punctilious about such things as teeth-cleaning and so on. It may well be that in Old Testament days, and in village communities in New Testament times, there was a good bit of neglect of personal cleanliness, but the influence of Greece and Rome was certainly on the side of washing, and by the first century A.D. bathing must have become common among educated and civilised Jews. We hear of a Roman bath not far from the pool of Siloam, and we also hear that the famous rabbi Gamaliel, a contemporary of St. Paul, did not object to using a Roman bath at Acco (Acre), while there are remains of public baths in several parts of Palestine. When about 165 B.C. Antiochus Epiphanes, to the horror of strict Jews (see Maccabees), built a gymnasium at Jerusalem, there was certainly a public bath attached to it, and no doubt this stadium was still in use in the days when Christ was in Jerusalem, though no Jew would have gone near it, partly because of the objection Jews had to practising athletics naked, partly because pagan ceremonies were usually connected with such stadia, and the games held in them (see Sports and Games).[1] Yet apart from Gentile bathing arrangements, it should in fairness be recognised that the provisions in the Torah for ablutions and lustrations were to a large extent sanitary and not simply ritual regulations. Anyone who reads Leviticus must see that behind the regulations for ceremonial washings

[1] The Greek passion for gymnastics was not at all well understood by outsiders especially Asians. Anacharsis the Scythian (perhaps Tartar), visiting Greece reports: 'In each city there is a place set apart in which the Greeks act insanely day after day!'

is something much more than the mere survival of primitive taboos, in fact a sense that disease has a real connection with dirt. It may indeed be affirmed that the Law of Moses was much more aware of this connection than most Christians were in the Middle Ages.

20   Male
water-carrier

Since the Roman bath was such a widespread institution, and was to be found almost everywhere in the provinces of the Mediterranean into which the Christian movement spread, it seems worth giving some description of its main features, and of the regulations by which it was governed. The Romans in early times only had a weekly bath, though they washed their arms and legs daily. The warm bath only came in gradually, and at first it seems that the bathroom was a primitive sort of place next to the kitchen, so that hot water could easily be carried into it. The invention of a centrally heated bathroom, with a supply of hot water, is said to have been the work of one Sergius Orata, about the year 70 B.C. By the time of Cicero (d. 43 B.C.), although the young were accustomed to bathe in rivers in the open air, just as they do today in many countries, the use of warm baths, with hypocausts or hot-air chambers under the floor seems to have become general, and already there were municipal wash-houses, open to the public for a small

21 Female water-carriers, Palestine

charge. Besides these municipal baths there were
others, built and maintained by private enterprise, and
sometimes the State leased out baths to private tenants, who conducted them instead, but in this case the
State enacted by-laws as to the number of persons to be
admitted free, the hours of opening, and the height at
which the level of the water was to be kept. Although
in general the sexes were separated and even adults
prohibited from bathing with children, in certain instances mixed bathing was allowed, and it led to grave
scandals. In the earlier empire it became general, but it
is significant that the good emperor, Hadrian, one of
the best rulers the world has ever known, abolished it,
and this prohibition was especially enforced by the emperor Alexander Severus, who forbade any institution

for mixed bathing to be opened in Rome. At first, the baths were only provided for the lower orders, and the upper classes had private baths in their own houses, but later on this voluntary restriction disappeared, and it is surprising, and in some ways an extremely modern feature, that persons of high rank availed themselves without scruple of the State bathing establishments. Thus we find that the mother of the Emperor Augustus went to one of them, and later on the emperors themselves were to be seen making use of them along with their humbler subjects.

Until fairly late in the days of the empire the baths were open from sunrise to sunset. The charge for admission was a *quadrans* (the smallest Roman coin, and the equivalent of nearly ½p perhaps). Sometimes on special state occasions the baths were opened to all without charge, and in certain cases strangers and foreigners were admitted free. The entrance fee might also be remitted as a reward for merit, as in the case of ex-servicemen. The baths could be closed on days of mourning, and one emperor forbade their use on religious festivals, a very 'sabbatarian' regulation. The usual time for a bath was the eighth hour or thereabouts, and in the public baths their use before that hour was reserved for invalids. At first one bath a day was considered enough, but as time went on, some people bathed four, five or even seven times a day. The procedure was not unlike that of the modern Turkish bath. There was a warm room, a sweating room and a cooling room, and sometimes people had a vapour bath followed by a cold douche. The room with the cold bath was frequently used for undressing, though some baths had separate changing rooms. The views of physicians varied as to the order in which the different temperatures were to be applied to the body, and in addition to the water, oil was also used, and the skin was scraped with an instrument called a *strigil* to massage the skin and remove sweat and dead epidermis. The warm room or *tepidarium* was simply a room in which to sit and be anointed, and so it was often highly decorated and served as a sort of club-room. Invalids and persons with a delicate skin used sponges and towels instead of strigils. The heating arrangements of the large baths included an elaborate system of boilers. Some of the great public baths erected by emperors, such as those of Caracalla or Titus, are enormous, and most costly and ornate in construction. Indeed the tepidarium of the baths of Caracalla, which of course is much later than the first century, reminds us of a cathedral nave. Remains have been found in Italy of two double-action pumps made of bronze, which show a high quality of workmanship, and which were used to pump up water from the reservoir into a bath. The design was that of an Alexandrian engineer called Ktesibios, and consisted of alternating plungers, raised and lowered by a rocking-beam. Bronze stop-cocks have also been found, which were used for controlling the supply of water from the cisterns to various parts of a building. It is clear that this sort of domestic engineering was surprisingly advanced.

DRAINS AND SANITATION

This seems the right place to speak of drainage. Sewage disposal by means of drains is at least as old as the ancient civilisation of Mesopotamia, and has been found at Nineveh, and in Crete the Minoan civilisation had a very complete form of it. The drainage system of Athens was also very advanced and seems to have included sewage farms. But the sewers or *cloacae* of

Rome were regarded by those who knew them as specially admirable, and wherever the Romans went they introduced their drainage works, just as they did their aqueducts and roads. The Cloaca Maxima at Rome was famous, but it was only the chief of many similar sewers, and into these large underground channels, with their stone or brick walls, were poured a number of much smaller drains, conveying the waste water from the baths as well as the sewage from private houses. Indeed the sanitation of the Romans was much better than that of many a medieval city, and probably better than that of London at the time of the Great Fire.

Roman lavatories often had running water. At Pompeii every house had at least one toilet convenience, and in some cases two. Cesspools were cleared by carts, as with us, during the night. It is difficult to say whether the sanitation in Palestine was as good as in other provinces. Probably it depended on the locality. Areas where the Romans or Greeks had put up buildings were better served than where there were only the cottages of Syrian peasants. We ourselves know how sanitation varies from village to village in rural parts of England, and what a struggle the public health authorities have to improve it.

It is not the case that sanitary regulations were not as strict among the Jews as among the Romans. Of course, in Roman cities such as Caesarea, Roman drainage systems were introduced. There was at Caesarea, in fact, 'a regular system of drainage into the sea, apparently similar to, but more perfect than that of any modern town.' But there was also a certain amount of good drainage and disposal of sewage even in Jerusalem, especially in regard to the Temple area, and in every town and village there were certain sanitary rules, mostly based on the Torah, which were strictly attended to. Thus cemeteries, tanneries and indeed any industry which might be prejudicial to health, had to be removed at least fifty cubits outside a town. Bakers' and dyers' shops and stables were not allowed to be on the ground-floor under the dwelling of another person. The principle of isolating contagious disease was, as we know, strictly observed in the case of persons suffering from leprosy. Although a good many side-streets were very narrow, and resembled the pictures of Eastern streets which we so often see, the main streets were in those days wider than those of modern Eastern cities, which have largely been rebuilt in a bad way, and we know that the practice of declaring a building-line in each street was observed by many local authorities, and no edifice projecting beyond it was allowed. There were also by-laws regulating the building of houses. For instance, the principal entrance to a shop might not be through a court which was common to two or three dwellings, and neighbours were not allowed to have windows looking into the courts or rooms of others. The flat roofs had to be constructed of some hard substance, and must slope a little, so that the rain water could drain off through pipes into a cistern. Each roof had to be surrounded by a balustrade at least three feet high, and strong enough to bear the weight of a person. (This, one fancies, was not often observed. It certainly is not today in old Jerusalem!) It was also an offence against police regulations to have open wells or pits, or rickety or unsafe stairs or ladders up which the public had to climb, or to keep a dangerous dog about the house if not under control. Watch-dogs, mostly of the pi-dog variety, were probably as common, and as noisy, then as they are now!

LIGHTING

Here again we are dealing with a situation which obtained in towns right up to almost modern times, namely the absence in side streets of any proper illumination. In the first century, as in the eighteenth in England, there would be some sort of lighting, probably in the form of oil lamps, in the main streets, but even these would not always have been well lit, and we can to some extent reconstruct the situation from our own experiences in the black-out, where only a few lamps were allowed to remain, and these with a rather feeble and restricted light, and we know that in the eighteenth century there were link-boys carrying lanterns, who accompanied vehicles, and especially sedan chairs. Probably there were similar persons in the streets of the cities of the Roman Empire during the first century. Candles were known, and were made either of wax or tallow with the pith of a rush known as *scirpus* for a wick, and they continued to be used by the poorer classes long after oil lamps had come into general use for wealthier persons. Candles were also used in funeral processions. Oil lamps or lanterns seem to have been of many patterns (25). Indoor lamps were sometimes hung in chains from the ceiling of the room, but they generally stood on a lamp stand, and this explains the reference in the gospels to a lamp being placed 'upon a stand that it may give light to all that are in the house'. Such a stand in most small Jewish houses would seem to have been just a plain pedestal with a flat top, but wealthier Jews and indeed all well-to-do Gentiles had almost as many different patterns of lamp stands or brackets as Victorian England, and the curious thing is that a good many of the Victorian patterns were copied from Roman moulds, probably

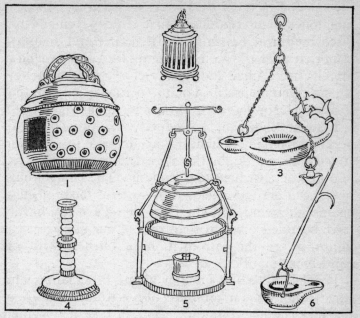

25   Groups of lamps, etc.

1. Portable lantern
2. Lantern for hanging or
   standing
3. Hanging lamp

4. Candlestick
5. Hanging candle-lamp
6. Small portable lamp, with
   bracket for suspending

owing to the nineteenth-century interest in the discoveries at Pompeii. Thus we have examples of a lamp
suspended in a basket from a chain held in the hand of
the statuette of a small boy, or a sort of tree bracket
with two branches rising from a stand in the form of
a rock on which is seated a figure of Silenus pouring
wine from a wine skin into a cup. Another pattern is
a rectangular decorated stand with a column in the
middle, topped by four branches, each with a lamp
suspended at its tip. This looks like a sort of table-
centre. Such devices were known as candelabra, and

the making of them was a recognised trade which is mentioned in inscriptions. A first-century Roman lamp discovered near Ely in Cambridgeshire and doubtless imported after the Roman conquest of East Anglia is attached to a small statue of Victory, and has a New Year's greeting inscribed on it—perhaps a present sent to an official on service in Britain by his family in Italy.

Evidence shows that a great city like Antioch had an organised system of lighting, at any rate in the main streets, and no doubt this would have been the case also in Rome, Athens and Ephesus. The lamps would have been oil ones enclosed in lanterns for protection against the wind, but the light they gave can hardly have been less efficient than that of our old street gas lamps before the introduction of burners with incandescent mantles.[1]

People talk easily enough about fires, lamps and stoves among the inhabitants of the Roman empire of the first century, but they seem to take for granted that they were all lit in some way or other. Yet how were they lit? There were no matches, there were no gas burners, still less were there any electrical devices. We have to face the fact that fires were kindled by (to us) rather primitive means, and that once lit it was a disaster to let them out. They had to be continually stoked, and watched, and from them torches were lit, with which lamps, stoves and lanterns were lit in their turn. People would borrow fire from one another, and from the central and sacred hearth of the household would be taken embers to light braziers in other apartments.

[1] Oil for these lamps is said to have been a certain sort of inferior olive-oil, exported from North Africa, where it was also used for lamps in the streets of such great cities as Sabrata and Leptis Magna.

But how was the first kindling done?
Mainly, it must be supposed, by strike-
a-light sets comprising flint, steel and
tinder. We know that this was done
among the Jews, at any rate in regard
to the temple, because in 2 Maccabees
10³ we can read about it, and what
happened then may well have also
been done in private dwellings.¹ Oddly
enough, we have no pictures of
surviving relics of such devices, but
references to them show that the
Romans also employed flint and steel.
In ancient Egypt, the wooden fire-drill
seems to have been in general use,
and there is said to be no record of
the use of flint and steel; but among the

26 Torch-bearer

Greeks the use of the burning glass to collect the rays
of the sun and to ignite tinder was not uncommon, and
in Mesopotamia it seems likely that flint and steel were
used.

There are hints as to the use of flint and steel
for ignition in Pliny's writings, and an epigram of
Martial seems to suggest that the use of sulphur
matches was known, though not of course tipped
with any mixture that could be struck and set on fire.
They would have had to be ignited with the flint and
steel.

Torches seem to have been made of wooden staves
or twigs bound together by a spiral cord, and then
stuffed with vegetable substances soaked in resin, wax,
pitch or oil (26). They were used, as well as lanterns
after sunset to guide folk about the streets, and a torch,

¹ The first classical reference to flint and steel is said to occur
in the writings of the Roman poet Lucretius, first century, B.C.

kindled at the fire of her parents, was carried before the bride at Roman weddings, by a boy.

It is worth recording here that various kinds of smokeless fuel were in use, and, in the absence of chimneys and central heating, no doubt much in request. Sometimes the wood was dried and scorched without actually being made into charcoal, sometimes it was soaked in water and then dried, and sometimes it was smeared with an oily mixture.

POTTERY

The making of earthenware vessels is, of course, very ancient, and there is not a great deal that need detain us at this point, since, unless one is writing a book on ceramics, one set of ancient pottery is very much like another. The main point which may be of interest to the reader is the consideration of how the industry of pottery-making was organised. Both in Palestine and in other parts of the Empire there were of course a considerable number of individual potters, whose industry was domestic, just as it is in parts of Palestine today. But in addition to this, pottery-making was beginning to be organised on the basis of what we should call factories, and there were certainly groups of potters who worked together, perhaps under a single employer, or there were state kilns, where jars, tiles and bricks were made under the auspices of the Government. In the case of these larger potteries, the products were stamped with the name or place of the industry, so that jars have been found marked in this way, and also tiles. Anyone who visits museums where pottery of the Roman Empire is displayed will see that there were a great many different kinds of wares, some of them highly glazed, some of them beautifully painted. Indeed a good deal of the high-class work

27   Group of pottery from Jerusalem, first century

1. Beaker with handle
2. "Fish-plate", i.e. vessel with small depression in middle for collecting the oil
3. Teapot-shaped vessel known as a *guttus*. The rouletting pattern on it was done mechanically, with a toothed wheel
4. Elbow-joined water-jar. The original was of terra-cotta ware, rather like red Samian, but it is a very stable pattern; jars of the same sort are in constant use today, and are sold by the hundred outside the Damascus gate
5. Mass-produced vessel known as a Megarian bowl (because the original type was believed to have come from Megara)

which came out of the potteries during the first century was as good as some of that which is made today, and perhaps in some cases even better, though we do not find very much which can compare with the beautiful and delicate porcelain of the last two hundred and fifty years.

In the Rockefeller Institute Museum at Jerusalem may be seen, among other first-century exhibits:

(i) A decorated beaker with the maker's name on it, showing that it was imported from a workshop in the Po valley in Italy.

(ii) A large urn of the Herodian period, possibly the sort of ablution vessel mentioned in the story about Cana.

(iii) A cup of terra-cotta red material, with an inscription showing that it was made at Puteoli in Italy by a potter called Naevius and his workman Primus.

(iv) A teapot-shaped vessel known as a *guttus*, with spout. It is covered with a roulette pattern, which was put on mechanically by a rouletting wheel. It was probably used for filling lamps.

(v) A piece of mass-produced pottery—known as Megarian bowl, because the original type was believed to have come from Megara in Greece.

(vi) A pottery brazier, with rest for cooking-pot. This might have been the kind of brazier at which Peter warmed himself in the courtyard of the High Priest's house.

(vii) A 'fish-plate', i.e. a plate of a well-recognised pattern with a circular depression in the middle of it into which the oil in which the fish was preserved could drain.

The amphoras referred to on page 108 were very largely the products of the island of Rhodes, where there was a flourishing and highly organised industry. Every jar had on its handle the stamp of its origin, the name of the maker, and the date, i.e. the name of the local magistrate for that year. These details were evidently for tax or licensing purposes. The rose stamped on the jar was the badge of the island of Rhodes.

Glass-making probably goes back to (at least) 1500 B.C. The older way of making glass vessels was to mould the glass round a metal core. But at the beginning of the Roman period glass manufacture spread from Egypt to Rome, and at the same time certain important changes occurred. First, it was found out how to make transparent glass. Previously glass had been opaque. Second, it was discovered how to *blow* glass. Finally, the making of glass at the capital led to its manufacture becoming standardised throughout the provinces. Some window-frames with fragments of glass are said to have been found at Herculaneum, and bronze window-frames also (rather like our Crittall frames), which must have been fitted with glass.

In Antioch it appears that the poorer classes contented themselves with locally made pottery and did not buy the more expensive imported wares. This was probably true of the peasantry in most of the provinces.

The commonest type of imported Roman pottery was what is known as Samian. It is familiar to anyone who visits British museums where Roman pottery is shown, and is a shiny terracotta coloured ware, originally made at Arezzo in Tuscany, and thence spreading to all parts of the Empire, so that it would have been just as well known in Jerusalem as in Britain. A good picture of a Samian bowl is to be seen in *Everyday Life in Roman Britain*.

Works of art in bronze were of course quite common, and certainly as good as anything made today, and very likely much better.

MISCELLANEOUS SMALLER ITEMS

We have grouped together under this heading a
number of conveniences which are not so much
machines as useful and handy tools and minor items
of furniture, the existence of which shows to what an
extent the world into which the Christian movement
entered had succeeded in effecting an adjustment to
life.

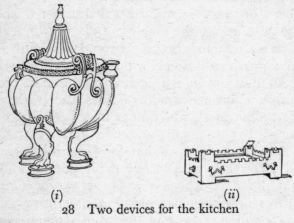

(i)   (ii)
28   Two devices for the kitchen

(i) Authepsa or urn
(ii) Caldarium, or apparatus for keeping food warm

Hot water was, with first-century people as with us,
and important matter, and apart from the system of
supplying it to baths, there were other smaller devices
for making and keeping it hot for table purposes.
Figure 28 shows one of these, called an *authepsa*, which
was a kind of urn for heating water, not at all unlike
the Russian *samovar*. Hot and cold water had to be
available at dinner-tables both for mixing with wine,
and for washing the hands. The *authepsa*, as will be
seen, looks rather like a Victorian urn in pattern, and
one has every reason to believe that the design of the

29   Roman carpenters at work

1   plummet   2   set-square   3   adze   4   chisel

latter was copied from that of vessels found at Pompeii,
since our great-grandmothers lived not long after the
publications of discoveries made there in 1831 and
succeeding years, and these got into popular books in
this country. The *authepsa* was not used for actual
cooking. For this purpose people had either the *aenum*
or bronze cauldron suspended from a chain, or the
caccabus or ordinary saucepan. Then there was also the
caldarium, which was on the same principle as our
'sluggard's delight', but used a charcoal brazier instead
of a methylated spirit lamp. The picture shows it as
a quadrangular object with four corner turrets (28).
The brazier was in the middle, and the sides and
corners were hollow and filled with water, which could

30   A Palestinian carpenter

also be drawn off by a small stop-cock. The vessels
containing the food which it was desired to keep hot
were stood on the top. Jews who wanted to keep things
hot on the Sabbath, when the labour of cooking was
prohibited, sometimes used the haybox.

Shower baths were invented by the Greeks. We
have a picture of one in use, and doubtless such things
continued into the days of the Roman Empire.

A number of carpenters' tools are represented on
a first-century tombstone, and from this and other
similar pictures we get a good idea of the saws that
were in use, and we also see the employment of
the plumb-line. A carpenter's adze was very much the
same then as it is now, and the ones employed by the
chair-makers of the High Wycombe district to this day
and in present-day Jerusalem (old city) are evidence
that such tools are not easy to improve upon. Door

keys and nails seem much the same as ours in many instances. Doors were swung open and shut with hinges of metal in the same way as ours, but they were sometimes worked by a dowel fitting into a socket, and this was not so good as it was more likely to creak.

Kitchen utensils were numerous, strainers, spoons, forks, knives of all sorts, ladles, sieves, filters, grills for

31 Woman weaving baskets (again of a very stable pattern, probably unchanged in twenty centuries, and still in use)

standing over an open fire, bellows, and so on. We have representations of stoves for which charcoal was the ordinary fuel, just as it is in many Italian homes even today. We have also a representation of a farmhouse dresser with its furniture, just in fact the sort mentioned by Cato in his book on the farm. Wicker baskets (Kophinoi) of the type shown here were commonly used for gathering fruit, and their exact counterparts can be seen on sale in Jerusalem (old city) today—hand-made in the Suq. The mechanical water-wheel we have given under the heading of machines, but the older and simpler pole-and-bucket elevator for water was in general use everywhere, in Palestine and in other Roman provinces alike. Wooden casks very similar to the ones in use today were employed for the storage and conveyance of fruit, grain or wine. The staves of these casks were usually of pitch-pine, but the stronger casks were bound with iron hoops, and others with rushes or osiers.

Walking-sticks were in general use among the Greek population of the Mediterranean, but not apparently among the Romans, except in the case of elderly persons, and officials who carried some sort of ceremonial staff or wand.

Women had all sorts of pins and brooches, and even nail-files and forceps for plucking out superfluous hair,

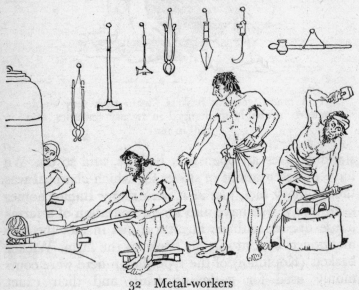

32　Metal-workers

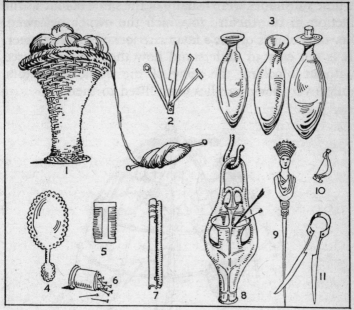

33   Group of toilet articles

1. Spools of thread
2. Manicure set (very modern in appearance)
3. Three unguent phials
4. Hand-mirror
5. Double-sided comb
6. Pin-box
7. Pen-sheath

8. Green glass cosmestic set with twin pots for paint, and kohl stick and brush (original in a Jerusalem museum)
9. Pin with ornamental top
10. ?Hair slide or brooch
11. Pair of scissors

and ornamental backscratchers, in case one got an unwelcome visitor under one's clothes. In the first century they already used umbrellas and sunshades, the latter in the garden, but also especially in the amphitheatre, where the awning did not always keep off effectively the hot rays of the Mediterranean sun.[1]

[1] Awnings of exactly the same construction of those illustrated by Daremberg and Saglio, are in use today in the Suq at Jerusalem, just inside the Damascus Gate.

These sunshades were usually of the same colour as the faction in the theatre to which the owner belonged, i.e. the colours of one's favourite jockey or charioteer. It is not easy to understand how they could be used without blocking the view of the other spectators, unless very long handles were fitted to them.

34 Slave with drying frame for clothes

A little homely touch is given by the discovery of some dog-collars inscribed with the names of the owners. These, however, will not have been Palestinian, since, as has been explained elsewhere, only puppies seem to have been allowed as children's pets by the inhabitants of Syria. Romans, however, kept and bred a variety of dogs, some of them for sporting purposes.

COSTUME

If we look at pictures or statues representing people of the first century, we are reminded at once of the visitors from India whom we see in the streets of London or of university cities at the present time. They wear loose garments, often draped over one shoulder, and they do not appear to use sleeves, buttons, collars and cuffs, and trousers or 'plus fours'. They avoid in fact what were rather scornfully called forty years ago

35 Man carrying bed

'tubular garments'. We do, as a matter of fact, find that some Romans in the army wore the equivalent of trousers or shorts, and we find the latter called *bracae*, which is obviously the equivalent of 'breeks' or 'breeches'. But in general, a crowd in the Mediterranean world during the first century may have looked a good deal like a crowd in Calcutta or Bombay. It is a little dangerous to draw general conclusions from costumes seen in Palestine in the nineteenth century,

36 Usual village type

37 Showing Jew wearing the great tallith or prayer-shawl, over a skull-cap

because Arab and Turkish influence may have altered them to some extent, and so far as we can judge, the dress of the people in the first century in Syria can only be described somewhat cautiously. It is safe to say that the head-gear was *not* a large scarf rolled into a turban, such as may be seen in India today, especially in the case of Moslem clergy. More probably (except in the case of people wearing Persian caps, which were rather like, though not exactly the same as, the modern fez or tarboosh), it was a skull-cap with a napkin folded into a long band wound round the edge of it; or perhaps the same kind of head-dress that is worn today by Bedouin Arabs, that is to say, a *Kaffiyeh*, a piece of cloth about a yard square, of either cotton, linen, or silk, folded diagonally and laid on the head so as to screen the eyes and protect the cheek-bones and the nape of the neck, and held in its place by a ring of some corded material (36). In the Gentile Mediterranean, however, if a head-dress was worn, it would most likely have been some sort of hat made of straw or felt, probably with a brim, and it is more than likely that some people in Palestine wore hats rather than scarves on their heads, though strict Jews certainly objected to wearing Gentile hats. (See 2 Maccabees 4^{12}.)

The description of the dress of a Jew which we find in the Talmud is, of course, somewhat later than the age of the New Testament, but since conservative Jews were very careful about their costume, it is not improbable that it represents the average type of orthodox Jewish dress during the first century, and if this is so, then the latter must have been very much as described below. The passage gives a list of essential articles of clothing which it is lawful to carry out of a house on fire on the Sabbath day. The list is in two parts, for men and for women, and runs as follows:

Male

1. The *haluk*, a long under-garment, which might be of wool.
2. The *nikli* (ἀνάκωλος), a short under-garment.
3. The *kolbur* (κολόβιον), a linen under-garment with short sleeves or no sleeves at all.
4. The *hazor* or girdle.
5. The *punda* or purse.
6. The *miktoran* (*amictorium* or amice), a breast-scarf.
7. The *ma'aphoret*, or head-scarf.
8. The *piljon*, or cap.
9. The *koba*, or hat.
10. The *sudarin* (σουδάριον) or scarf over the hair (? a *kaffiyeh*).
11, 12. The *abrition*, or breeches.
13, 14. The *subrikin*, or pants.

15, 16. A pair of stockings, or *empiljjot* (ἐμπίλια).

17, 18. A pair of sandals or shoes.

Female

1. A short under-garment or *kolbur*.
2. A long under-garment of linen, called either *baldinajja* or *klanidja* (χλανίδια).
3. A robe around the body, the *istomukhvia* (στομαχάρια).
4. A girdle or pirzomata (περιζώματα).
5. A coloured girdle or *zonarim* (ζωνάρια).

These, as will be seen, have in many cases names which are the equivalent of Greek words, so we may infer that the garments in question were similar to those worn by Gentiles. Some of the items are plainly alternatives (e.g. linen for summer, woollen for winter), and it will be seen that a *cap* is specified. It is significant that no Arabs ever wear hats with brims, and the tarboosh is really the development of a conical cloth cap (it is now a sign of respectability, and used to be the mark of a Turkish subject). I think we may conclude that the first-century Jew wore much the same clothing as on this list, and that the head-scarf was normal. It looks very much as though the great *tallith*, which has now become the proper prayer-vestment in the synagogue, was originally the normal head-scarf, and that to show one's 'Jewishness' it was made compulsory to put it on in addition to one's other clothes, as one does today. If you wear a hat (e.g. a top-hat as some London Jews do) you drape the *tallith* over your shoulders, but if, like so many eastern male Jews, you wear a skull-cap, then you put the *tallith* over your head, and look at once much more like your Arab neighbour (37).

The Talmud also gives directions as to the order in

which the garments are to be removed in order to take a bath, giving much the same name to them. These Jews of the Talmud, at any rate, had adopted one Roman custom, that of always putting on and removing the right sandal *first*—a genuinely superstitious practice.

We will now proceed to describe the costume of Mediterranean people in detail, and it will be natural to try to tell what might have been seen in Palestine. We can leave out for the moment the dress of Roman officials, which would have been the same in all provinces, and we can also omit the uniforms of the Roman soldiers, which we have dealt with elsewhere. Let us take the most ordinary dress of the great mass of the people, the *am haaretz* or proletariat, or as they are called today, the *fellahin*. These were labourers or agricultural workers, and for the most part not very strictly orthodox Jews in their habits, either as regards dress or the eating of *kōsher* food or keeping holy days. In addition to the small *tallith* (about which see below, and over which they may well have been careless) their costume would have consisted of five articles, to wit, a long cotton shirt, a leather or stuff girdle worn round the waist, a head-dress as described above, shoes or sandals, and a cloak made either of goat's or camel's hair, or some sort of coarse sackcloth. This cloak had no girdle and varied slightly in pattern. It might be of two forms, either: (1) a heavy, sleeveless cloak worn for protection against rain and cold, and used as a coverlet during sleep, or (2) a long-sleeved overcoat. The former would be about seven feet from right to left, and four and a half feet from bottom to top, and at each top corner it would have a slit through which the hand and wrist could pass. It might be plain, or with stripes of varying colours, woven in it, or it might have ornamental strips sewn on to it. The other form of over-garment was more like a cassock, worn open in the front and without a girdle. It would have wide sleeves, and it would be about the same length as the shirt worn underneath it. In general the long-sleeved coat was the mark of officials, priests and educated and wealthy persons, while the cloak was worn by country-dwellers such as shepherds. The under-garment mentioned above also varied a good deal in pattern and extent. As worn with other garments it was more like a nightshirt with sleeves, or with holes at the top corners for the arms, and worn with a girdle so that it could be girded up for rapid movement. Sometimes, however, it would be little more than a waist-cloth, leaving the upper part of the body bare, but wrapped tightly round the loins and reaching to the knees. This would be the sort of garment worn by boatmen, fishermen and outdoor labourers, and anyone wearing it would technically be called 'naked' (as we find Peter is in John 21[7]). A larger form of this was a plain sheet wound round the body with one end flung over the shoulder and worn with or without a girdle: this reminds us of the young man, who was captured by the police in the garden of Gethsemane, but wriggled out of their clutches. (It is also rather like the uniform costume prescribed for wearing by Moslems making the Mecca pilgrimage, as I have seen for myself at Beirut.) For indoors, or for working in shops, the under-garment would be the shirt or tunic with sleeves, worn with a girdle. There would be a slit about a foot in length on each side of the skirt to allow for freedom in walking, and there would be an opening for the head sometimes cut into a V-shape down the front; but when the garment was new, it was probably sold, as it is today, without any such opening. The reason for this is still, as probably of old, partly to show that it is new and not second-hand, and partly to allow the purchaser to make the opening for himself of the size that he wants, and to wear it plain or ornamental as he pleases. Another variation that we find is that the long tunic was sometimes divided into two parts from the belt downwards, and the bottom sewn up, except for a hole at each corner for the feet to pass through. This would provide the wearer with a pair of loose baggy trousers, and it was apparently the practice to wear them trailing down, to indicate that one was a person of leisure, though labourers or messengers would draw them up and tuck the folds under the belt, and this would be another way of 'girding up one's loins'. The girdle served several purposes. It not only drew in the tunic, making it neater, but it provided above the tunic-waist a sort of bag in which objects could be carried, such, for example, as food like lentils, literally 'measured out into one's bosom' by the shop-keeper. Tucked into the girdle itself might be a sword or dagger, or, in the case of the scribe, a case for hold-ing reed pens, and a box or ink-horn for writing fluid. (See 'ink'.) In a hot, dusty country, a scarf or napkin was folded round the neck to keep the collar of the coat from being soiled by perspiration, and this was also used to wipe the face and the back of the hands.

Present-day Jews and Moslems often wear a close-fitting, brimless cap, much lighter than a beret, and this is probably a custom of great antiquity. It is risky to make too clear generalisations. Peasant dress until recent times has been very conservative, and in India today, while there are many persons who have adopted European costume, there are equally many others who still dress as Asiatics. While, therefore, it may well be that many Jews, especially those living outside

38 A small tallith or sacred under-garment

Note the tassels and the star of David. The texts inscribed on it in Hebrew are too small to be decipherable. This is a modern tallith, but it can be little different in essentials from those worn in the first century A.D. except in colour. New talliths are sold without the slit for the head to go through, and are cut afterwards to suit the size of the wearer. It is said that very many Jews of the present day have given up wearing them

Palestine, adopted the fashions in clothing, jewellery, headgear and hairdressing which prevailed in the Hellenistic world of their day, and introduced them into Palestine, there would be plenty of others who would indignantly refuse to dress like Gentiles, and in any case the important under-garment with its tassels would be an obligation. This garment, the *small tallith* (38), was directed to be worn by every male Jew next to the shirt. It was of purplish-blue[1] cotton, and had four tassels, and it seems to have been regarded as a solemn badge or sign of the separation of the people of Israel from the rest of the human race. The *large tallith*, which is today seen only as the prayer-shawl worn by Jews in the synagogues, was a piece of white cotton or wool about two yards square, with a black border or tripes, and a cord attached with eight threads and five knots, symbolising the number of the commandments in the Law or Torah.

The dress of women so much resembled that of men as to make interchange of garments possible. The two chief differences would seem to be that the women's garments were

[1] Lydia at Philippi may have been in request as the supplier of dye for small talliths.

39 Cotton-cleaner

more elaborate and brightly coloured, while the head-
dress was different, and consisted mainly of a large veil
of varying pattern, though sometimes a cap with a horn
on the top of it would be worn, with a veil attached to
the top of the horn. In this case, the veil of a widow
would be black, that of other women white. If the villa-
gers have kept their traditional dress, then the women's
dress was certainly very colourful, with a ground work of
some colour like maroon, blue or apricot, and a breast-
plate of another colour and stripes of the same sewn
on to the skirt; the breast-plate and stripes being 'of
divers kinds of needlework', sometimes very elaborate.

We can obtain some idea of Syrian dress from the
mosaics discovered by the American archaeologists at
Antioch on the Orontes a few years ago. In these there

is a marked distinction between the dress of the
country-dwellers and that of the townsfolk, and
although the pictures are not all of first-century date,
it seems likely that there was not a great deal of change
between the dress of the average person in the time of
the martyrdom of Ignatius, A.D. 110, and that prevailing in A.D. 50, the days of Paul and Barnabas. One
peasant is represented in a rose-coloured tunic and
long black boots or buskins. Another mosaic shows
a negroid fisherman with a yellow waist-cloth and
yellow helmet carrying two fish baskets, one at each
end of a pole. As the baskets are yellow (straw?) we
may assume that the helmet is a straw-hat, and perhaps that the waist-cloth was of some unbleached
material. A slave carrying a packet and a pannier is
dressed in a very short white garment of some light
material. Artisans and manual labourers wear a short

40   Spinner

white tunic with girdle, and
an attachment only to the left
shoulder, so that the arms,
legs and right shoulder are
bare, though some have both
shoulders covered. Most male
peasants have a short tunic
with sleeves, and long boots,
and apparently stockings.
As this is the costume of the
local peasantry round about
ruined Antioch to this day, it
may well have been that worn
in the first century. The boots
are not worn by townsfolk,
who use lighter footgear, so it is
safe to assume that they were
meant to protect against mud

and dung. People of a higher social class in these
Antioch pictures have a long tunic with sleeves, and
some other figures show their nationality perhaps by
wearing a *toga* (Roman) or a *chlamys* (Greek). The
women wear a long tunic with sleeves, sometimes
richly embroidered, and covered by a cloak with a
hood, the cloak being red and the coiffure white. What
about dress materials? Wool and flax were certainly
known. Cotton garments (39) are mentioned expressly
by a Greek writer of 350 B.C., and silken garments are
referred to in the book of Revelation (Ch. 18, v. 12).
We may take it generally that in the New Testament a
himation means an outer garment and a *chiton* an under-
garment. To say 'Don't take two *chitons*' is therefore
like saying 'don't trouble to take a spare vest—you
won't be long away from home'. But names of garments can be very confusing. The Roman soldier's
military cloak was called a *sagum*, but in the Greek
New Testament it is sometimes called a *chlamys*, sometimes a *himation*, while St. Paul's cloak is called a
phelonē. Clearly there were quite a number of different
patterns.

It would never do to describe Gentile dress in the
first century without saying something about the *toga*.
This garment was the distinctive city dress of the
Roman citizen, and its use was forbidden to foreigners (44). The Emperor Augustus was exceedingly strict
about its being worn in public, especially on state
occasions, and it was considered disgraceful for a
magistrate to appear on the bench without it. In the
country it might be discarded, and this was a relaxa-
tion hailed with delight by many, since the toga was
a large and rather heavy woollen wrap, and must have
been somewhat of an encumbrance, especially in summer. The *toga praetexta* was one which had a purple

stripe round its margin. This ornamentation was at first given to boys who were free-born—thus St. Paul could have worn it. Subsequently it was worn also by certain magistrates, though not by all. It was often bestowed by the Senate as a badge of distinction. It is quite correct to represent Pontius Pilate as wearing it on the judgment seat. Sometimes a dark-coloured *toga* was worn as a sign of mourning, and at the other end of the scale there was the *toga picta*, which was a very splendid garment, and had, in addition to the purple hem, a quantity of golden embroidery. It was worn by victorious generals at triumphs, and later by most of the emperors.

(For details as to the putting on of the toga see *Everyday Life in Roman Britain*.)[1]

Sandals, whether Jewish (41) or Gentile, were of various sorts, but usually flat soles of leather, wood or dried grass, with loops attached, and with a leathern thong which was passed through the loops, and by means of which the sandal was strapped to the foot. For indoor use, slippers of black or coloured leather would be in use, and out of doors it was sometimes the custom to walk barefoot. In a hot climate, close footgear naturally make the feet hot, and lead to chafing, so sandals are best; but anyone can see that under such conditions the feet get very soiled and dusty, so that washing the feet is by no means a mere ceremony, but is of practical importance. Observers in India say that they have seen Indian women wash the feet of their guests on occasion, and wipe them with the hair of their head, apparently as a sign of deference or courtesy.

[1] It is said that the normal North-African garment called a *barrican* is virtually a toga, and may have survived in pattern from Roman days.

41   Shoe-maker in Jerusalem (old style)

There were three main sorts of Roman footgear:
(1) The *calceus*, which was a regular closed boot with
a sole and an upper; (2) The *caliga*, which had a sole,
but an open upper consisting of a series of thongs,
giving ventilation to the foot. The *caliga* was made of
tanned hide, but there was another sort which was
called a *pero*, made of untanned hide; (3) The *solea*,
which was a mere sandal, with only a sole, a toe-strap
and a strap across the instep. It is said that differences
of rank were shown by different sorts of boots. This
was during the Republic, when the plebeians were
distinguished from the patricians by their footgear, but
it is plain that some such distinction continued under
the Empire, for we find as late as three hundred years
after Christ a ceiling-price fixed by an imperial edict

for the different grades of footgear. Of course we do not know the exact value of money at this time, but it has been thought probable that a patrician *calceus* cost about eighteen new pence, the *calceus* of the senator about twelve new pence, and the *calceus* of a man of equestrian rank about eight new pence, and below these there seems to have been a *calceus* for the ordinary Roman citizen. The patrician *calceus* was of red leather, but its use is a little vague, since it was not worn by all patricians, nor by patricians only, but strictly by magistrates of high rank on great public occasions, almost as the insignia of orders are worn in this country.

Peasants and country people seem to have worn a kind of shoe called a *crepida*, which was a cross between a boot and a plain sandal, and often had a heavy sole studded with nails. The upper was not generally complete, but there was more protection for the foot than in an ordinary sandal. Another distinction which should be noted was the use of different kinds of footgear in stage plays. In tragedies a high boot (a *cothurnus*) was worn, with a thick sole and a high heel, in order to increase the stature of the actor and to make his appearance more impressive. For the comedy actor there was a different sort of shoe called a *soccus*, a kind of loose slipper which made it easy for the wearer to dance. There was also in use a warm felt slipper called an *udo*. The sandal is, of course, the most primitive type of footgear, but among the Romans sandals and slippers were reserved for indoor use, and to wear them out of doors, except, perhaps, in the country, was thought effeminate. It was, however, quite in order to wear sandals or slippers when going out to an evening meal. When you lay down at the table, your host's slave or your own attendant came along and took off your foot-gear, so that you could be easy and comfortable. If you had a conveyance, such as a *cisium* or a litter, you could put on your sandals before starting, but if you could not afford this luxury, you walked to your entertainment in boots and carried your indoor shoes under your arm, and the customary phrase for preparing to take leave of your host was 'to ask for one's sandals', just as a man in the eighteenth century might order his coach or his sedan-chair.

42 Roman civilian hair-style (male). (*From a crystal figurine at Jerusalem, probably of the Emperor Vitellius*)

How did people wear their hair? We usually see Romans of the first century strictly clean-shaven, and with their hair short, though not with partings. Indeed, the Roman aristocrat usually seems to have worn his hair combed straight forward from the crown to the forehead (42).[1] Boys usually had their hair cut short and combed in the same way, unless they were either boy slaves waiting at table or boys employed in some temple service, in which case the hair was long. Fops and fashionable young men sometimes had their hair waved or curled. Seneca says that they would rather have the State in disorder than their hair out of curl, and they used curling tongs and all kinds of hair oil. Among the Romans, for men to wear their hair long was a custom which went out three hundred years before Christ. If Roman officials were clean-shaven,

[1] As did many European gentlemen about the year 1800.

how did they manage to shave? The answer is provided by the specimens of iron or steel razors which have been discovered, and an illustration of some of which is given (84). In a grave relief we have also what appears to be the representation of an old man actually being shaved (43). Shaving soap was not available, but

43   Old man being shaved
(*From a drawing in a Jerusalem museum*)

one can safely assume that people had found out how to soften the beard with hot water, and very likely they also used oil. We know that the Romans had discovered by the first century how to make tempered steel, so it is quite likely that some of their razors were really sharp. The dressing of women's hair was much more elaborate, and there were many ways of doing it. In good social circles it was considered bad form to use artificial arrangements or waving, but this convention seems to have been relaxed during the first century A.D. under the early Empire, when a poet says that there were as many ways of ladies dressing their hair as there were bees in Hybla. Old-fashioned women who were matrons seem to have worn the hair in a high mass on the crown. There is a picture of the daughter of Titus, the man who besieged Jerusalem, showing it done in this way. Another, of a niece of the Emperor Augustus, shows her with ringlets coming down on to the shoulders and a row of curls over the forehead with three hair curlers actually in position, and a fillet of beads bound over the top, to keep the hair tidy. Others show close-fitting hats, or possibly hair-nets, in both cases not at all unlike some that are worn today. For young women a very common way was to bind the hair back in a plain knot and to run a plait over the top of the head in front, a fashion again well known in our own day. Both men and women dyed their hair. Men sometimes dyed it black, sometimes blond. Women dyed their hair black, but especially auburn, and were at pains to cover grey hair. False hair was sometimes used to add to the coiffure. Wigs were also used by both sexes, especially blonde ones, and remains of them have sometimes been found even in the catacombs. Hair for these purposes was imported (so we read) from Germany and even from as far as India, which perhaps means Southern Arabia. The hair was fastened up with hairpins and combs, the latter being made of box-wood, ivory or tortoise-shell. Hair-bands might be made of gold set with jewels, and even some hair-nets might be made of gold thread. Men do not seem to have parted their hair, though women sometimes did, and sometimes caps were worn with lappets covering the ears and two strings for tying under the

44 Roman civilian dress in first century

chin. Girls appear to have altered the dressing of their hair after marriage. Towards the end of the first century most wonderful structures came to be erected on the top of women's heads, but this would not have been the case with women of wealth and fashion who had maids to wait on them. Twice in the New Testament and once or twice in the early Greek Fathers we find Christian women warned against such elaborate customs. Cosmetics were used certainly as far back as the times of ancient Egypt, and they persisted among the Greeks and Romans. It seems likely that there was quite as much lipstick in use in the first century in the Mediterranean world as there is in the western world today. When we come to speak of beards we approach the subject of hair-dressing in Palestine. It seems probable that to be clean-shaven was not the custom in that country, but that most men wore beards, and that the hair was long rather than short. There is also evidence that the moustache, which is so common a feature among Hindus, was by no means unknown in first-century Palestine. The shaving of the head and also the practice of letting the hair grow excessively long were both ways of showing that one had taken a vow. We often read in the Bible of the long-haired Nazirites, and we read of St. Paul having his head shorn in the performance of a vow.[1] There seems evidence that in

[1] The shaving of the head was also practised by the Egyptians, who rather despised people who wore their hair long. Egyptian grandees often wore wigs. The Hebrews, like the Babylonians,

this shaving the topknot was retained, making the man look rather like a Brahman priest in India. Women wore ear-rings, and also, as in India today, nose ornaments. The commonest and most usual female head-gear seems to have been some kind of scarf or veil fastened to the fillet, and strings of coins were used as ornaments. It was considered unlucky to lose any of these, so it is thought that the 'lost coin' of the parable was possibly one of these ornaments.

MEALS AND FOOD

It is only when we come to inquire carefully into the facts, that we find how elaborately the world of the first century organised its meals. We hear of Christ going to dine with a well-to-do Pharisee, but we do not realise how much preparation was involved in such a dinner. There were, no doubt, as there are today, considerable differences between the way in which meals were served in Jerusalem, Athens and Rome, but the organisation of the Mediterranean under the Empire makes it likely that among well-to-do and fashionable people, and especially among Hellenistic as distinct from Palestinian Jews, dining customs from Rome would tend to spread into other parts of the Empire, so that in Palestine it would have been possible to find people living in much the same way as if they were in Rome. Of course this would be chiefly true of Gentiles, and especially of persons in the government service, such as Cornelius, the centurion of

---

and the modern Bedouin, regarded long hair as actually an ornament. Readers will remember how the Jordan Camel Corps were known as 'Brigadier Glubb's girls', because of their long plaited hair. Strict Jews wear side-curls because in Leviticus 19[27] they find a prohibition against 'rounding off the corners of the head', i.e. trimming of the hair.

the Augustan band, but there would, of course, also
have been the great difference, that Jews and Gentiles
would not approve of eating together, and Jews
especially, unless very low-class peasants, would only
eat *kōsher* food, i.e. food prepared in a special way, by
draining the blood out of the meat. There were also
certain classes of food designated as unclean in the law
of Moses, and as these might be eaten by Gentiles but
not by Jews, this would make it difficult for Jews and
Gentiles to share a meal.

We will begin, therefore, by seeing how a Roman
like Pontius Pilate or one of his officers would have had
meals served. For the Roman there were usually four
meals in the day. The first was a small morning meal
often taken by schoolboys at cockcrow, and it was
called *jentaculum*. For these lads it consisted of a kind
of pancake, but for adults the meal consisted of bread
spread with honey or dipped in wine, and sometimes
bread and cheese, followed by a few dates and olives.
For grown-up people, this would be usually at the
third hour, and not later than the fourth. No doubt
abstemious people might drink milk or water, but the
usual drink was wine, perfumed or scented (rather like
the modern vermouth). The next meal was about
noon. The early Romans dined in the middle of the
day, but by the time of the Empire what we should
call late dinner had come in, and the midday meal was
known as *prandium*, or, as we might say, 'luncheon'.
This was taken about the sixth hour, and the menu
varied from a piece of bread to a quite elaborate meal,
with either hot or cold fish, fowl, butcher's meat,
vegetables and fruit; but the meat was not of a very
solid character, more of the nature of sweetbreads,
pig's cheek, lamb's heart and so on, and sometimes the
meat of the previous dinner served either cold or hot.

45 Roman dinner scene

If wine was drunk, it was often heated, and being usually thick and syrupy, it would be mixed with water. The third meal, known as *merenda*, was originally rather like our four-o'clock break for tea in factories, and was confined to workmen, but later, if *prandium* happened to be very small, or got left out altogether, *merenda* would be a sort of postponed *prandium*. The principal meal of the day came normally at the ninth hour, and was preceded by the bath. It could be as early as the eighth hour in summer, and it was called *cena*, and was a very long affair. The famous writer, Pliny the Elder, says he used to spend as much as three hours at *cena*, and sometimes it was spun out until late at night, indeed until it was time to go to bed, which was, of course, much earlier than with us, or with French and Italians of the present day, because the Romans got up at daybreak; but ceremonial meals or drinking parties could go on until midnight or even the early morning. For ordinary people, meals would be served in the main living-room, but very wealthy persons built a separate dining-room.

Let us see what went on at a dinner-party. The number of guests invited would usually be nine. There might be fewer, but it was considered bad form to invite more, and sometimes a guest might bring with him an uninvited person known as an *umbra* (the word means shadow), if the number were one short. It was the fashion to dress for dinner, not, of course, in the way we do, but by putting on light, richly ornamented and coloured robes. Only the vulgar rich changed the robe in the middle of dinner, unless it was demanded by some religious ceremony taking place. Special sandals were usually put on when dining out, but the slave who attended the guest and who waited on him at table would take them off and keep them until the time came for going home. (See page 96.) The table, of a circular, semicircular or horse-shoe shape, did not always have a table-cloth. Each guest had his seat pointed out to him by an attendant, but one did not sit down, but lay on a couch, which was either shaped so as to curve round the table, or was in general pattern rather like one of the so-called day-beds which were made in the time of our Charles II. In this case it would stand more or less at right angles to the table, and in any event, one would lie in the same direction, so that the head of the individual would be next to the table, and the feet at the end away from it, which would make it easy for the slave to come up and take off and put on the sandals, and would leave a clear passage up the middle, for the waiter to put the dishes on the table. As soon as the guests were reclining, water was brought round to wash the hands (you will remember that Simon the Pharisee omitted this when he asked Christ to dinner, and so acted discourteously). The hands were then wiped with a towel. This was often provided by the host, but sometimes the guest brought it along with him, in order to carry away in it the presents which were often given to guests at entertainments. Table-cloths began to be used at about the end of the first century. From a quotation in a speech, it seems that many people then said grace—'we invoke the gods'. The meal itself was in three parts. First what we should call hors d'oeuvres, accompanied by wine diluted with honey. Then the *cena* proper, which on ordinary occasions constituted the whole dinner, and consisted of three separate courses, each of which was brought in on a tray, generally of wood, but sometimes of silver. The arrangement of the dishes was made with considerable art; indeed the accounts remind us of the coloured plates in some editions of Mrs. Beeton's cookery book. Between each course the tray was taken away and the table was wiped down, and any bits that had fallen were gathered up. Then the tray was brought up again. The guests ate with their fingers, just as they do in places like Arabia today, except in the case of soup, eggs and shell-fish, when they used a spoon called a *cochlear* or a *ligula*. Consequently the guests had to wash between each course. Forks did not come into use at table until the second century, though they were employed in kitchens. Sometimes the food was served ready to pick up, but at other times it was carved at the open end of the table, and delivered to each guest by a slave. Written menus appear to have been in use. After the *cena* proper was finished, the table was removed, and what evidently corresponded to 'grace after meals' was said. This consisted in throwing certain offerings to the gods on to the hearth, where they were consumed by the fire, and if the behaviour of the elements was favourable, a slave then announced that the gods were propitious, and there was a short period of silence out of respect for the gods.

After the grace there came the dessert, or 'second tables', consisting of various sorts of pastry, with fresh and dried fruits; and this was followed by the *comissatio* or drinking party, in just the same way that the wine is passed round at dessert during a modern dinner, or in college after those assembled have retired to the combination room.

At important dinner-parties there would be musicians,[1] and sometimes a sort of cabaret, with girls to sing and dance; on other occasions cultivated hosts would read aloud. A Roman satirist indicates that it was often a nuisance when authors would insist on reading from their own works. After-dinner speeches were not the fashion, but there could be shows by gymnasts, and comic turns given by jesters and comedians.

The first century in Roman circles seems to have been a time of very elaborate cookery. It has lately been pointed out that a special cookery book was composed by a man called Apicius, who lived about A.D. 25. Pliny says that he had a peculiar recipe for making pigs' livers a great delicacy, which involved feeding the animals on figs, and giving them wine to drink sweetened with honey. He had an unusual way also of preparing a savoury dish made of the tongues of flamingoes. Perhaps for us the most important fact about him is that he was the inventor of the omelette. Seneca complains that he corrupted the youth of the Empire by weaning them away from the study of

[1] The commonest musical instrument appears to have been the double-flute, but there were also stringed instruments of a simple character, and percussion was known. We hear of timbrels (i.e. tambourines of a sort), and in Palestine at any rate the drums were earthenware vessels with a skin stretched over them, used for dances, but never as in Africa, for spreading news.

philosophy through the delights of the kitchen. This
grumble from a serious-minded man sounds rather on
a par with a modern complaint that youngsters prefer
to go to the cinema rather than go to church. The
good dinners served in some circles are to be balanced
by the (perhaps rather one-sided) description given in
Juvenal of a meal given to poor clients by a mean-
spirited rich man who keeps all the best dishes for himself, and serves his guests with mouldy bread and bad
water, fresh-water fish caught in the sewage works on
the Tiber, and cooked in rancid oil, with crab instead
of lobster, and inferior brands of wine in broken cups.

On Jewish cookery the following facts may be noted.
Meat was usually eaten only on festival days, just as
among Moslems today it is specially eaten on the feast
commemorating Abraham's sacrifice, the Aid el
Kebir. Many vegetables were eaten raw (e.g. small
cucumbers). Lentils or greens were boiled in water or
oil. Corn-porridge was made with water, salt and
butter, and many kinds of cakes were made from
crushed and malted grain. Meat was usually boiled,
though the passover lamb was, of course, roasted.
Roasting was at an open fire with a spit. Cane and
beet sugar were as yet unknown, so, for sweetening,
raisins and figs, honey and dates were in use, honey
especially being employed in the same way that we use
sugar. There was a considerable variety of fruits,
grapes, mulberries, dates, pomegranates, and various
sorts of nuts. Fruit was often dried and compressed, as
is still the case with dates and figs, such as we have
imported to us from the Middle East.

Milk was often kept in skins like wine. Besides skins
(or as we might say 'leather bottles'), wine, especially
by Gentiles, and by Jews who had adopted Gentile
habits, was decanted into a long narrow-mouthed

cylindrical vessel called an *amphora*, which ended in a
point. The *amphora* was useful for keeping the wine
cool, because the point enabled it to be plunged deep
in sand or earth, or even in an ice-box, but if it was
taken out it had to be put on a stand. Our illustration
shows a two-horse dray with a large wineskin on it, and
men running off the wine into *amphoras* (68). This
picture, however, comes from Italy. Dinner-parties
sometimes had wine-flavoured with myrrh or other
spices (as we should say 'mulled wine'), and the wine
was kept in ice until the company were ready to drink
it. A kind of beer was imported from Media and
Egypt. It is said that fruit and nuts were always eaten
on New Year's eve for luck. Nuts were much used for
flavouring. Fish-curing was extensively practised, and
the way of doing it had been known for many centuries.[1] There was a regular industry on the shores of
the sea of Galilee for salting down fish and packing
them into barrels, and the products were sold not only
in Palestine but as far west as Rome. Pickled roes of
fish were also a known delicacy. Cream was sometimes
served as a separate dish in wooden vessels, with
honey.

Meat-eating in antiquity was so often associated
with sacrifices that one might almost say that every
slaughtering tended to be a sacrifice. Some blood from
the victim had always to be taken to the altar. This is
the reason why St. Paul has to give explicit directions
to the Corinthians about meat sold in butchers' shops,

[1] The pious fishermen of Tiberias are said to have once entered
into a combination not to fish on *any* of the days of the feasts of
Passover and Tabernacles, instead of on some of them. Result, a
serious shortage of fresh fish, never very plentiful inland at the
best of times, so that the public had to fall back on salt fish, or go
without altogether.

not only because for a Jew it had to be *kōsher*, that is to say, drained of blood, but because it would also be unclean for a Christian, whether Jew or Gentile, if it had previously been offered upon the altar to any deity.

The custom of lying down to meals is said to have been introduced into Roman circles after the Punic wars, and to have come from Carthage. If this is so, it must have been a Phoenician and therefore an oriental practice, and it would not therefore be surprising to find it among the Jews. A *triclinium* has been found in one of the Herodian palaces, but it need not have been common. But in Old Testament times it was the fashion for people to sit around a table either on the floor or on stools or chairs, and the custom, in New Testament times, of *reclining* is said to have come round into Palestine from Greece, after the conquests of Alexander. Be this as it may, the meals we read about in the Gospels are often served in the same way as Roman meals, at a *triclinium*, and this is the only way of understanding the episodes in the house of Simon the Pharisee and at the Last Supper, though Christ speaks of '*sitting* at meat'.

As to meals themselves in Palestine. There were usually two formal repasts, one at midday and one in the evening. Breakfast was slight and informal, and there was no break at four or five p.m. It is unwise to take the various articles of food described in the Old Testament as giving a correct picture of what was eaten in the time of Christ. By that period even the food of the masses had become much more varied and extended than in the time, say, of Elijah. In addition to corn, rice was now being grown in wet places, though it had not yet reached the popularity that it did later under the Arabs. Much of the food was vegetarian, but small pieces of mutton were cooked together with rice, wheat or barley groats, just exactly as they are today, and the fat tails of the Palestinian breed of sheep had for long been a favourite luxury. But again many of the modern vegetables were as yet unknown. There were, for instance, no tomatoes, no squashes and no pumpkins, though there was certainly some kind of gourd, probably the still popular water-melon, which may be seen on sale by the hundred outside the Damascus Gate at Jerusalem. There were horse-beans and lentils, and various sorts of cucumbers and vegetable marrows. Onions, leeks and garlic were just as much in request as they are today in all Mediterranean lands.

As to fruits. Bananas were not yet known, and only the citrus among fruits of that species. There seems some doubt whether the apricot and the prickly pear had yet been introduced, but there were dates, figs and pomegranates in plenty, then as now.

By far the most important tree cultivated in Syria was the olive. Olive-yards were in the first century much more numerous than they are today, when after Turkish rule, in which every tree was taxed heavily by a rapacious government, many were cut down or destroyed.[1] They have been described as 'meat and butter to the peasants of Palestine'. One tree in full bearing formed a very large part of the food of a single family. Instead of butter it was the oil of the olive which was used to make a relish for cereals. The rations of a body of workmen employed in Old Testament times are quoted as 20,000 measures of wheat and 20 measures of pure oil. The same kind of rations would have prevailed in the first century. It is worth

[1] It is good to see what extensive planting of olives and vines is going on today both in Jordan and Israel.

noting that the Arabs call old olive trees 'trees of the Romans', meaning that they were planted in the days of the Empire. The wild olive grows naturally, and can be grafted from a cultivated tree. A good tree in full bearing will yield in a season as much as ten to fifteen gallons of oil. In an olive-yard it does not follow that all the trees are the property of the same person, since each may belong to a different owner. The harvest has always been in early October, and no one is supposed to start clearing the trees until a date has been appointed by the local elders. One can see how inconvenient it would be in a yard where there are (say) ten different tree-owners, if picking began on different dates. The work has always been done by women and boys, partly by beating the trees, partly by

46   Olive harvest

47   Olive press as
(An old disused one, exactly like this, was

worked by hand
seen by the author in a cave at Bethany)

shaking them. In the Torah it is expressly forbidden (Deut. 24[20]) to go over the same tree twice. After the first picking, the residue is to be left for the poor, who may come afterwards and glean, on the same principle as gleaning in the cornfields. Gleaning of all kinds was also permitted for resident aliens, who, not being citizens of the country in question, would have no ordinary property-rights. (This explains the case of Ruth in the Old Testament.) The olive harvest (46) was the last crop of the year, and came before the Feast Tabernacles. Some of the olives were preserved in salt water and eaten as food, just as we eat them today at dinner-parties, where they usually come first as appetisers. But the bulk of each year's crop was taken to the olive presses. We have described one of these in the chapter on machinery, but all presses were not so elaborate, but were more primitive. After the crushing of the fruit into a pulp, the latter was divided and some of it was put into bags, either canvas or horsehair, and the oil trodden out by the feet of women and girls, but the rest, indeed most of it, was put into small baskets, and these were then piled on the top of one another, and put in a large wooden press (47) worked by a lever or screw.[1] Sometimes presses were driven by water-power. After the oil was drawn off, it was allowed to stand, until the sediment had settled, and it was then stored in cisterns of stone or cement, or in jars kept in cellars. It should be noted that Gethsemane means

[1] I saw a very old olive press in a cave at Bethany, worked with a screw, and in the Museum at Jerusalem a still older stone one (perhaps 1600 B.C.) for hand use, like a small cistern with two compartments, one shallow and the other deep, with a hole connecting the two. The olives would be crushed in the shallow part by a stone held in the hand, and the oil then drained down through the hole into the deeper compartment.

48 Putting wine into jars

'olive press', and there must therefore have been an olive press in the neighbourhood of the garden, as was often the case.

Although interdicted to Moslems of the Middle East, wine in antiquity was an almost universal drink (48), and the cultivation of the vine is one of the most important occupations in the Mediterranean world. The vine is grown in a number of different ways: sometimes it is trained over a trellis, and sometimes over props about the height of a man; at other times it is made to climb a tree. The most usual method is to let it trail over the ground rather like a vegetable marrow, and then to prop up with forked sticks the branches which are bearing clusters, so as to keep them off the ground. The plants are put far enough apart to allow a plough to pass between the rows. At the end of the fruiting season the vines are pruned as severely as we prune rose-trees, so that each vine is reduced to a trunk and a few branches, and all dead wood is cut out, thus ensuring a vigorous growth next year. Trunks of old vines become thick like those of trees. Vines can be grown on irrigated ground, but usually they are planted on hill-sides, and have to get along without artificial watering. To protect the vine-yards against thieves, foxes and other pests, watchmen are employed, and this means that vineyards usually have some shelter, either a little tower, or a booth rather like a summer-house.

Green grapes can be eaten as early as June, and are sometimes made into a slightly acid and cooling laxa-tive drink. The vintage proper begins in July, but extends as late as September, and is a time of great social merrymaking. The pickers eat vast quantities themselves, and say that for some curious reason it makes no difference to their appetites for ordinary meals. Besides being eaten raw the fruit is spread out to dry into raisins, or crushed in a wine press. After the extraction of the juice the latter is sometimes boiled until it becomes like thick treacle, and is used as a sweet relish, but the ordinary procedure is to put it into vats to ferment. The above gives a general idea of the vine-culture and vintage as they existed in the first century.

The main fig-harvest, in September, like that of the olives and the vintage, was a time of considerable social activity, and parties of people would gather and picnic out of doors for the occasion.[1] There is a curious tradi-

[1] I myself once sat under a fig-tree in the valley of the Kidron with an old Arab, and watched his son and grandson climbing about the trees harvesting the figs. The fig-tree in Jewish folk-lore was sometimes identified with the biblical Tree of Knowledge.

tion, which may indeed be a true one, that the circumstances under which Nathanael first saw Christ were connected with the fig-harvest. Preachers have often said that it was probably when Nathanael was at prayer under a fig-tree that Jesus saw him, but the other story, being less edifying, may contain the correct account of the episode, for it says that Nathanael was at the time in the company of some young women of none too steady character, and was recalled to more sober things by the piercing glance of the Rabbi as he passed by the little group.

At the time of Elijah there were no domestic fowls in Palestine, but by the time of Christ, keeping chickens had become usual, geese were already known, and ducks were beginning to become popular. Turkeys, being creatures of the New World, were not known or bred until after the discovery of the Americas, but pheasants were probably known, and a variety of other edible birds, such as quails, pigeons and partridges. Quails at times may be counted in thousands, and partridges are fairly common all over the country.

Details about corn-growing are given in the chapter on country life.

One curious and sinister fact about market-gardening may be mentioned in conclusion. Strabo reports that Jewish speculators deliberately *limited* the size of the date-palm plantations which they controlled, in order to keep up the price of dates.[1]

A few words should be added as to the use of milk.

[1] Date-palms occur in the Jordan valley; they need a damper, hotter climate than the Judaean uplands. Although some dates were on sale in September, the date harvest seems to come later, and the fine dates I saw growing at the southern end of the Sea of Galilee, just where the Jordan emerges from it, were not ripe even on 23rd September.

It would be interesting to know who first discovered the value of animal as distinct from human milk as a means of nourishment. So far as the first century goes, we can record that camel's milk at that date was known and used as far west as Rome, and one part of it to three parts of water was considered a good drink. Virgil held that cow's milk should be reserved for the calves, and that goat's and ewe's milk was to be preferred for human beings. In this respect modern dietitians would probably agree with him. It is certain that some Roman emperors controlled the price of milk. Asses' milk was used as a cosmetic by Roman ladies, who employed it daily to keep away wrinkles. Poppaea, the wife of Nero, had a stud of 3000 she-asses to provide her with a daily milk bath.

Chapter IV

COUNTRY LIFE

AGRICULTURE has been for many hundreds of years
the principal occupation of the peoples of the
Mediterranean world and the Middle East.
Although in the period we are considering the cities
were growing, and eating up the country around them
just as they are doing in England today, by far the
largest area of the land was still under cultivation.
Everybody knows how in the Gospels there are many
illustrations in Christ's teaching drawn from the life of
the countryside. What is not so generally known is the
extent to which the long experience of cultivating the
soil was stored up and transmitted. The tradition of
farming in an organised manner in the Middle East as
well as in Egypt, goes back for thousands of years, so
that what we find going on in the first century A.D.
only comes at the end of a very long line of activity.
There seems, however, one marked difference between
the Mediterranean countries and Palestine, namely
that in the former the experience came to be written
down. Very likely something of this sort happened in
Egypt,[1] though our knowledge of the secular literature
of that country is still somewhat patchy, but we do
know that upwards of fifty Greek authors contributed
to the development of what we may call agricultural
science. Unhappily not a single writing by any one of
these has survived. It is possible that a curious volume
called the Geoponica, divided into twenty books,

[1] It has been alleged that maxims regarding agriculture have
been found among some tablet-collections in the libraries of
ancient Mesopotamia.

which was compiled somewhere about 800 years after Christ at the request of one of the Byzantine emperors, contains extracts from these lost books; but of course we cannot be sure.

On the other hand, the writings of the Romans on the subject have by no means all disappeared. We still possess, first the poems of Virgil known as the Georgics, and then four prose writings on the business of country life, two of them at least by practical men. First we have 162 chapters from Cato the elder, an extraordinary medley, consisting as it would seem of notebook jottings made on his estate, but containing valuable hints for estate management, including the farm, the olive garden, and the vineyard. These are put together without any sort of method, and are mixed up with medical prescriptions, charms for mending broken limbs, cookery recipes and prayers—making, in fact, the sort of household notebook that some of our great-great-grandmothers used to compile in manuscript in parts of England like rural Sussex. The second volume consists of the three books by Varro, a successful soldier, farmer and politician, who was also the best scholar of his age. Both these works belong to the century before Christ. The third work, by a man called Columella, in thirteen books, seems to have been written down about ten years after the Crucifixion. It is much more minute in detail than the others, but the author is less familiar with his subject, and is a theorist rather than a practical man. Besides the foregoing, an entire book in Pliny's Natural History is given up to matters connected with the work of the countryside. We can see then that in the countries into which the Christian movement spread there was a very highly organised system of farming.

It is probable that in Palestine until the British

introduction of mechanised farming in the Republic of
Israel the ways of the country people had altered very
little in the cultivation of the soil between the first
century and the nineteenth. The same simple tools
would have been in use, and the same methods
adopted in sowing, reaping and harvesting. It is fairly
easy to get a picture of these, so we will give here some
specimens which will show what farming looked like in

49 Ploughing in Palestine with primitive wooden plough

the days when Christ walked about the countryside of
Palestine (49–52). The ploughing is done, as will be
seen, with a very simple plough, drawn either by an ox
or two oxen (sometimes by an ox and an ass yoked
together) (49). The sowing is by hand, and the grain
is scattered in just the way that is described in the
famous parable of the sower. The reaping also is done
by hand with a primitive kind of sickle, sometimes of
flints set in a wooden frame, though sometimes of iron
(it is worth remembering that steel in the Mediterranean was just being invented and brought into use
by the Romans in the first century A.D.). The threshing

and winnowing take place on a special threshing-floor
with a hard bottom.

The procedure in growing a cereal crop in Palestine
ran somewhat as follows. The year divided itself into
two fairly clear portions. From mid-October to mid-
April came ploughing, sowing, harrowing and weed-
ing. From mid-April onwards came reaping, carrying,
threshing and storing. If there was a gap between the
end of the latter and the beginning of ploughing, it was
amply filled up with the details of the vintage. Two
methods of sowing were in practice. Either the seed
was scattered on unprepared land and then ploughed
in (this seems to be implied in the parable of the
sower, since 'weeds' and 'stony ground' can hardly
mean soil which has been prepared and dug over), or
else the ground was first ploughed and then the seed
scattered, and covered up either by rough harrowing
or cross-ploughing. In Egypt the former plan was
adopted, since the sowing took place after the Nile had
left the soil moist, and all that was needed afterwards
was to cover it up either by dragging bushes over it or
driving domestic animals backward and forward so as
to cut up the surface and also dung it. But this all
seems very crude and primitive, and one imagines that
only the poorest peasants went on doing it after ox-
drawn ploughs had come into use. The time of sowing
was one of anxiety because of the usual uncertainty of
the weather. It is said that the first to be sown were the
pulse crops, beans and lentils, then the barley a fortnight later, and then after another month the wheat.
Sowing was done mostly with a basket, but careful
farmers, it is said, took trouble to put the seed into the
furrows in proper rows. Grain for the spring or early
summer was sown during the period corresponding to
our month of February. The young crops were ex-

posed to many dangers: first, the east winds of March and April, then hailstorms, various kinds of weeds, mischievous birds, insect pests and fungus. Perhaps the worst enemy was the locust. Harvest time always varies from district to district even in our own temperate climate, and in a land like Palestine with very varied altitudes and temperatures it varied a good deal

50   Reaping in Palestine

more. It is said that on the average it began with the barley, and this was ready near Jericho about the middle of April, but on the coastal plains ten days later, and in some of the higher areas as much as a month later. Then a fortnight after this came the wheat. The harvesting of the two corn crops lasted about seven weeks, and the cutting was done with sickles (50), as described above. Although the reaping was mostly done by the farmer and his family, they

51   Threshing and

usually had to hire extra labour, and gangs of harvesters went around from district to district according as
the grain ripened. The usual provision for feeding such
labourers in the field had to be made, and we read of
parched corn, and of bread dipped in vinegar. But by

winnowing (Palestinian)

this we must not understand the sort of vinegar we use, but either a sour, over-fermented wine, or over-fermented palm-juice. These were commonly used with food as a relish, and the food was dipped in them. The diluted liquid was used as a drink by the poorer classes and by soldiers, both among Jews and Greeks, and this accounts for the guard at the foot of the Cross having some handy, which could be mixed with a drug and given to persons undergoing execution. This diluted drink was called *posca*, and one general ordered his troops, who were Ethiopians, not to drink anything else. A writer on veterinary surgery says that *posca* and oil are good for healing wounds, and we know that this combination was used by the good Samaritan in the story, to dress the wounds of the man who had been beaten up by brigands.

Palestinian harvesters do not seem to have set much value upon the straw, as they wasted a good deal of it. Some crops were plucked up by the roots, and then threshed as they were. The one essential in threshing was to have a good, hard, smooth threshing-floor,[1] and this would be out of doors, so that the wind could carry away much of the refuse. Bean crops were often beaten out with sticks or flails, but in the case of a large corn crop, the sheaves would be spread and then cattle driven backwards and forwards over them, while at intervals the sheaves would be lifted up and turned over with a fork (51). The more thorough and elaborate way of threshing was to use a machine, which was drawn by an ox or oxen yoked to a pole. The winnowing was done by hand, and very often at night, when there was more wind. First the grain was thrown into the air, generally by a large fan or shovel. After that it was sieved. Finally it was collected into large heaps (52) ready for carting to the barn. To prevent anyone from purloining any of the grain, the owner might sleep beside it after it had been winnowed. As in the

[1] Many of these threshing-floors can be seen from the air as one flies over Palestine.

case of our own neolithic ancestors the storage often took place in pits underground, the openings to which were very carefully covered up. There were the usual festivities at the time of harvest, and these were gradually associated with religion. So much for Palestine.

52   Sifting grain

In Italy, on the other hand, it is clear that a well-ordered farm was rather like the same sort of institution in England before the introduction of machinery. Varro gives a very good description of a large farm-house, and it seems to have been very much like the Roman villas described in *Everyday Life in Roman Britain*, to which the reader is thus referred.

Piecing things together from the writers we have mentioned above, we find that rural economy is divided under two separate heads, first, the art of tilling the soil, and second, the management of stock.

53 Women grinding with hand-mill

Varro goes into great detail over the different kinds of soil, its colour, its consistency, whether crumbling or tenacious, and its composition, whether clayey, sandy, chalky, gravelly or stony; and he also discusses its natural vegetation, i.e. whether it grows grass or weeds more easily. He seems to have known (and this is rather surprising) the difference between acid and alkaline soils, just as a modern botanist does, and he also describes in great detail methods of draining land, either by open ditches or by underground land drains.

As to labour, there were three classes, the free labourers who were usually hired in gangs, slaves who were not under restraint, and slaves who worked in chains under the control of a gaoler. Naturally there was specialisation in the various crafts, so that (as with us) there were what we call skilled and unskilled labourers. The skilled ones were the vine dressers and pruners, the ox-drivers and ploughmen, and the stablemen. The unskilled were those who did digging and spreading manure. Pliny describes a plough invented not long before his time which had two small wheels. Great emphasis is laid upon the number of

times that land should be ploughed, varying from two
to nine. The plough was usually drawn by oxen,
though sometimes by asses or mules. (In the case of the
Jews, there was actually a prohibition, not regularly
observed, against ploughing with an ox and ass together.) Although with a one-handed plough the
ploughman's other hand was free to use the ox goad,
it was not used very much, as it was found that if a
young steer was pricked by it, he was apt to become
restive and unmanageable. The usual thing seems to
have been to stroke the back with the rod of the goad
just as one used to see it being done fifty years ago in
Sussex. The animals were allowed to rest at the end of
each furrow, but not to stop in the middle of it. When
unharnessed, before being tied up in the stall they were
carefully rubbed down, allowed to cool, had their
mouths washed out with wine, and were then given
a drink of water. The normal length of a furrow was
supposed to be 120 feet. Anything longer was considered too much strain for the oxen. As with us, there
was great competition over ploughing straight and
uniform furrows.

The writers above-mentioned give very careful
instructions about the different sorts of manure, including bird guano, with which they are quite familiar,
and also instructions for the making of compost heaps,
to which are to be added ashes, road scrapings, and
sweepings from the house, as well as leaves, hedge clip-
pings and straw. They know well the system of
manuring by penning and feeding sheep upon a limited
space of ground, the quantities of dung to be used for
spreading on different kinds of land, and also the use of
marl, containing a large quantity of phosphate of lime.

Sowing was mostly by hand, and the grain was
sometimes raked in, and sometimes ploughed in. The

seed seems to have been cast out of a three-peck basket, and Pliny mentions that the sower had to drill himself so that his hand kept time with his stride, in order that he might scatter the seed with proper uniformity. The practice of selecting seeds according to size and quality, and grading them, was in use, and, what is still more remarkable is that these Roman scientific agriculturalists had already discovered the value of soaking the grain in chemical mixtures to protect it from being eaten by pests, especially a small beetle, probably a weevil. After the sowing came the harrowing, which was often done at two different periods. In addition to this, when the land was weedy, a grubber, or *irpex*, a strong plank set with iron spikes, was dragged over the ground, and sometimes wicker hurdles fitted with teeth were used for this purpose.

There does not seem to have been any kind of spraying at this period, and since there was always a good deal of trouble from various kinds of root pests, caterpillars, spiders and mice, the chance of the farmer's crop failing was still considerable. Small rodents could be trapped, and birds snared, but the enemy dreaded above all others, whether in the vineyard or the cornfield, was a sort of blight called *robigo*, and this was regarded as the work of a malignant sacred being, who had to be propitiated by an annual festival called the Robigalia. This kind of thing reminds us remarkably of India.

In Palestine there was the added terror of locusts, and, as we know, it is only now that government entomologists[1] have begun to try to tackle this serious

[1] I had an interesting talk with the Jordan Government entomologist at Amman, who showed me examples of the old and new ways of dealing with a horde of locusts, and described how the Arab Legion had recently tried bombarding a flight of these pests.

problem in the parts of the world where it occurs, whether by sprinkling insecticide on the crawling locusts from aircraft such as helicopters, or by exploding small shells among the clouds of insects as they fly. The ancients knew none of these devices, and there was little that they could do except to light large fires, and to hope that the locusts, being suffocated by the smoke, would fall down into the flames.

The corn was reaped as soon as it had become uniformly yellow, without waiting for it to be dead ripe, so as to avoid the loss that would be caused by shaking, and to forestall the ravages of birds and other creatures. Indeed there was a saying that it was better to reap two days too soon than two days too late.

Threshing was done both in Syria and throughout the Mediterranean on a threshing-floor. This was of a circular form, slightly raised in the centre so as to let moisture drain off. The surface was sometimes of beaten earth compressed by rollers or pounded with rammers, or better still it was paved with hard stones or pieces of potsherd. On this surace the ears of corn were spread out and sometimes beaten with flails, especially when it was only the cut-off ears that had been brought in, but when the ears were brought in on a stalk the sheaves were spread out and trodden either by the feet of men or, more usually, of animals, especially oxen, which were driven backwards and forwards, yoked to some kind of threshing-machine. This latter would seem to have been of two sorts, either a board made rough underneath by having pieces of iron or stone attached to it, or what was called a Punic (that is to say African or Phoenician) *plostellum*, which was a set of toothed rollers with a platform of planks on the top of them, on which stood a man who guided the ox team (51). Close by the threshing-floor there

was always a large shed or barn, and here the crop,
when carried wet, was dried before being threshed.
There were various ways of storing the grain. In many
places the corn was put into pits, sunk in soil which was
found to be perfectly dry, and then lined with chaff,
and sealed up. Varro says that wheat in the ear can be
preserved in such pits without harm for as much as
fifty years, and millet for a hundred. But modern

54   Mule-driven corn-mill

scientific experiments have shown that such seeds very
rarely retain their vitality for as much as forty. There
were various devices for keeping away vermin. The
store-houses were often built of brick, with very thick
walls and no window, only a hole in the roof. The
walls of such granaries were sometimes plastered inside
with a kind of stucco mixed with a chemical which was
believed to be a protection against pests. Others
sprinkled the corn with preservatives. We do not know
what they were, but it is clear that they could not have
been injurious to human beings, or that if they were,
the ancients did not detect it. As a matter of fact, some
farmers considered the use of lime in granaries under

any form to be injurious, and of course if the corn were sprinkled with a fluid preservative immediately before being housed, without being allowed to dry thoroughly afterwards, it must certainly have gone mouldy.[1]

We learn from our authors that there were a surprisingly large number of varieties of seed corn, and they were favoured by farmers according to their characteristics, one sort having very heavy weight and a shiny surface, another being particularly white, but rather light in weight, so that more had to be grown to get a big crop. In the same way the millers graded their flour, generally into four sorts, finest double dressed, best first flour, seconds, and bran. We don't hear anything about the extraction-rate per cent, but it is quite likely that something was known about it. A sort of porridge was known, and also how to make starch, both for medicine and for use in the kitchen. Oats were not grown with any advantage in the Mediterranean, because the climate was too warm, but Pliny says that oatmeal porridge was a national dish among the German tribes, and he also says that oatmeal soaked in vinegar is a good remedy for spots on the skin.

Among the leguminous crops we find reference to the bean, which was sometimes ground into meal and baked into cakes, and even made into porridge for temple offerings. There were all kinds of fodder crops, not least that which we know as lucerne, which is so far from being a modern discovery that it was known in Persia before the battle of Marathon. It was regarded as the best fattener for lean cattle, and so nourishing, and capable of being cut repeatedly during the same season, that it was calculated that a single

[1] We have seen an illustration of an ancient form of *silo*, a device which was apparently known to the Carthaginians.

juger of lucerne would supply enough food for three horses for a whole year. Hay was also made. The knowledge of rotation of crops was already available, and was applied to the laying down of meadow pastures as well as to arable land. When an old meadow grew mossy it was treated with a top dressing of ashes, just as today we use lawn sand.

55   Roman baker's oven

The second part of scientific agriculture divided itself into the management of sheep, goats, swine, cattle and horses on the one hand, and that of poultry, game, fish, bees, and a number of small animals and birds on the other.

The farmers of the first century knew perfectly well how to produce new breeds of sheep by crossing, and they did this not only for mutton, but also to obtain

certain tints of wool. Both Varro and Columella detail
the points of good animals, whether sheep, goats, pigs,
cows or horses, and, in regard to the latter, the method
of telling the age of a horse up to seven years old. In
every case except that of goats a warranty of a good
and healthy condition was required by law of the
seller, but it is curious that goats when sold were never
warranted in good health, because they were believed
to be always more or less labouring under fever.
Castration was used in the case of sheep, cattle and
horses. Stallions were used for racing and in war, but
geldings for road work, as they were naturally more
safe and tractable.

There were two sorts of asses, the common domestic
donkey, and the wild ass or onager, which was common in Lycaonia and Phrygia, countries visited in one
of St. Paul's missionary journeys. These latter were
easily tamed and very good for crossing. We have no
record of the price of various breeds of horse, but the
best breed of ass appears to have fetched as much as
£500 on the market, and a team of four, upwards of
£3000; but, of course, the ordinary farmer could not
afford blood stock of this kind, and had to be content
with more ordinary breeds. The animals were very
hardy, did not get ill, were easy to feed, and capable
of putting in much hard work. There were two sorts of
mules, *hinni*, which were the offspring of a stallion and
a she-ass, and *muli*, the progeny of a male ass and a
mare. Mules were used chiefly for drawing travelling
carriages, but also as pack-animals and for ploughing.

Cheese-making usually began in May, and the
method was much the same as now practised. Curiously enough, goat's cheese was regarded as the most
digestible, but far less nourishing than that made from
cow's milk. It is odd that butter, though mentioned by

Varro, does not seem to have been common as an article of food.

Poultry-farming was a most lucrative occupation, and was widely practised under the early Empire, and it included not only domestic fowls, but also guinea-fowls from North Africa, pheasants and peacocks from the Middle East, and geese and ducks; and the practice of shutting up birds to fatten was already in vogue. Smaller birds such as quails, ortolans, doves, thrushes and blackbirds were also kept in aviaries for food, and in some places there were enclosures for hares and rabbits, as well as for various species of deer. Bee-keeping was evidently very popular as may be judged from the space which Virgil devotes to it, and by the minute instructions to be found in the agricultural writers. The honey, as we have seen, was important for sweetening purposes, in the absence of cane or beet sugar. The methods of bee-keeping, even in small details, differ very little from those of the present day, though our entomology is more advanced. Hives were of various material, mostly brick, but sometimes of wood, wicker-work or bark, and even earthenware, though the latter was not favoured because it was easily affected by changes of temperature. Cork bee-hives were accounted the best. The strange example of a bronze bee-hive has been found near Pompeii, but we think it must have been open to the same objection as an earthenware one, as it must have been rather too cold or too hot for the bees. In the swarming season the device of making the swarms settle by tinkling sounds was already in use, and sometimes the bees were induced to alight by having dust thrown over them, or by rubbing the branch of a tree with some sweet-smelling or sweet-tasting substance. In the Mediterranean climate it was possible to harvest the

honey three times in the year. Whatever may have
been the practice in Palestine, elsewhere such curious
fare as snails and dormice were eaten, and the snails,
which were of special varieties, were sometimes preserved in an enclosure called a *coclearium*, and were
even fattened by being shut up in a jar with special
food, a mixture of wine-must and flour! Dormice of a
special variety (not our native English ones) were a
great luxury, and at one time their use was even forbidden by law. They too were kept in a special enclosure, planted with acorn-bearing trees for their
food, and supplied with holes for their nests, and
they were fattened up in jars of a special pattern,
where they were fed upon chestnuts, walnuts and
acorns.

Gardens. We ought to try to get the position clear
about these. The gardens or *pardes* (Gk. *paradeisos*,
and so 'paradise') of the Mesopotamian grandees were
not gardens in our sense of the word; they were parks
for the preservation of game for hunting purposes. So
the garden of Eden was really a park. The ancient
Greeks had kitchen gardens and orchards, and also
herb gardens, but they do not seem to have cultivated
flowers as we do. They grew them for the table, and
planted them side by side with the vegetables. Sacred
groves had sweet-smelling trees and shrubs, apparently
for the benefit of the gods, who perhaps liked to walk
in them in the cool of the day; but in Athens flowers
were grown for making garlands, and so for profit, and
not because they looked nice out of doors. Still people
evidently liked having them in their houses, and there
was a considerable trade in such things as roses and
violets: but the range of flowers appears to have been
small. The idea of pleasure gardens proper seems to
have come from the East, although today the *pardes* in

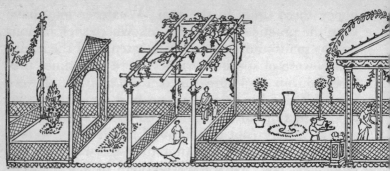

56 Roman

Asia Minor means any enclosure for growing things. In Esther, Ahasuerus entertains his guests in his garden attached to his palace. The Romans adapted some of these Eastern ideas, and laid out formal pleasure gardens to their houses, with striking results (56). Thus, in front of the portico of the residence there would often be a *xystus*[1] or formal garden, divided into shapes by tiny box edging just as in some of our old English gardens. Flower-beds were sometimes arranged so as to form terraces with sloping sides covered with creepers—these were doubtless imitated from the hanging gardens of Babylon, of which we hear so much. Then there were lines and avenues of large trees of all sorts, and clipped hedges of evergreens. It was the Romans who developed the practice of topiary gardening—i.e. of cutting shrubs into the shape of birds, animals, etc. It is indeed surprising to learn how much we today owe to the Romans in the layout of the gardens of many of our famous country houses. The

---

[1] Whether the *xystus* in old Jerusalem was a sort of Herodian public park, or whether in addition it was used for sports, does not seem clear; but it is probable that it was both.

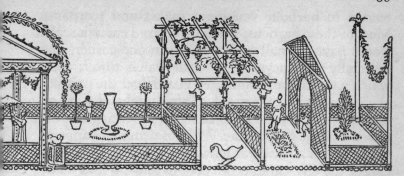

garden

ideas came in from Italy at the time of the Renaissance.[1]

In New Testament times we have to imagine that in
the various provinces into which the Christian movement came there were gardens of the Roman type
belonging to well-to-do citizens who had adopted the
fashionable style of gardening. In Palestine itself, however, we should have encountered, in the hill-country
of Judaea, and around and in Jerusalem, gardens of
rather a different sort. These were conditioned by the
nature of the ground, and were enclosures made by
dry-walling, partly to keep the soil from washing away
in heavy rains—this is called terrace-cultivation, and
is a very ancient practice in all mountainous countries
—partly to prevent trespassing by thieves or destruc-
tive animals. Each stone dyke made for the latter
purpose would have a hedge of thorns, possibly prickly
pear (this is not certain), planted on the top of it, and
this was a good protection against intruders, but

[1] It is interesting to note that the city-dwellers of the Roman
Empire in the first century, though often poor, made a colourful
display with window boxes as people often do in England.

tended to harbour venomous snakes and scorpions.
Most of these gardens, when on a large enough scale,
would have a small hut or booth in one corner, and
especially in vineyards, a small watch tower, from
which a watchman could keep guard over the produce
of the garden or vineyard. There might also be an
olive press or a wine press in it, for squeezing out the
olive oil or the grape wine. At Jerusalem there appears
to have been a royal garden in the valley on the south-
east of the city close to the pool of Siloam, and many
rich citizens would also have extensive pleasure gardens. A rose-garden is referred to in Isaiah 35. These
hillside gardens were supplied with water from springs
or reservoirs, and the water was pumped up the hill-
sides by primitive devices. Other gardens were in more
level country, outside the city. Josephus mentions one
abounding in rivulets of water, which used to be
visited by Solomon, and is, I believe, still shown on the
site of a modern pleasure resort not far from Jerusalem.
Round Joppa there were deep wells, from which the
water was drawn by mules winding up buckets fastened to a revolving wheel. The water thus secured was
stored in large tanks and let out at intervals through
sluices into channels through the gardens.

Country life was brightened by country sports such
as hawking and hunting, and by fairs held at the time
of great festivals, very much the same as those with
which we are familiar, with stalls where useful articles
could be purchased, but also with plenty of side-
shows, such as marionettes, acrobats, rope-walkers,
jugglers and fortune-tellers.

Chapter V

ROADS AND TRAVEL

THE conditions of travel in New Testament times were practically the same as those which prevailed in Europe up to the beginning of the nineteenth century. Until railways were made, mechanically drawn or propelled vehicles invented, and air routes laid out, the only ways of getting about the world were on foot or in a vehicle which was either carried, pushed or pulled by human beings, or in a vehicle with wheels which was drawn by animals—unless you rode on the animals. In some ways the position was actually worse in the year 1800, because under the Romans a number of fine and well-metalled roads were constructed and maintained throughout the Empire, whereas at the beginning of the nineteenth century macadam roads and the steam roller had not come in, and the existing thoroughfares were often very badly kept in repair. One has only to read the stories of road travel by coach and horse in the eighteenth century, to realise how bad the roads were, full of pot-holes, badly drained and often neglected. Side roads hardly existed, and in any case rarely had any bottom to them.

Now the Romans had a very definite method of constructing their roads, and this was so good that some of the thoroughfares they laid down still have the same metalling today. Thus, there is a piece of one still to be seen on the top of the Pennines today near the Lancashire border, and another in the Forest of Dean, in Gloucestershire. (See *Everyday Life in Roman Britain*.)

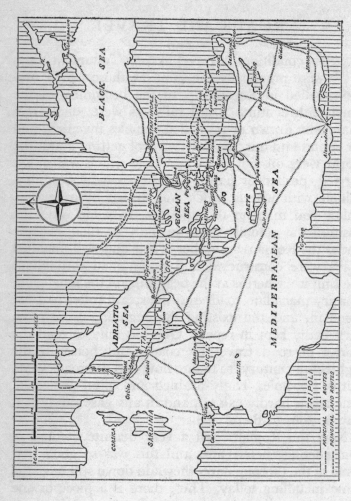

57   Map to illustrate travel in the Mediterranean world of the first century A.D.

The expense of constructing these main trunk roads must have been enormous, but they were built with great solidity, and carefully maintained, made indeed, as has been said, 'to last for ever', so that to this very day they survive entire and level in some parts of Europe. In the absence of railways or air service, it must be obvious that these roads were of vital importance to rapid communication and unity of government. I saw one in Palestine for moving troops from Caesarea to Tiberias and back, which ran straight across the plain of Jezreel, and through the Megiddo gap.

The roads were usually raised some height above the ground, and went in as straight a line as possible over hill and vale. They were made of three separate layers of materials. The lowest, called the *staumen*, was of stones mixed with cement—concrete in fact. On the top of this was laid what was called *rudera*, or as we should say rough core, consisting of gravel, rubble, rough stone or broken pottery. The top structure was not as in our case granite macadam, but what in the north of England we know as 'sets', that is to say large stones accurately fitted together. In the neighbourhood of cities there were on each side raised side-walks protected by kerb-stones, and the road itself had a camber, so that water would drain off into the gutters. In some cases the streets were paved with large pieces of lava, in fact with 'crazy paving'. In what we should call built-up areas it was necessary to afford foot passengers a dry crossing, since in the narrower streets there was often less camber, and also people tended to throw waste water from their houses into the streets, so that they were frequently full of muddy pools. Stepping stones were therefore placed between the two side walks at convenient intervals, with just enough room for the wheels of wheeled traffic to run freely between them. Market places were not paved like the streets, but often covered with large slabs of marble.

Records show that manuscript-drawn maps existed for the use of travellers and that they were copied and obtainable in shops. There were also in existence a certain number of guide-books for the use of tourists. One of the largest of these was composed by a man called Pausanias for people travelling in Greece. It is in effect a sort of Baedeker or Murray's *Guide to Tourists*, and as translated by Sir James Frazer it takes up two considerable volumes. No doubt similar works were in existence for travellers in other interesting areas. An important official under Augustus had a large map made of the new Empire, and a detailed gazetteer was also compiled by this orders. Nero sent a surveying expedition of army officers as far as the Upper Nile.

The object of the Roman road system, as has been said, was to connect all individual districts and provinces as closely as possible with the Imperial capital, but to keep them as much as possible separated from one another. This not only prevented combination for revolt against the Government, but also promoted the spread of what we may call Roman Kultur. The road system made it possible for easy trade with the capital, so that new inventions in the way of furniture, and new fashions in clothing, could spread easily from Rome into the provinces. It also made for centralisation in finance and for unity of administration. In the same way a new idea or a new movement could spread more easily to Rome than to a neighbouring province, but once it reached Rome and obtained a foothold there, it was easy for it to extend into a number of different provinces.

Seasonal conditions affected routes of communication in that age rather more than they do today. It is true that we hear of Atlantic liners being deflected out of their course by the danger of running into icebergs, and of roads and railways in the north of Britain being occasionally blocked by snow-drifts, but on the whole our mechanical transport is rather less affected by the weather than the transport of ancient times. We know that big liners can cross the Atlantic in very heavy seas, but it is said that sea-travel in the Mediterranean was only regarded as perfectly safe between 26th May and the 14th September, while the sea was considered to be closed to traffic entirely from the 10th November to the 10th March. There were two uncertain periods—from the 10th March to the 26th May, and from the 15th September to the 10th November, when it was unusual to send out fleets of warships, though privately owned merchant ships might take the risk, and one Roman emperor was so anxious about the corn supply to Italy during the winter that he guaranteed a higher rate of profit to the merchants, and agreed to insure their vessels against loss by storm, but it is uncertain whether even in this case merchant ships would have agreed to risk the voyage from Alexandria to Rome, and probably any journey that was taken would be a shorter one, from North Africa or from Sardinia. Armies were occasionally, in times of urgency, taken across the sea in winter. It was done twice about fifty years before the birth of Christ, once by Julius Caesar and once by Pompey. Occasionally special voyages were also made by ambassadors, or by people who had urgent business at the capital. Thus, Philo and four other Jews sailed from Alexandria in the winter of A.D. 38–39, and Philo mentions that they sailed in the middle of the winter, and had a bad voyage, but it is pretty certain that as far as they could they sailed round the coast. From Alexandria this would naturally take a long time, because unless you took the summer route straight from Alexandria to the Straits of Messina, and then up the Italian coast to Puteoli and Ostia, you would have to cut across the Mediterranean to Rhodes, then across the Aegean round the southern tip of Greece and finally across the Ionian Sea to the Straits of Messina, and neither of these routes in winter could be regarded as anything but risky. The only other alternative would be travel round the coast from Alexandria to Philippi, hugging the coastline all the way, then go overland to Dyrrachium or Aulona, and then to take the short cross-channel route to Brundisium, and finish the journey by road from there. There would also be a slightly less safe route in which you coasted round as far as Rhodes, and then struck south-west as far as Salmone in Crete, and so round the southern coast of that island till it was possible to turn north-west, and cut up the coast of Achaia until you could get across the Ionian Sea to south Italy. It will be remembered that when Paul went this way, a northerly gale drove the ship out of her course, and wrecked her on the island of Malta.

The same difficulty had to be faced in travelling by road. Ordinary persons, in crossing mountainous districts, as for example parts of Asia Minor, avoided travelling by winter and waited until the spring. Thus the important city of Caesarea in Cappadocia was cut off from Athens completely in a severe winter, and so also from Rome, and it appears that many roads were blocked even in a mild winter, so it must have been floods as well as snow which caused the suspension of traffic. No doubt the Romans were doing their best to remedy this by building their principal roads as much as possible on causeways, but the fact that even in the fourth century A.D. the main road from Caesarea in Cappadocia was still impracticable in winter would suggest that they cannot have been entirely successful.

Another point to be borne in mind is that if you have to depend on sailing ships, you cannot be sure that the wind which conveys you rapidly in one direction will be equally favourable on your return journey. For example, it was possible in summer to travel very quickly from Alexandria to Ostia, but the wind would be dead against you on the return journey, so that you had to go back by a different line of route. There were four main recognised ways of getting from Palestine to Rome: (1) By sea from Sidon to Puteoli; (2) by sea to Corinth, crossing the Aegean from Miletus; (3) overland to Ephesus, then by sea to Corinth (in both the latter cases the journey from Corinth would be continued from the western harbour to Brundisium); (4) by land to Troas and then across into Macedonia, where the land journey was possible by a good Roman road, the Via Ignatia to Dyrrachium or Aulona, and then across the Channel to Brundisium. It is said that the first of these four was the favourite route, and that there was a splendid and regular service of passenger ships between Alexandria and Puteoli. This was the main route for the conveyance of corn from Egypt to Rome. Italian wheat, unless subsidised, did not pay as a crop in competition with Egyptian wheat, and in any case there was not enough of it, and the Emperor knew that his life depended upon keeping up the supply. If he didn't, his army would mutiny and the civilian population would riot. This corn trade was therefore a State business and was carried on in State ships, and because of its vital character the province of Egypt was kept very closely under direct Imperial administration, and the whole supply of corn available for exportation was earmarked for the central government, and was only allowed to be diverted to any other centre of population by special permission of the Emperor in times of famine. There was no doubt a considerable amount of private trade between Puteoli and Egypt, but the corn trade was a government monopoly and completely state-controlled. The eastern journey was easier at some seasons than others, best of all in midsummer when there was a west wind, but the pilots or shipmasters were very skilful in steering their vessels so as to make harbour with accuracy. One of the best times for getting back to Egypt and Palestine was either for forty days from the 20th July, or thirty days from the 1st August, when there was a north-westerly stream of air known as the Etesian winds.[1]

The bulk of the trade with Italy at the time of Christ seems to have gone into the port of Puteoli, and it was only after the time of Claudius that the Portus Augusti harbour at Ostia was developed, until by the time of Trajan it had come to supersede Puteoli as the headquarters of commerce with the east, but even in New Testament times it is said that most of the heaviest goods went straight through to Ostia. Ephesus was the great port for dealing with the produce of Asia, though Smyrna and Miletus competed with it for the trade. Ephesus was in fact regarded as the capital of the province of Asia, and it was the custom for the Roman

---

[1] I think our aircraft on my return journey must have had to fly in the face of these Etesian winds, because I remember the captain circulating his report somewhere near Crete, and saying that we were losing time because we were flying against a head wind.

governors of Asia to land and enter upon their duties there first. Nearly all heavy merchandise travelled between Rome and the Aegean round the southern tip of Greece, because before the Corinth canal was made everything had to be transported by land and across the isthmus of Corinth, and this, of course, added to the cost of carriage. It is said that Nero had an idea for a ship-canal through the isthmus, but for some reason the scheme was abandoned.

It is not at all easy to get any accurate figures as to the time which these various journeys took, since the ships were generally merchantmen which were liable to vary their course and to put in at harbours on the way, where they might be kept waiting to unload or to take in cargo. We have some knowledge of the time taken by Imperial despatches, but since there was, as we shall see, no regular postal service for private persons, letter-carriers travelling for the latter were often liable to be delayed and interrupted, so that there is a great difference between the time taken by individual letters over the same route. One sent to Cicero in Rome from Syria took a hundred days, and another fifty, and the latter seems to have been the usual time taken over the same route by Imperial despatches. About a hundred years after the time of St. Paul a business letter written in Italy arrived in Tyre 107 days later by private transport, even though sent in the most favourable season.

As to overland routes. These naturally had to be used at the time when the seas were not open, and even then short cross-channel passages could not entirely be avoided. Thus the Imperial service of despatches to the eastern provinces, including Syria, went round by Macedonia and Thrace, a very long journey, as will be seen from the map, unless a crossing was possible from

Brundisium to Dyrrachium, and then there would be the little crossings of the Hellespont or the Bosphorus. Of course, for many provinces, even when the sea was open, the overland route would be shorter. So it was worth while to keep it in an efficient condition all the year round, and the Imperial couriers seem on the whole to have preferred it, and unless the weather was too bad, messengers between Rome, Syria and Egypt, as well as messengers to the province of Asia, made the two crossings at Brundisium, and at Neapolis, the port of Philippi. Sir William Ramsay gives the following figures of times and distances:

Rome to Brundisium . . . 360 miles
Brundisium to Dyrrachium . . . 2 days
Dyrrachium to Neapolis . . . 381 miles
Neapolis to Troas . . . about 3 days
Troas to Alexandria via Antioch and Caesarea . . . about 1670 miles.

(This list is abridged)

Imperial couriers are said to have taken 63 days by the northern route to travel from Rome to Alexandria, and 54 days to travel from Rome to Caesarea.

The *cursus publicus* or courier service seems to have been first definitely organised by Augustus. It would take too long to give all the details, but the main facts are these. The emperors retained the supeme management in their own hands, delegating the work to their own freedmen, and appointing a sort of 'Minister of Transport'. The use of the conveniences attached to it in the shape of vehicles, horses and inns, was restricted mostly to imperial officials, and licences for other persons to take advantage of it were rarely issued. Even government servants had to obtain warrants from the emperor's secretariat to make use of the post. Each stage had a supervisor in charge of it, with a staff of workmen under him, to repair the roads, vehicles and rest-houses, and to attend to travellers. All these persons received a salary from the treasury, and were not allowed to demand any recompense from travellers for their services. Seneca mentions that the coaches had a conductor who travelled with them, chiefly to see that the postilions did not steal the horses, but brought them back in good condition to the places from which they started. There was a standard list of those persons regularly entitled to use the posting service, and each traveller could take with him one servant to look after the baggage, and there were always two or three guards attached to every vehicle of any size to see that none of the valuables were purloined, and to protect travellers against highwaymen. There were two sorts of transport, the express service or *cursus velox*, which employed the fastest horses, and the *cursus clabularis*, or heavy transport, which was mostly for goods traffic. Vehicles on the latter usually had four wheels, and were of strong make, and they tended to be drawn by oxen, rarely by horses. Their maximum burden was fixed by law at 1500 Roman pounds. Mules, asses, and even camels were also used for drawing these wagons. No one was allowed to use more than two of them in one day, and private persons could only do so by special licence. The cost of the service seems to have been apportioned between the central fiscus and the provincial funds or, as we might put it, between the taxes and the county rates. In general, the postal service of the emperors was not of much direct benefit to the ordinary public: on the contrary its maintenance was something of a burden to citizens who were already heavily taxed.

What were the usual means of getting about? As to

62   A Mediterranean sailing ship

ships, we learn that by the first century A.D. the craft
of shipbuilding had so much improved that vessels of
quite a considerable size were being constructed (62).
An Alexandrian corn ship could be 180 feet in length,
with a tonnage of 1200, and as to passengers, we know
that Paul sailed for Rome in a ship which took 276,
while Josephus travelled to Rome in a ship which
carried as many as 600. Nevertheless, it is said that
there was not much improvement in design over the
more ancient vessels. Ramsay considers that there must
have been a great deal of useless length and waste of
space in the high bow and stern, which stood far out
above the water, so that a disproportionate length of
the whole ship stuck out as compared with that part of
the keel which was submerged. Ships were sailed
usually by one big sail on a single mast. This made it
hard to shorten sail, and so to adapt navigation to the
force of the wind; and leverage with one sail and one
mast must have been tremendous, for the straining of

the mast would gradually rupture the timbers of the ship and so make her leaky. It is true that a few other small sails were sometimes used, a topsail, and a storm-sail, and sometimes small sails at bow and stern, and we read in the story of the shipwreck in Acts that an *artemon* was rigged up after the ship became disabled, and this seems to have been a small foresail set on the bow, where there was often a small mast. In general, however, only the one big sail was used. Warships were much more independent of the wind, because they were generally impelled by oars, but in order to make them easy to manoeuvre they were lightly built, so that they were not very seaworthy on long voyages, nor had they much storage-room for provisions and equipment.

Under ordinary circumstances, therefore, passengers went by the larger trading ships, and regular services for passengers only may not have existed. Clearly, however, there must have been special passenger ships for the use of pilgrims at the time of festivals. It is well

63   A Mediterranean galley

known that the Jews of the Dispersion were not supposed to live more than a maximum of ninety days'
journey from Jerusalem, and thousands of these would
have been able to go to the Passover only by ship, for
the land journeys in many cases would have been too
slow. It may, therefore, be regarded as certain that
pilgrim ships would be run for the benefit of Jews, and
would make non-stop journeys, charging passenger
fares in accordance with the convenience thus provided. But since Jews were fair game for extortion,
harbour officials and shipowners made as much money
out of them as they could, and it is rather significant
that Imperial edicts issued in favour of the Jews expressly mention their right to have unimpeded freedom
to make the journey to Jerusalem. This throws some
light on the journey of Paul mentioned in Acts 20 and
21. He was known to be an unorthodox Jew, and he
had charge of a sum of money raised at Corinth for the
benefit of poor Jews in Jerusalem. It was not unlikely
that orthodox Jews might use the opportunity to
murder him at sea. He did not, therefore, make the
attempt to reach Jerusalem in time for the Passover by
the ordinary pilgrim ship, but went to Philippi, observed the Passover there, and then went on quietly by
easy stages so as to reach Jerusalem in time for
Pentecost. There is one interesting problem raised by
the statement in the account of the storm in the
the Mediterranean in Acts 27, where we read that the
sailors 'used helps, undergirding the ship'. There has
been some doubt as to the correctness of this translation. What exactly did the sailors do? On the
analogy of what was done in the case of Egyptian
ships, it seems more likely that the 'helps' were in this
case ropes running from stem to stern and tautened,
which were used, it is agreed, in order to prevent the

ship from 'hogging', i.e. breaking her back. Such a device, it is said, has been used on sailing ships even in modern times.

As in our own day, navigation by sea was rendered safer by the provision of lighthouses. One of these, as we know, survives on the top of the cliffs at Dover, but this seems to have been of Roman brick, whereas the lighthouse at Alexandria was a splendid affair, built of marble, with a beacon in the top continually burning (64).

64 Lighthouse at Alexandria

By road, long journeys would naturally be by horse or carriage, though a great many persons would go on foot, and it seems to be clear that foot passengers could travel about sixteen to twenty Roman miles a day, and that travellers, when driving, averaged four Roman miles per hour, with a regular day's journey of about twenty-five Roman miles (half as long again as the journey of a foot traveller), though the pace of vehicles naturally depended upon the amount of luggage, the weight of the vehicles, and the quality of the animals drawing it, so that some faster travellers went double distance, and a few even four times as far. Couriers on horseback travelled anything between five and ten miles an hour, and so could do about fifty Roman miles per day. This would give about fifty-four days for despatches from Rome to Alexandria, and forty-six from Rome to Caesarea in Palestine. But couriers were undoubtedly soldiers, and picked men at that, and therefore were probably hardy and capable of much endurance. Ordinary travellers did not go anything like as fast.

Places of entertainment and lodgings (65) were certainly to be found in numbers along all the main roads, but they varied very much in quality, and it is said that in many of the less civilised provinces they were dirty, badly kept, badly managed, with leaky roofs, and generally uncomfortable, and it is known that inn-keepers in general had a bad reputation, and that their houses were often used for immoral and criminal practices. The private traveller, therefore, unless he was fairly well-to-do, would have rather a bad time. Government officials and soldiers on the march could claim the right to free billets, and some municipalities built hostels specially for their reception.

A few further details about inns and restaurants may

be of interest. Inns along the great main roads were not a State affair, but were built mostly by neighbouring proprietors as a speculation, and leased to a tenant landlord or managed by slaves. They usually had

65   Inn scene

stables attached to them. At some centres of traffic there were several inns, and they competed for customers in a very modern way, by advertising. The accommodation at these inns was not of a high quality, but it may be reckoned cheap. One writer, Polybius, tells us that the inclusive charge rarely exceeded half *as* (apparently a copper coin). There were no separate items on the bill, as in most of our hotels, and it was advisable to inquire beforehand as to the charges. There is a picture in relief at a place called Aesernia which shows a landlady reckoning with a departing guest. The dialogue between them is actually given in detail, so we can learn what the customary charges were: bread and a pint of wine, one *as*; meat 2 *asses*; provender for the customer's mule, 2 *asses*; and apparently a charge for the use of the toilet (or something worse). Restaurants abounded in Rome, but they appear to have been frequented mostly by slaves or

66   Beggar by wayside

low-grade individuals, and were far from luxurious. A wall-painting at Pompeii shows what one of them was like. The customers sit on stools at a three-legged table, and from their costumes are probably sailors and fishermen. Many of these places were what we should call disorderly houses, and were certainly frequented for immoral purposes (this may explain the final item on the bill). It is to the credit of the Emperor Claudius that he gave orders for the closing down of them altogether in Rome, but as in modern

London and New York, night-clubs and speak-easies have been found very difficult to abolish, so in Rome the *popinae* and *ganeae* (as they were called) were soon open again, if indeed they were ever closed. The Emperor's edict soon became a dead letter. Nero (of all people!) tried controlling them, by ordering that they should only sell vegetables and cooked meat, but whether this had any effect is not on record. It would be like making an order that a licensed public-house in England must only sell groceries, and sounds like an early attempt at 'prohibition'. Tiberius had previously tried just the opposite plan, and had forbidden them to sell any cooked provisions, apparently with the idea of making them unattractive, and so driving them out of business.

In what sort of vehicles did you travel on the roads? It is evident that some people went in litters (67), with poles carried on the shoulders of men (as in the case of the old sedan-chairs in England), but there were certainly wheeled carriages of various sorts (68). We read of the eunuch who was treasurer to the Queen of Ethiopia, travelling up to Jerusalem in a 'chariot', but this can hardly have been the ordinary racing chariot (which, like a racing motor-car, or the driver's vehicle behind a fast trotting horse, had no seat and only room for one man), since the eunuch was sitting down and reading while he was being driven along, and there was room in the carriage for somebody else to sit beside him and talk. We must assume, therefore, that in this case he was probably travelling in a larger vehicle, with perhaps four wheels, rather like the carriage in which the rich old lady is represented as travelling in Kipling's book, *Kim*. There was also in use among the Romans a sort of gig, a light open carriage with two wheels, capable of carrying two persons, a driver and

67   Transport. Litter with escort. Note the first-century
tombs in the background

a passenger. This was called a *cisium*, and it was drawn
either by a single horse or mule, or by a pair. We hear
of a messenger travelling fifty-six miles in ten hours in
a *cisium*, part of the journey being done at night. These
gigs could be had for hire, and were kept for that purpose at posting stations along all the great roads, and
in some places we find that they were stationed on a

kind of licensed cab-rank. This was certainly the case at Pompeii, where the locality in the city took its name from it, and there must have been similar cab-ranks at Rome, so that when Paul landed in Italy he could have hired a *cisium* to drive him to the capital. From legal records, we learn that the drivers of these hired vehicles were subject to penalties for driving without due care and attention, and they were reckoned to be very fast. They would have been no use in a place like Jerusalem, or indeed in any hill-towns with narrow streets, but on the ordinary main Roman roads they were common. Besides the *cisium*, there was also an *essedum*, which had no seat for the driver, but was driven by the traveller himself, always with a pair of horses, and this vehicle again could be hired at posting-houses. Sometimes it was highly decorated, and generals and even emperors did not mind using it.

There were several other different kinds of vehicle in use in addition to those already mentioned. Thus there was a cart or wagon with solid wheels supporting a flat wooden platform. It was usually drawn by oxen, though sometimes by mules, and was the equivalent of our lorry for conveying market produce. Large baskets of wicker could be placed on the platform for conveying such things as vegetables. This cart was called by the Romans a *plaustrum* or *plostrum*, and there was a larger variety of it with four wheels, called the *greater plaustrum*, which sometimes had wheels with spokes, and also a body of open work rails so that it was very much like some of the older farm wagons. Then there was another kind of carriage called a *reda* which could take a fair number of passengers. This had four wheels, and several seats like a charabanc, and it also carried luggage. It was probably covered, and though usually drawn by two horses or mules, could some-

68   Group of vehicles

times be driven by four horses for greater speed, so that
it was really rather like one of the old stage-coaches.
It is believed to have been invented in Gaul, and to
have been taken over and adapted by the Romans. A
covered wagon with two wheels was called a *carpentum*.
Another vehicle used by the Romans was called a
covinus. This probably did not operate in Palestine, but
as used by the Romans was rather like the *reda*. The
name comes from the Celtic, and the original was used
by the Belgae and also by the Britons as part of their
armed forces, since the spokes of the wheels were
furnished with long scythes or sickles for mowing down
the enemy. The *essedum*, mentioned above and adopted
by the Romans as a means of rapid transport, and, like
the *cisium*, probably kept for hire at post-houses, was
originally a British war chariot, and Caesar says that
the army of Caswollan had about 4000 of them. The
striking difference between these and the chariots of
the Egyptians and Greeks was that the front of the car
and not the back was open, so that the driver was able

69   Street café

to run along the pole to the extremity, discharge his
weapons, and then run back quickly into the cover of
the car itself. It seems to have come into common use
for civilians about the time of Nero, and Seneca

mentions gilded *esseda* as being in use among fashionable ladies.

The rough hilly country of Central Palestine was not very suitable for large wheeled vehicles, and wagons were not much used except in the level coastal plain, where they seem to have differed very little from the Roman ones just described, the ordinary carts having two wheels of solid wood, and the larger wagons four wheels with six or eight spokes.

The litter, a specimen of which is given here, was no doubt of more than one pattern, but the general principle on which it was constructed was probably constant, i.e. it provided for a person to be carried by bearers. Julius Caesar restricted its use to certain persons and certain specific occasions, and all through the first century it was only people of a particular rank who were allowed to ride in it, presumably because it gave the occupants an air of arrogant authority, and encouraged an enervating luxury.

In the chapter on machines we give examples of early forms of taximeter for calculating distances and fares in hired vehicles.

It is worth adding that sea-travel was more extensive than we are apt to suppose. During the first century one Roman (a Greek) sea-captain sailed down the Red Sea and across to the Malabar coast of India and round into the Bay of Bengal and returned to write a record of his voyage for the benefit of traders. Only thirty years after the writing of the fourth Gospel, Graeco-Roman merchants had sailed as far as China. Mr. Charlesworth records that a statuette of the Hindu goddess, Lakshmi, has been unearthed at Pompeii.

The finding of the boy Jesus in the Temple precincts, as conceived by J. J. Tissot.

Tissot, who during the nineteenth century made a prolonged stay in Jerusalem, is thought by some to have over-Orientalised the architecture of the Temple in his imaginative reconstruction; but there can be little doubt that his representations of the first century Jewish costume are substantially correct, certainly as far as the non-Hellenised observant Jews are concerned.

Air-view of part of the Jordan valley.

Note the dense, almost tropical vegetation of the lowlands, and the aridity of the flanking hill.

Inscription commemorating a Roman officer who
died at Jerusalem on active service.

Views of the ruins of Sebaste built on the site of the Samaria of King Ahab.

Note the Graeco-Roman architecture, and the evidences of the splendour created by Herod the Great, the
senate-house and forum, with a temple to the Emperor Augustus, and another to the fertility-goddess
Kore (the maiden).

Air-View of an Arab village in Palestine.

This gives very much the "feel" of first-century rural Palestine. Note the circular threshing floors and the darker patches of tilled ground, also the flat roofs of the houses.

Village scene in Palestine, with man winnowing.

After J. J. Tissot.

Group of typical Roman citizens from a mural monument.

Note the dourness of the faces of these tough farmer-soldiers, a genuine but harsh aristocracy, born to rule others.

Transport by camels, Bethany and Jericho road.

Palestine fisherman casting a net on the Sea of Galilee.

Old schoolmaster reading (lamp found
near Ascalon), first century A.D.

Leaden weight from Jerusalem, with
inscription referring to the inspector o
Weights and Measures.

Pottery lamp from Jerusalem, first century A.D.

Christ in an orthodox synagogue.

Tomb of Herod's family

So-called tomb of the Judges.

Reconstruction of the (Hellenistic type) synagogue at Capernaum, built in the first century A.D.

Statue of the goddess Athene the Virgin –
from the Parthenon at Athens.

Chapter VI

LETTERS AND LETTER-WRITING, BOOKS, ETC.

IN the first century A.D. there was no government collection, carriage or delivery, for private correspondence. The only public letter-post was provided solely for government purposes, and was carried by the elaborate system of couriers, referred to in the previous chapter. Anyone else who wanted to send a letter anywhere had to make private arrangements. This does not mean that there was not plenty of letter-writing. Judging from what has turned up in the various rubbish-heaps, more particularly in Egypt, and from the collections of letters written by well-known persons such as Cicero, there would seem to have been almost as much letter-writing as in the nineteenth century.

The material used for such letters was various. The papyrus sheet was obviously the most natural one. It was made from the stalk of a plant growing in marshy places, and we know of its use as far back as about 2600 B.C. The process of making the paper was simple. The pith of the stalk was cut into thin strips, and these were laid side by side in a row, till they formed a sheet of the desired dimensions. Next, another row was laid across these at right angles, and fastened to the first row with some kind of gum. A heavy weight was then pressed upon the two layers to flatten them and the sheet was dried in the sun and afterwards polished, one supposes by some kind of sandpaper. After that it was ready to be written on. The curious thing is that as recently as 1902 papyrus sheets were being made in

Sicily in exactly the same way. The workers there used a wooden mallet to beat the stems flat, just as the Roman scientist, Pliny, describes the process in his own day. It is said that this Sicilian papyrus is not so fine, white or close-grained as the old papyrus, and the industry is an artificial one, the product of roughly 200 sheets a year being sold only to tourists. It is estimated that two bundles of papyrus stalks are needed to make one (large) sheet about 10 in. by 8 in.—actually the same size as the sheet on to which this chapter is being typed. Good papyrus sheets were also made in 1913 out of a plant growing in the Botanical Gardens at Berlin. The size of a single sheet of papyrus in the first century varied a good deal, and for most documents, such as letters, accounts and receipts, a single sheet was enough. For longer texts, such as books, sheets were stuck together, end on, and made into rolls, measuring in some cases as much as twenty and even forty-five yards. We shall have more to say about this when we come to speak of books. Other forms of writing were on what are called *ostraka*, which are really pieces of pottery. When a pot was broken and the pieces thrown away, they were picked up by the poorer classes who could not afford to buy papyri, or tablets, and used for scribbling on, with the result that thousands of non-literary notes and messages have survived more completely than if they had been written on papyrus; for the latter, although fairly durable, does decay, especially if it gets damp, whereas earthenware if not exposed to extremes of temperature, is almost everlasting in durability. The *ostrakon* was beneath the dignity of wealthy persons, but it is recorded of a famous philosopher, called Cleanthes, that he could not afford papyrus, and so wrote on leather or on *ostraka*. *Ostraka*, in fact, were the cheapest writing materials possible, and you had to apologise to your correspondent for using them. One such apology runs: 'Excuse me that I cannot find papyrus as I am in the country', rather like saying 'Forgive this pencil scrawl, but I have no ink'. Of course, the *ostrakon* was no use for long letters, but it was all right for short messages, school-room exercises, and memoranda. For instance, if you were preaching a sermon you might write your text on an *ostrakon*, and we actually have quite a number of little fragments of pottery with a verse, or two verses, of the New Testament inscribed upon them. Among the very poor and ignorant, verses of this kind might have been used as amulets.

Besides these two sorts of material, we have also the leather or skin (parchment) mentioned above, and the wax tablet. Tablets among the Romans to some extent took the place of *ostraka*, where only a short message was concerned, but it must have been rather inconvenient to write permanent inscriptions upon them, because the surface was wood, with a thin film of wax (usually black) spread over it. The wax was written upon by a sharp-pointed instrument called a *stilus*, but it was quite easy to destroy or obliterate the writing by heating it or scraping it, and indeed when the message was done with, the tablet could be used over again by scraping off the old wax and pouring fresh melted wax over it; hence the phrase 'tabula rasa'. More permanent inscriptions were made on tablets covered with gypsum, or with a harder wax. A schoolboy could carry a single *tabula* suspended from his waist by a ring, and there is one vase-picture which shows tablets of this kind hung on the walls of a school-room. For the wood of such tablets people generally used beech, fir and box. More expensive materials were citron wood, or ivory. Only one side was covered with wax, and if two tablets were used, the wax was put on the inner side, and the tablets fastened together with wire hinges. There was a raised margin round each tablet to keep the wax surfaces from rubbing against each other.

Sometimes a number of tablets, as many as five, or even more, were fastened together, and then they were called a codex or a codicillus (from the latter word we get 'codicil', for the addition to a will). When a very large number were used, a handle was attached to them by which they could be hung up. Legal documents, and particularly wills, had the outer edges pierced with holes, and through these a thread or tape was strung, and its ends knotted and sealed. In this way nobody could open the codex without breaking the seal, and so forged insertions in the text were prevented. It is said that one of the common criminal offences was the forging of wills. It may seem to us odd that letters were so often written upon wax tablets, but such was the case, and if more than one tablet was used they would be tied together with pack-thread, and sealed, but naturally they were not very permanent, so that not many have survived (18). Two very old ones were discovered some years ago in gold mines near villages in Transylvania.

In Egypt some years ago, at a place called Oxyrhynchus, in the Fayum area, a rubbish-heap was dug up which yielded a great many papyrus letters, bills, receipts and short messages. Even though some of these may be dated a little later than the year A.D. 100 they are quite typical, and it may be interesting to look at a few of them. Thus, there is one from an Egyptian boy written to his father. He is evidently an extremely naughty boy and a perfect handful to his mother, who told somebody else, so he says, 'he drives me mad—do take him away'. The boy writes, of course, in very bad grammar, and spells just as badly, and he is annoyed with his father for not taking him to Alexandria for an outing, so he says, 'I will not write thee a letter, nor speak to thee, nor wish thee health. Send for me I beseech thee. If thou sendest not I will neither eat nor drink (a threatened hunger strike). If thou wilt not carry me, these things will come to pass.' He adds ironically, 'thou hast indeed sent me great gifts— locust beans. They deceived me and my brother as to the date of thy sailing.'

Another letter is from a lad whom we might describe as a National Service recruit. The boy appears to have gone into the marines, and he writes to his family from the first port of call to say that he has had a rough voyage, but that he prayed to the god Serapis, and came safe to land. Now he is delighted because he had received his first bit of pay from the Emperor, three pieces of gold, and he sends his father a little portrait of himself. There were, of course, no photographers, but there were artists who made a living in the neighbourhood of the docks, by painting people's portraits. He is just about to close the letter, when some of his mates, who come from his own home-town, ask him to add messages for them, and he does it much in the same way that Paul puts in all the salutations at the end of his letter to Rome. He hopes, 'if the gods will' for quick promotion, and then he addresses the letter (which has to go to a town in the Fayum) by rather a a roundabout way, first from the garrison where he is stationed (at Misenum) to the garrison of a special cohort, and then to the accountant or paymaster to the cohort who has to forward it to the man's own village.

Side by side with this we can put the message quoted by Caiger as sent by a boy to his father (apparently concerning his school report), 'Don't fidget about my mathematics, for I'm working hard.' Caiger also quotes two nice little messages, one from a fond mother to her son: 'Do not forget, my child, to write me about your health. You know how anxious your mother is about her boy'; and the other from a lad called Sempronius to his younger brother Maximus: 'I hear you are not very obliging to mother. Please dearest brother, do not vex her. If any of the youngsters disobey her, give them a clout on the ear. You are the eldest at home now, so you are in charge. You mustn't mind my writing to you like this.' One copybook text quoted by Caiger, and written on an *ostrakon* used as a school slate, has added to it a schoolmaster's comment on the writing: 'Enoch, don't throw your pen about.'

But it is not only letters of human interest that turn up, but business letters—as has been said, tax collectors' demand notes, death certificates, burial club receipts, and so on.

Thus, we find one written about the time of the martyrdom of St. Peter, i.e. about A.D. 60 from a small farmer in Egypt to an official of what corresponded then, one supposes, to the (provincial) Ministry of Agriculture. Apparently the farmer has to register the animals in his possession, for he says that he wishes to make a return of the number of lambs in his possession in the twelfth year of Nero Caesar. He says he has twelve, and he adds, 'and now I enrol those that have been born since the last return, i.e. of the young of the same sheep, seven lambs. And I swear by Nero Caesar that I have kept nothing back.' What the penalty was for making a false return history does not relate, but it is interesting to see that this document was countersigned by one of the clerks employed by this Ministry official, saying that he has noted the total of seven lambs. Bureaucracy does not change.

A receipt found among Egyptian business papyri runs: 'Asclepiades to Portis, greeting. I have received from you the rent for the field I leased to you . . . and you now owe me nothing. (Written at the dictation of the above by Eumelus, who was asked to do so because Asclepiades writes rather slowly.)' A clear case of the professional letter-writer, who may still be seen at his job outside the passport office on the Arab side at Jerusalem. Caiger cites a list including a butcher's bill, an invitation to a wedding feast, a ticket of membership in an athletic club, and an inventory of household goods, and finally a certificate signed by a grocer undertaking not to sell eggs *below* the controlled price!

The *graffiti* or casual inscriptions, as casual as those carved by schoolboys on the top of their desks or the scrawls inside choirboys' service books, often reveal the humanity of the masses during our period. Caiger quotes the scribble of some disgruntled builder's labourer on the walls of a Maccabaean mansion in Jerusalem: 'To blazes with Simon's palace says Pampras.' He also quotes the inscription found on a wall: 'Brunettes for me. I always did like blackberries', plainly the work of some adolescent girl-hunter; and finally, election slogans exactly like our own: 'Vote for Publius Furius as duumvir, he's a good man', and 'Fuscanus for alderman'. So apparently they did have municipal elections!

Sometimes we find very short love-letters, and here comes in a curious reflection upon the statement made in the Book of Revelation that the number of a certain wicked emperor was 666. It would appear that the use of figures to conceal somebody's name was quite a common practice in the first century, for one message scribbled on a wall at Pompeii runs: 'I love her whose number is 545', and another one, which is said not to be later in date than A.D. 79 runs: 'Amerimnus thought upon his lady Harmonia for good. The number of her honourable name is 45 (or, if another reading be taken, 1035).'

What did people use for writing purposes? The pens were usually reed pens, sharpened with a knife in the same way as the old-fashioned quill pen (18). The best reeds for this purpose came from Egypt. The ink used was of various kinds. Some was made by collecting soot from the walls of a specially constructed marble furnace, in which pitch pine was burnt. The soot was then mixed with glue and dried in the sun, so as to make ink blocks which could afterwards be diluted. Another kind was made with vinegar instead of glue, and another, imported from India, was very likely the same as what we know as Indian ink. These sorts of ink were, however, more used by painters than writers. Ink for books (*atramentum librarium*) had gum instead of glue in the proportion of three parts of soot to one of gum, with an infusion of wormwood, to protect the manuscripts from being eaten by mice, by making them bitter. Although this ink was thicker than ours, more like printer's ink, and also durable, it was easy to wipe it out before it was dry, and to leave the papyrus or parchment clean. A sponge, therefore, was one of the regular possessions of any scribe. Inkstands have been found at Pompeii with pens beside them (18). One inkstand actually had some ink in it which, though thick, was still fluid. It is said that this thick ink did not take very well on parchment, and it is therefore possible that, as early as the first century, people knew how to make ink out of galls and oxide of iron just as we do, since such was certainly made in the second century, and manuscripts which may be first-century, in which it was used, have been found at Herculaneum, the ink on them having been analysed.

We also know that sepia, the black fluid from the cuttle-fish, was used as ink, especially in Africa, and a writer towards the end of the first century mentions the use of coloured inks, and also gold ink for illumination. Invisible ink was known. One poet advises writing love-letters with milk, for this, when dry, would be invisible, unless the papyrus was sprinkled with charcoal dust, which would stick to the milk, throwing the letters in relief, while it could be brushed

75 Specimen of *uncial* writing

away from the rest of the page. Another writer suggests the use of a white gum from a plant for the same purpose, while a third mentions that an ink made of gall alone is invisible until a sponge is passed over it dipped in a solution of copper sulphate, when it turns black. Some of the inkstands which have been found were double, and evidently used, as in our day, for black and red ink. They were of different shapes, round or hexagonal, and of different materials, sometimes metal, sometimes terra-cotta, and two of the inkstands shown in the picture will be seen to have rings with which they could be fastened to the girdle.

The two main types of writing were: (1) uncials,

(2) cursive. Uncials are so called from 'uncus' a hook, because the letters look rather like curved hooks inscribed on the papyrus. 'Cursive' is a flowing hand in which all the letters and most of the words are run together. An illustration of uncial type is given here (75).

BOOKS AND LIBRARIES

As we have already said, the book of the first century was a manuscript roll made of sheets sewn together end on, and was hardly ever in pages. Copying was a regular trade or craft, and scribes were naturally very numerous. Allowing for the large number of illiterates, and for the slowness involved in copying, the number of books in existence was considerable. Sir Henry Bell says 'there must have been a fairly large reading public, and an active book-trade. And certainly there were municipal libraries of standard works, though only for reference purposes, not for lending out.' One rich Roman is said to have had a library of 62,000 manuscripts. Private collections of books began at Rome quite a long time before the first century, and much earlier we have record of great public libraries both in Babylon and in Egypt. The great libraries in Alexandria are said to have had between them something like 600,000 scrolls, and books in foreign languages were brought there and translated into Greek, so as to provide a uniform record in one standard language. It is probable that the Greek version of the Old Testament which we call the Septuagint was made in this way. In Italy, people like Cicero spent much money on buying manuscripts, and by the beginning of the first century it had become the custom for all well-to-do persons to have one room in the house reserved as a library, and elegantly furnished and decorated, and it was fashionable to make a pretence of learning by having a library, even if one never read the books. Nero's tutor, Seneca, writes unfavourably about the rage for book-collecting. In one house excavated at Herculaneum in Italy a library was found fully furnished. Round the walls it had cases for keeping the rolls, and these were all numbered, and in the centre of the room there was a rectangular case. It is surprising how little space the manuscripts occupy, for the room was so small that a man by stretching out his arms could touch both sides of it, and yet it contained 1700 rolls. We read of the existence of municipal and provincial libraries at a number of different places.

In the absence of printing, the composition of a book often involved the employment of a small army of scribes and secretaries, to whom the author dictated. Sometimes one copy was loaned or hired out for copying, and works existing in a single copy could be multiplied in this way, either by a single scribe or by a person dictating to one or more scribes. The problem of correcting mistakes was great, and it was not always carried out very well, so that errors are repeated again and again by copyists, who were often slaves, and had no personal interest in producing an accurate text. We can hardly be surprised that scholars who have to edit the text of old books from the first century, whether they are gospels and epistles, or works by ordinary Greek and Latin authors, often have a hard task to determine the true reading of some passages.

It is said that most booksellers would seldom produce more than 500 copies of any single work, but the variety of works was considerable and even included novels, usually written in Greek.

Nine different sorts of papyrus material are recorded by Pliny as in general use. The first and most important was the royal, or *Augusta*, which was about half of a metre in width. The *hieratica*, about one-fifth of a metre in width, came next. Then there was the *amphitheatrica*, so called because the factory at which it was made was near the amphitheatre in Alexandria. A cheaper papyrus was made at Sais and was a good deal narrower. The *emporetica* was coarse packing paper. The *charter Claudia* was made under the patronage of the Emperor Claudius, and was not only extra strong material, but could be used on both sides. Egypt, however, seems during the first century to have had a monopoly of the manufacture of all papyrus. Writing was usually in columns, so that one sheet of papyrus had only one column on it. For letters, one used either one sheet, or a sheaf of strips fastened together with thread and when folded up, sealed at the end.

DISTRIBUTION OF NEWS

It is difficult for us who enjoy the benefits of radio and newspapers to understand the state of a society which was almost completely devoid of any written medium for spreading news. Of course, in a society where large numbers of people are illiterate, anything like a news-sheet or written notice is useless, and in this connection it is important to remember that news-sheets with a large circulation are also impossible without a mechanical printing press. It would seem that in England newspapers did not immediately follow the introduction of printing, and probably only began in the eighteenth century, and even then only a limited number of people were able to read them, because we still had no universal elementary education. The position, therefore, in the time of Queen Elizabeth I, must have been rather worse than in the first century A.D.

in the matter of news? How then was it spread? We
naturally think of the spoken word, but if one depended upon the unofficial use of this, one would
simply get gossip and rumour. One imagines that there
must have been some way in which the State guaranteed that important announcements were accurately
made, and important news correctly given. We can
perhaps see the vestiges of this in the curious office of
the Town Crier. The latter seems today to be little
more than a picturesque survival with a loud voice,
who at some seaside resorts announces forthcoming
events such as dances and flower shows, and cries
property which has either been lost or found. It seems
likely, however, that the office of crier was once much
more important, and that the crier's business was to
take the place which is now filled by the B.B.C. news.

In the first century A.D. we can imagine that important messages would be delivered from place to
place either verbally or in manuscript form by means
of runners. But the government must have had some
other device as well for making sure that the public
knew any facts necessary for the discharge of the duties
of citizenship or the transaction of business, or any
momentous information about public events. We find,
therefore, that there was an institution among the
Romans known as the *album*. This was not a book, as
with us, but a notice-board or tablet (either dark with
white letters or white with dark letters—we are not
certain which), put up in a public place in Rome so
that all persons might have sight of its contents. It was
in fact like the *official notice board* which appeared in
this country outside police stations and on police
telephone boxes during the Second World War, and as
with these, so with the Roman *album*, there was a heavy
penalty for anyone who removed, defaced or destroyed

it. Cicero tells us that the *pontifex maximus* used to write certain chronicles upon the *album*, and the word seems to have been used for any tablet which contained a public announcement. In a good many cases it was the same sort of thing as the lists of town councillors and justices which may be seen on an official notice-board outside any municipal buildings. But this does not get us very far. What we should like to know is whether the Roman government had any machinery for ensuring that the public got daily or weekly news about what was going on in the province or city, or in some other part of the Empire. We do know that in Jerusalem there was an attempt at the circulation of some kind of news-sheet. It is mentioned in Rabbincal records, but it does not appear whether it was a private venture or whether it was issued by the Roman government or by the high priests. It is a serious thought that at the first Easter there might have been an issue of this, which has long since ceased to exist, and in which there could have appeared a notice of the execution of Jesus of Nazareth. The sheets, of course, were manuscript, and, therefore, unless a very large body of scribes was employed, the actual circulation must have been relatively small, but scribes were, of course, numerous, and, as in India, the professional letter-writer would be available in any market place or at a city gate. We are given to understand that the publication of these news-sheets was prohibited on the Sabbath except for the purpose of making official pronouncements such as the issue of priestly or Imperial edicts.

Dissemination of news among the Romans seems to have been rather meagre. My information is that the *Acta diurna*, perhaps rather like the *London Gazette*, were issued in manuscript form and posted up, and contained rather more than official notices: for instance, events in important families, sporting results, etc., got in. But there is no evidence that copies were distributed to the provinces. It is believed that a certain amount of news 'received through official channels' was made public by announcement at the assemblies held in the various cities, but that the Emperors stopped this. Curiously enough, a certain amount of ephemeral news which we find today in newspapers, or hear over the wireless, got put down in permanent form in inscriptions. This is evident from the rather curious wall-inscriptions in some of the streets of Pompei, which are of the nature of advertisements for goods, or testimonials for individuals.

The percentage of literates in the population was probably much higher than might have been expected, so it is quite likely that the notices on the albums and other public inscriptions were read and understood by a great many people.

Chapter VII

VARIOUS MATTERS OF BUSINESS AND ADMINISTRATION

WEIGHTS AND MEASURES

WITH the Jews the most ordinary unit of weight was the *shekel*. We have no record of its exact size before the period of the Maccabees, but at that time the Jewish shekel amounted to 218 grains, and the Phoenician shekel to about 224. Smaller weights were the *beka* or half-shekel, and the *gerah*, which was one-twentieth of the shekel, and the principal larger weights were the *menah*, which may have been anything from 50 to 100 shekels, and the *kikkar*, which weighed 3000 shekels. The Phoenician equivalent of the latter weighed about 96 lb., and when we read of a crown weighing as much as this, we must realise that the article in question was not worn by a human being, but by an idol in the form of a man, and was, therefore, of colossal size. *Kikkar* is translated 'talent' in the English Bible, but we must remember that the *talentum* (Greek *talanton*) varied in size, the Attic being about 57 lb. in weight.[1] The word *menah* or *mna* passed from the Phoenicians to the Greeks, who called it *mana*, and thence to the Italians, who pronounced it *mina*. This is the 'pound' of the New Testament. The Greek *mana* varied a good deal in different

[1] The Jewish *talanton* was very large and heavy, more like a cannon-ball or a kerbstone (there were perhaps two shapes) and its estimated weight was about 40 kilograms. It is hardly surprising that a lazy person might prefer to bury it, or pack it up and put it away. The *mna* was a very large flat coin, perhaps six inches in diameter, and also inconveniently bulky.

times and in different places. The Romans from the earliest times used the copper *libra* or pound both for money and for weight. It appears that pieces of copper were cast in Italy of the weight of a pound and of its various fractions, and although the standard of Roman coinage fell rapidly, the weight continued unchanged, and the Roman *libra* as a weight was exactly the same under the Emperor Constantine the Great as it was in the time of Christ; indeed it has been said that the dominion of the *libra* as weight was as durable and extensive as the dominion of Rome herself. This must have been of great advantage in every province of the Empire.

The measures of volume vary, of course, in name as between Palestine and the other parts of the Empire. Thus, the *ephah*, which is said by Ezekiel to have been equal to the *bath* in volume, seems to be the same as the Greek *batos* mentioned in Luke 16[6], and the *seah* and the *kor* seem to be the same as the New Testament *saton* and *koras*. The *seah* was about one-third of an *ephah*, and the *kor* contained ten *ephahs*. The *seah* and *ephah* were usually employed in measuring dry substances, but the *bath*, and its smaller units the *hin* and *log*, were fluid measures. To get the whole of the equivalents right we must consider that the *log* was very nearly an English pint, that the *hin* contained twelve *logs* and the *bath* six hins, or about eight and a quarter gallons. The *seah* was nearly one and a half pecks, and the *ephah* was three times this volume. The *kor* contained ten *ephahs*. Other measures were the Latin *modius*, which was correctly a vessel containing two gallons, and usually translated 'bushel' in the New Testament. This *modius* was the standard measure used for corn rations. Then there was the *metreta*, which is translated 'firkin' in John[6], and which was a jar containing nine gallons. The water pots at Cana, therefore, contained anything from eighteen to twenty-seven gallons apiece. The *choenix* held about a quart, and since a labourer could be hired for a denarius a day, we can judge that the statement that he could get one *choenix* of wheat or three of barley for one denarius indicates that his daily corn ration was a quart of wheat or three quarts of barley.

Weights and measures had to be of the correct standard, and were stamped with the name of the controller who passed them for use. Thus, we find at Jerusalem a lead weight in the museum inscribed:

ΑΓΑΘΟΚΛΕΟ(Υ)C ΑΓΟΡΑΝΟΜΟΥΝΤΟC
'while Agathocles was Controller of weights and measures' (72),

and another inscribed:

TIMINNIOC KPHTIKOC
'Timinnios the Cretan';

another inscription runs '(made) in the year when Euphemius was magistrate and Apollonius controller of the market'.

RATIONING AND FOOD-CONTROL

When Paul went to Rome, would it have been necessary for him to have the equivalent of a ration card or identity card? This question is by no means an extravagant or foolish one. From the earliest times it was considered the duty of the Roman government to secure the supply of cereals for the population. In times of scarcity the State went in for bulk-buying, and then re-sold to the citizens through the corn market (to which it guaranteed supplies) at a moderate price. The market was under the control of an officer of State called an aedile. With the decline of agriculture in Italy, and the increase of the urban population, the government had to buy more and more, and since the price went up, it soon became impossible for the poorer citizens to purchase at the ordinary retail price fixed by the State. At first this difficulty was met by the liberality of rich private citizens, but from 123 B.C. onwards there was a regulation made by which every citizen was entitled to a certain ration of wheat per month, probably five modii, about ten gallons English, at a little over half the market price, the difference being made up out of the treasury. This, as we can see, was virtually the same as the modern food subsidy, and the ration was granted to fathers of families as such, and not confined to the poor, but was a basic ration to which any male married person was entitled, whatever his income. Each citizen had, however, to apply for his ration in person, and snobbery would thus deter a good many people from presenting themselves at the local food-office! Various modifications were made in this law from time to time, and at one period it was temporarily suspended, but it was soon restored, as the suspension was most unpopular. From the time of Julius Caesar onward the further step was taken of supplying corn *free* to all citizens, a very socialistic step, comparable to the modern supply of free milk in schools, or of free education. It was said that this free ration of corn cost the State one-fifth of its revenue (perhaps £700,000 a year) and, of course, this had to be made up out of the taxes in the usual manner. It can well be seen how easily such a system was open to abuse. The first thing, therefore, that Julius Caesar did was to order a list to be made of all the persons in Rome who would be entitled to this free ration, and to exclude from it all who could not prove their Roman citizenship, and the chief reason for this was that during the civil wars a large number of aliens who possessed no claim to the Roman franchise had settled inside the city boundaries in order to get the benefit of the ration. The number had grown to 320,000, and it was now reduced to 150,000. But even of these, only the really destitute were allowed it free. There was, in effect, a means test, and the indigent had to have special tickets, others having only an ordinary ration ticket entitling them to buy at the controlled price. This prudent regulation was discontinued soon after the death of Julius Caesar, and Augustus doubled the number of free tickets for a time, but later cut it down once more, and even thought seriously about abolishing the free list altogether, in the interests of Italian agriculture. In the end he kept it on, and even made the whole distribution free during times of famine. After that, the only variation made by the Emperors was as to the controlled price at which the corn should be sold to those not entitled to the free ration. Later still each citizen entitled to a corn ration was given a permanent ration ticket or *tessara*, which he could even sell, or bequeath by will, and the ration once more became free to all, without any means test. Thus, we see that when Paul came to Rome he would have had to supply evidence of his citizenship in order to get any corn, except, perhaps, in the black market. He would thus have had to produce some sort of certificate or identity card (issued to him, perhaps, originally at Tarsus), on showing which at the local food-office he would have been given a *tessara*, unless, of course, being a State prisoner, he was supplied direct with a prison ration. It will, however, be recalled that during part of the time in which he lived in Rome, he did so in his own hired house, and in this case he must surely have applied for a *tessara*. It seems hardly likely that so good a business man as a Jew usually was would have bought his corn for more than the controlled price, if he could have avoided doing so.

We also note that a Roman Jew got extra rations of grain and oil on a Friday, to avoid complications over the Sabbath, and that since some Jews objected to receiving Gentile oil, they were allowed to claim the equivalent of the oil-ration in cash.

TIMES AND SEASONS

Reckoning of time is one of the things in which the first century differs from our own, and here also there was a difference between East and West. In Palestine the Orientals as distinct from the Romans reckoned each day as beginning at sunset, and continuing until the next sunset. (Hence the phrase in Genesis—The *evening* and the morning were one day.) This is still the practice among most Syrians who are not westernised, so that if you are told that you are invited to a meeting on a Tuesday in the evening, you must be careful not to arrive on Tuesday, but on Monday evening. This accounts also for the fact that the Jewish Sabbath was always reckoned as beginning on the Friday at sunset, and ending on Saturday at sunset. The day itself, from sunrise to sunset, was divided into twelve hours of day-light, the first of these beginning at sunrise. This did not mean that the hours were, as with us, of the same length all the year round. Indeed, it would not have been possible to compute them as containing sixty minutes in winter, for the hours in fact changed in length every day, and there was no constant or fixed duration for each of the twelve divisions. Noon was the sixth hour, not, as with us, the twelfth hour, and if a boy had to be in school at nine, he would have said that school began at the third hour. The night was divided into three watches by Jews, but the Romans divided it into four, evening, midnight, cock-crowing and early morn, but the Jews also used the expression 'cock-crowing' and there was a special benediction or prayer to be said at it. The Romans also had a variation as between summer and winter in the length of the days, yet did not reckon the day from sunset, but from dawn, so that their way of speaking was different from that of the Jews, and it has sometimes been held that in the Fourth Gospel the days are reckoned in the Roman way, whereas in the other gospels they are reckoned after the Jewish manner.

The division of an hour into minutes and seconds goes back to Babylonian times, and passed on westward from Mesopotamia, and it was certainly known to the Jews. Nevertheless it is extremely unlikely that the bulk of the population of any Mediterranean country during the first century had any accurate ways of measuring the time in small units. In this respect their world differed greatly from ours. No transport timetables, calculating arrivals and departures in minutes, was in circulation, and nobody could make precise appointments with doctors or dentists. It must have been very inconvenient for busy people, but no doubt life went on in a much more leisurely fashion than in our day, and if you had a business interview in prospect with a great man, instead of being told to arrive at 9.10 or 11.20, you turned up with a crowd of clients and just waited your turn. It was only wealthy persons who could afford mechanical clocks as private possessions. Other folks merely knew of the smaller divisions of time when they lived near some time-telling instrument.

Now what devices were there for telling the time?
The clock with wheels is of course a much later invention, probably medieval, but the *solarium* or sun-
dial and the water-clock were both in use in the first
century. Dials seem to have been invented in Mesopotamia, and may well be very ancient, and there is
a clear mention of one in 2 Kings 16^{10}, while Herodotus definitely asserts that the Babylonians not only
invented the concave dial and also the ordinary sun-
dial, but also introduced the division of the day into
twelve hours. But we do not really know the shape of
the dial referred to in 2 Kings. Under the circumstances it seems likely that if any time-measuring
devices existed in Palestine they were most likely to
have been the sort of dials known as gnomons. On the
other hand the Greeks seem to have invented the
water-clock, in which time was reckoned by the level
of a liquid in a bowl, down the side of which were
marked divisions. The water was released a drip at a
time in the same way as sand from an hour-glass, and
indeed on the same principle. Wealthy Jews might
have bought and used such instruments, and Romans
certainly used them. There would very likely have
been one in Pontius Pilate's house, and in the house of
the Roman governor at Caesarea. The Romans began
by using the sun-dial or *solarium*, a specimen of which
was introduced at Rome twelve years before the war
with Pyrrhus (i.e. about 290 B.C.), but since this was no
use on overcast days, one of the Scipios had a water-
clock erected in a public place in 159 B.C., and this
indicated the hours of both day and night, and was
probably made on a large scale. Nevertheless, since
these *clepsydrae* (as they were called) soon got out of
order, the *solarium* still continued to be the commonest
form of time-keeper, and Augustus had a magnificent

one erected in the Campus Martius, which must have been there when Paul visited Rome. *Clepsydrae*, however, were used in military camps to measure accurately the night and day watches, since no one could rely upon sunshine for these, and *clepsydrae* were also used in law-courts to regulate the length of counsel's speeches, since there was a regular limit to the time allowed for the prosecuting counsel (two hours) and for the defending counsel (three hours). In one exceptional case, however, the prosecution was allowed

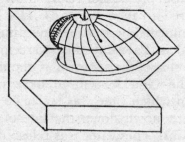

76   Roman horologium

six, and the defence nine hours. Pliny in one of his letters says he was allowed to address the bench for five hours! We don't know whether *clepsydrae* were used in the trials of Christ or Paul, but there are signs that in the trials of the latter long speeches were permitted, and it is fair to assume that they were timed in this way.

The most elaborate water-clock of which we have any record was one invented by a certain mathematician at Alexandria in 135 B.C. It could hardly have been used except by very wealthy persons, but rich Jews could have afforded one. In this case the water was made to drip upon wheels which were thereby turned, just as in the case of an overshot mill-wheel, of which it was a miniature form. The movement of the wheels elevated a tiny statue holding a rod which pointed to the hours marked on a pillar, and it was capable of doing this for all periods of the year, but it is said that it needed frequent attention and regulating, and was much too complicated to be in general use. Public *horologiums* (76), as they were called, seem to have been provided for the benefit of those who had no clocks of their own, but only in larger centres of population. At Athens are to be seen the ruins of one large *horologium* which combined an elaborate *clepsydra* with a number of sun-dials.

Whether you were a Jew or a Gentile, you had in any case a calendar, and this was naturally based upon the monthly phases of the moon, so that the year with its four seasons was almost inevitably divided into months. But whereas with the Jews there was also the week, which they had inherited from the Babylonians, together with its seventh day as a Sabbath, with the Romans the division of the month was more a matter of days, so that on the one hand you had certain special days in each month marked out by a name, the *kalends*, the *ides* and the *nones*, all indicating some phase of the moon, while the rest of the month was described in relation to these, so that you had 'the day before the ides', or 'the second day after the kalends', and so on: and then on the other hand you had the division of each month into (i) days which were sacred to some divinity, and on which work must not be done, and (ii) days which were secular, and devoted to human business. The Roman year had 355 days, and of these 109 were sacred, and 235 secular, while eleven were divided between the gods and men. No doubt this determined eventually something of the form assumed by the calendar of the Christian Church, but the latter was also affected by the Jewish week, so that the month became divided up into four weeks, with the holy day on the first instead of the seventh day, and this was not entirely on account of the Resurrection of Christ, because the first day of the week was also a festival of the Sun, so that the Christians were able to take over a day that was already sacred.

We are so accustomed to reckoning time by the week that it is a little difficult to place ourselves in the position when the week was a new thing, and perhaps only just coming into use, and not accepted by everybody. How did it happen? As far as we can make out, it came in somewhere about the first century, as the result of the combination of two influences. On the one hand there was the growing tendency to associate different days with the power of different heavenly bodies or planets. On the other, there was the growing influence of the Jews, who, from whatever source they derived it (whether, as they taught, from Moses, or from the customs of Babylonia), certainly had a seven-day week with their Sabbath on the Saturday. It appears that the Sabbath coincided with the day which was under the influence of Saturn, and of this the Roman historian Tacitus said 'Of the seven stars which rule human affairs Saturn has the highest sphere and the chief power.' Hence, it would seem, even Romans who did not believe in the Jews' religion felt some kind of superstitious regard for the Sabbath. References in well-known Latin writers such as Ovid, Horace and Tibullus show that this was the case.

Anybody can see that the names of the days of the week in some languages of continental Europe show that they were called after the heavenly bodies. Monday (Lundi) is the moon's day, Tuesday (Mardi) belongs to Mars, Wednesday (Mercredi) to Mercury,

Thursday in French (Jeudi), Italian, and Spanish, is under the sway of Jove or Jupiter, and Friday in the same way belongs to Venus (Vendredi). When St. Paul in some of his letters speaks of people being enslaved under the *stoicheia*, for a long time it was uncertain what he meant, because *stoicheia* can mean 'the alphabet' or 'the rudiments of knowledge', and to translate the word in this way does not seem to make any good sense of the passages in Galatians 4³ and Colossians 2⁸ (which you can look up for yourselves, and where the word occurs). *Stoicheia* is, however, also used for 'the elements', in the sense of 'the signs of the Zodiac' or 'the planets', and if we use this translation we get very good sense. What St. Paul aims at showing is that until people become Christians they are enslaved by a belief in astrology, that is to say they think that the planets control the events of life from day to day, and, as he says, they observe days and months and seasons and years, and are always on the look out for lucky and unlucky, auspicious and inauspicious days and even hours, and therefore they have no real freedom, but are just puppets. How this worked we know a little bit from the books on astrology that were written. The poet Juvenal actually wrote a satire (No. 6) against ladies who regulate every action by their astrological books. There were astrological predictions made in connection with every Roman Emperor from the time of the Crucifixion to the martyrdom of St. Peter, and one whole poem called *The Astronomica* on astrology was written by a writer called Manilius (believed to be first century). He is not very well known, but Professor Housman, who wrote *The Shropshire Lad*, was a great authority on his work, and was the first to edit it properly. Mr. F. H. Colson has given a good example of the sort of guidance that

astrologers provided for the public.[1] (Although the
source from which he draws is a little later than the
first century, it is quite typical.) He takes the hour at
which he is writing, namely about 12.30 p.m. on a
Friday, 20th November. At this time of year the sun
rises about half past seven and sets shortly after four,
and the day-hours, according to Roman reckoning,
would then be about forty-three minutes each. At half
past twelve one would be in the eighth hour. Venus is
therefore the ruler of the hour as well as of the day.
What may happen to me at such a time? According
to the handbook quite a number of unlucky things. It
would seem that the planets rather enjoy tormenting
human beings. Thus my slave may run away (this is a
thing that is predicted in nearly all the astrological
books of the period, and no doubt corresponds rather
with your daily help not turning up in the morning).
Then I may fall ill or I may lose or break something,
or I may have a burglary, but the influence being that
of Venus, the burglar will be a soft womanish kind of
person, and will steal my earrings, and if my slave runs
away he will probably be found hiding with a woman
in a public house. It is a relief to know that although
the illness will be a serious one I shall recover. In about
half an hour one passes into the next or ninth hour of
the day ruled by Mercury (i.e. Hermes). In this case
the property stolen will be parchments or gilded vessels,
and the thief will be an educated or literary person.
The runaway slave will take refuge in a temple;
but alas, any illness contracted may end in death!

One may well judge what a relief it must have been
to be delivered from bondage to this pernicious nonsense by the clear fresh proclamations of the gospel.
Nevertheless, astrology dies hard. It has reappeared in

[1] In his very interesting book: *The Week*.

cheap newspapers during the past twenty years, and is sufficiently well-known for the B.B.C. to make jokes about it, with the expectation that listeners will understand the allusions.

Turning to calendars in general, an interesting one was discovered some years ago at Pompeii. It consists of a marble cube, rather like a large paper-weight, the sort of thing that could be stood on the writing-table in the billiard-room of a country house today, and it was evidently in use in a country house in the first century A.D. The four sides are divided by vertical lines into months, and information is given about each month in turn (including the name of the deity presiding over it), certain important dates, and notes on the work to be done on the estate in field or vineyard during the period in question. A much older calendar, of the tenth century B.C. found at Gezer, records the principal farming operations of the successive months. This kind of record must therefore have existed in Palestine in the first century, and is evidently a traditional one of great antiquity.

COINAGE

Although, as we shall see, there were manuscript documents in use corresponding to cheques and bills of exchange, many cash transactions, as with us, were in metal. The Roman Empire seems to have recognised two sorts of currency. *First*, its own gold and silver coins, which were issued by the emperor for the time being, who controlled the minting of them.[1] The gold

[1] An interesting commentary on the Book of Revelation is provided by a coin of the first-century Emperor Vespasian, representing ROME as a female figure seated upon seven hills. Another coin of the same emperor, issued after A.D. 70 is inscribed JUDAEA CAPTA, with a picture of a palm-tree, and on one side of it a male Jew in fetters, on the other a Jewess mourning.

consisted of (1) the *aureus* and half *aureus*, and (2) the
standard silver coin, the *denarius*, which is often
wrongly translated 'penny', where 'shilling' would be
much more appropriate. Coinage of a lower value was
minted under the authority of the Senate, and was in
brass or copper. In the time of Augustus it is said that
the ratio was 1 aureus=25 denarii=100 sesterces=400
asses. Such coins all had a universal range throughout
the Empire. Besides these, and in the *second* place, the
Government tolerated the circulation of local curren-
cies in the various provinces and municipal areas.
Hence it would be legal tender to pay in either Imperial or local currency in a given place; but it does
not follow that that local currency would be legal
tender outside its own area (77). Some years ago a
choirboy found some coins dredged up on Midsummer
Common at Cambridge. When I took them for him to
an expert, I was told that they were Egyptian coins of
c. 165 B.C. which were in circulation long after in the
province of Egypt. The explanation offered was that
since the small hoard was found in the river Cam not
far from the foot of the Castle Hill, it was probably
thrown into the river by a soldier stationed in the fort

77   Money-changers

above it, during the Roman occupation of Britain. He may well have been sent to Britain from a regiment previously stationed in the province of Egypt, and finding that some local Egyptian coins in his wallet were of no use in a garrison town in the province of Britain, cast them away in disgust.

The local coins in circulation in Palestine seem to have been eight in number, and they were mostly those coined in the neighbouring Phoenician cities, i.e. Tyre and Sidon. They were (1) the silver *talent* which was worth 240 *aurei*, (2) the *mina*, which was one-sixtieth part of a *talent*, (3) the *drachma*, which was small silver and worth about 9½d. of English money, (4) the *didrachma* or half-shekel, which was worth about 7½p of our money, and was the amount of the levy exacted each year towards the support of the Temple from all Jews of the age of twenty and upwards (this was probably a coin made in the time of Simon the Maccabee and still in use), (5) the *stater* or shekel, worth about 21p, which is the coin mentioned in the 'thirty pieces of silver' paid to Judas Iscariot, and (6) the *assarion* and (7) *kodrantes*, which were apparently copper coins, and the nature of which is somewhat doubtful. The smallest coin mentioned in the New Testament is (8) the *lepton*, a name which simply means 'thin' or 'small', and which is rendered 'mite'. This again would seem to have been a very minute copper coin of local mintage. An *assarion* may have been less than half a new penny, and this, it is said, was the price paid for two sparrows.

Money-boxes for small savings were in common use. One, made of red earthenware, was found in excavations at the baths of Titus, and contained 250 denarii. I saw red earthenware money-boxes of identical pattern actually on sale in the Suq at Jerusalem.

BANKING

It is natural to pass from an account of coinage and currency to consider what was done with it. Both the Jewish and Roman business worlds had organised banking systems. Under the early Greeks (and even much later), temples played the part of safe deposits, but in the early Roman Empire we also find regular banking establishments, sometimes owned by a number of partners. The function of such was first to arrange for the business of foreign exchanges, and second to enable people to make deposits and to draw upon them whenever necessary. Many persons entrusted all their capital to their bankers, and payment was made by manuscript cheques, for, of course, there were as yet no printed ones. Bank accounts were kept very accurately and were regarded by Roman courts of law as good evidence in cases where such was needed. Although there were no State banks, except in Greece (where the practice by this time did prevail), bankers had to be licensed by the local authority. This would have applied as much in Jerusalem as in Rome. The *argentarius* or *shulchan* as he was called, was also entitled to lend money, and the Greek custom of using bills of exchange was also in vogue, so that a banker in Rome might receive a sum which had to be paid at Athens or Jerusalem, and then draw a bill to be paid in one of those cities by a banker on the spot. Slaves were allowed to act as bankers on their own account with their own savings, presumably only by permission of their masters, but in general a slave was only manager of a bank for his master. Rates of interest for loans were rather high. The Jewish law distinguished between what it called 'increase', and 'usury', and only allowed transactions of the latter character with

Gentiles. Herod Agrippa borrowed a sum of 20,000 drachmas (say £800 to £1000) from a Jew at Alexandria, on a bill of exchange to be paid in Italy, and the interest and commission on this was at the rate of $8\frac{1}{2}$ per cent; but in the main the influence of the Torah was against such business, and in the first century not many bankers were Jews. In Rome very high interest was charged at an early date, but later it was lowered, first to $8\frac{1}{2}$ per cent, then to 4 per cent, but this regulation did not endure, and soon we find monthly interest being charged at 1 per cent per month. During the first century A.D. it stood at 8 per cent. Extravagant and luxurious persons were, however, charged sometimes as much as 10 to 24 per cent, and even 48 per cent, and this at compound interest.

Most Roman business men kept a day-book for jotting down disbursements, and a ledger with a credit and debit column.

If you had seen account books of Roman business men you might have found, besides the ordinary Roman numerals, some unfamiliar symbols. Thus until after the first centry

> 1000 was designated by ⋔
>
> 10,000 by (⋔)
>
> 100,000 by ((⋔))
>
> and a million by ⋈

Some fractions also had special symbols. Thus the 144th part of an *as*, called a semi-sextula, was shown as Ƶ

THE BUSINESS WORLD GENERALLY

It is said that at the time of Philo the number of
Jews in Egypt amounted to about a million, and that
at Alexandria they occupied two out of the five divisions of the city, and lived there under governors of
their own, almost in a state of independence. Their
quarter, called after the fourth letter of the Greek
alphabet, *delta* (possibly from its shape Δ), lay along
the seashore, and it appears that the supervision of
navigation, both sea and river, was entirely entrusted
to them. We learn that the provisioning of Italy and
indeed of the whole Mediterranean world thus became
the business of the Jews, and the export trade in grain
from Egypt, which we have mentioned elsewhere, was
(under Government) entirely in their hands. There is
a curious analogy indeed between the position of the
Jews at Alexandria and that of the great house of
Rothschild at the time of the battle of Waterloo.
During the troubles at Rome following the murder of
Julius Caesar the Jewish bankers of Alexandria con-
trived to obtain from their correspondents earlier and
more trustworthy political news than anyone else. They
thus managed always to be on the right side, whether
as supporters of Caesar or of Octavius, and they
gained, as may be imagined, the full advantage, both
political and financial, which resulted from such
policy, just as Rothschild managed to make his fortune
by buying securities on a falling market at a time when
the news of Wellington's victory was not generally
known, but had reached him privately by pigeon-post.

We have record of some of the imports and exports
connected with Palestine in the first century. Imports,
with the exception of wood and metals, were chiefly
luxury-goods and certain sorts of food, apples from

Crete, cheese from Bithynia, fish from Spain, wine from Italy, beer from Media, dresses from India, shirts from Cilicia, veils from Arabia, sandals from Laodicea, plates from Babylon, baskets from Egypt, jugs and basins from Sidon. Exports were almost entirely agricultural products such as wheat, olive oil, balsam, honey, figs, etc. It is said that the value of exports and imports was nearly equal, but that the trade balance, if any, was on the whole in favour of Palestine.

Rabbinical Judaism laid down strict regulations with regard to all commercial transactions. A wholesale dealer must cleanse his scales or measures once a month, and a retail dealer twice a week. All weights had to be washed once a week, and balances wiped every time they were used. In sales of fluids, an ounce had to be added to every ten pounds, to make up for waste or spilling, and half an ounce for every ten pounds of solids. A bargain was not to be considered closed until both parties had taken possession of their respective properties. If a purchaser could prove that he had been overcharged, or that a higher than the controlled profit had been made, he had the right either to return the article and have his money back, or to claim the balance in money, but he could not do so unless he submitted his claim within a certain specified time. The seller was similarly protected. Goods of different qualities might not be mixed in a sale, and for the protection of the public it was forbidden to sell wine in Palestine diluted with water, unless in some place where the usage was recognised. It is well known that much old wine was thick and sticky, and needed dilution, but to dilute it before sale was likely to open the way to grave abuses. No corn was allowed to be sold until the controlled price had been announced. There is no reference to the prohibition of secret commissions, but one Rabbi condemned tradesmen who gave presents to children in order to attract the custom of their parents.

Although Jews appear to have charged interest for loans freely to Gentiles, usually it would seem to have been strictly discouraged within the nation. One curious regulation runs that if a woman borrows a loaf of bread from her neighbour, she must fix its value at the time, since a sudden rise in flour might make the loaf returned more than that which was borrowed, and so the lender might get unearned increment. If a house or a field were rented, and the rent were not paid in advance, a higher charge might be made, but this would not apply in the case of an outright purchase. It was lawful within certain restricted limits to take a pledge for a loan and in the event of non-payment to sell it, but wearing apparel, bedding, a plough-share and all articles needed for preparing food must not be sold.

TRADE-GUILDS

There were certainly trade- and craft-guilds (*collegia fabrorum*) throughout the Empire, but it appears to have been necessary to obtain an Imperial licence to form one, and this licence was not infrequently withheld, if the Emperor was advised that a union in a particular area might be used as a means of organising sedition. Labour guilds in Palestine went so far as to regulate days and hours for working, and to insure their members against losses in the matter of ships or donkeys. Pliny wanted to found a guild or *collegium* at Nicomedia to extinguish fires—a sort of national fire-service—but (!) the Emperor stopped him because he said the Bithynians were too factious, and that it would only create another instrument of party-feeling, be-

tween members and non-members. The number of
these quasi-trade-unions varied considerably from
province to province, according as the government
deemed it advisable to license them, but they were
commonest in the Rhône valley, in the old Roman or
Latin *coloniae*, and in North and Central Italy. Some
of the guilds were those of artificers attached to the
fighting-forces. The *fabrica* was the name given as the
equivalent of our ordnance corps. Arsenals or *armen-
taria* certainly existed at an early date, though originally citizens were expected to furnish their own arms.

AUCTION SALES

The organisation of the public sale of goods was
quite well known in the first century, at any rate
among the Romans. The time, place and condition of
sale were announced either by a notice posted on the
album, or by a crier. Bidding was done either by word
of mouth, or by the sort of nods and hints which are
familiar to people who go to auction sales today. Payment had to be made to the person who supervised the
auction. The latter was evidently too dignified an
official to do the usual patter himself, but he controlled
the proceedings, and made entries in his books of the
sums due from the bidders, who signed an engagement
to pay the money to him, and whom he was entitled to
sue if they defaulted. Sometimes it was a condition
that payment had to be in advance. The supervisor
employed a *praeco* or crier to play the part of the
modern auctioneer. The *praecones* called out the bid-
dings and made the usual facetious remarks to amuse
the company and keep the bidding brisk. They were
not generally educated men, but freed slaves of a low
social grade, and the Roman satirists make fun of
them. Yet, as so often happens, a job of this kind was

extremely lucrative, and a *praeco*, if he did not mind
being looked down upon, could become quite a rich
man.

PROCEDURE IN LAW COURTS

It will be remembered that when there was a disturbance at Ephesus over St. Paul's preaching, the
town clerk appeased the people by pointing out that
the disturbance was likely to bring the city into dis-
credit, and that if the Jews really had any grievance
'the courts are open, and there are deputies. Let them
implead one another'. It is clear, therefore, that the
Romans, who have always been famous for their legal
institutions, had evidently established throughout the
provinces of the Roman Empire a proper and uniform
system of law courts. It is reasonable to inquire how
the proceedings in these courts were conducted. To
give full details would obviously take up too much
space, but some of the general points may be noted.

A plaintiff *summoned* his opponent to appear in court.
If he refused to go, the plaintiff could call any by-
stander to witness the delivery of the summons and its
refusal, and he was then entitled to use force to compel
the defendant to appear, if he shirked or raised any
objection. But he had to provide transport for the
defendant if sickness or old age hindered him from
going, though the transport need not be luxurious, e.g.
there need not be cushions in the car or litter. There
was a curious ritual when the plaintiff delivered the
summons. He was supposed to touch the ear of the
witness as a symbol that he was making him listen to
the terms of it, whereupon the defendant could either
settle the matter at once out of court, or accept suit in
person, or he might employ an advocate, the equivalent of our solicitor or counsel, to appear on his behalf.

The payment of advocates was graded by the income of the person who engaged one. If there was no settlement out of court, the parties to the suit had to appear in an appointed place, and state their case. If one was present and the other not, the case was against the absentee. The proceedings were not continued beyond sunset, and if they were not finished then, the court rose, and the parties had to find bail for future appearance. Another piece of ritual was that if the case was a property dispute, either the whole of the property or some representative part of it had to be produced in court. Thus if it was a dispute about the ownership of a flock of sheep, one animal, or at least a lock of wool had to be brought in. If the dispute were over a piece of land, house property, or a ship, then a turf or a brick or a piece of the ship's timber had to be brought in. The first hearing, before a praetor, might end in an immediate decision, but if the assignment made by the praetor was not accepted, further bail was demanded by him from both parties, and the case was sent for trial by a judge. The trial might take place within two days, though there might be an adjournment, in order to call further evidence, or bring a foreign defendant from a distance, or on account of the serious illness of one of the litigants. Actions might take place *in rem*, that is to say to establish some kind of property right or privilege, or *in personam*, to deal with an injurious act or tort, such as breach of contract on the part of a certain person or persons. Modifications in procedure were made in the course of time, and in the end Roman law settled down to two main kinds of trials, those in the praetor's court, which we might call a court of summary jusrisdiction, and those in the judge's court; but under the Empire the distinction between a praetor and a judex largely ceased, and the various officials of the Empire, such as local governors, decided all cases themselves, though this may not have come into full effect until after the first century.

So far we have been dealing with what we should call civil suits. What we call criminal actions, as with us, only very slowly developed into a separate branch. A *crimen* in earlier days was regarded as an offence against religion and the gods. Later a *crimen* was defined as an offence not against a private individual, but against the State or community.[1] If there was dispute as to a contract or the ownership of some individual property, this was a matter for a civil action. But if it was a case of robbery or murder, then there was a penalty inflicted by the State. In the case of theft, not only was the value of the stolen goods recoverable, but a penalty twice or four times the estimated value of the stolen goods could be awarded as compensation. Murder of course did not admit of full restitution, so it was natural for the penalty to be much heavier. Hence the practice of capital punishment.

PUNISHMENTS

This section is bound to be an unpleasant one, but it cannot be left out without unfairly toning down the picture of social life in the first century. We have to consider that the world of that day was on the whole a cruel world, and that its punishments of criminals tended to be brutal. Cruelty unfortunately is a blemish upon human life which is hard to eradicate, and anyone who considers how the Tudor Christian King, Henry VIII, treated the Carthusian monks for refusing

---

[1] cf. the much later, though probably inherited, definition of a murder (in English law) as 'against the peace of our Soverign Lord the King (or Lady the Queen) his (or her) crown and dignity'.

to acknowledge the Royal Supremacy can hardly judge the age of Tiberius and Nero to severely. Almost everyone knows the story of how, by Nero's orders, the Christians in Rome were dressed in fantastic costumes, tied to stakes in the Imperial Gardens, and then burned to death by having their clothes soaked in inflammable material and set on fire, while the Emperor, dressed as a jockey, drove about looking on, and amusing himself with his friends. Even supposing that this is not an exaggerated account, things were perhaps not always quite so bad. Nevertheless, there was little pity for the condemned criminal. We shall see in the chapter on the public games how some convicts were given a chance to fight for their lives, and perhaps to witness a battle to the death in the arena was no more revolting than to go to Smithfield to see men hanged, drawn, quartered, or burned in public, as did our Christian forefathers. Perhaps the worst type of execution was that by crucifixion. It was not only rough and cruel, but it involved a lingering torture, since the victim was left naked, and exposed to the pitiless rays of the eastern sun and the attacks of insects, suspended by nails driven through hands and feet. Small wonder that kindly women sometimes subscribed to provide doped drinks to be given to criminals before the execution began. Nor was crucifixion rare. It is said to be heard of first among the Phoenicians, and was an oriental form of execution, but it was adopted by the Romans, and by the first century had become a normal way of dealing with those convicted of crimes of violence, as normal as was our cat o' nine tails. Moreover it was sometimes inflicted simultaneously on large numbers of offenders, especially in cases of rebellion against the government. There is a record of as many as 2000 victims being crucified all at once. Titus, during the first Jewish war, crucified on one single occasion so many prisoners that the supply of wood ran short.

Scourging seems to have been of two kinds. The Jews scourged with a rod, thirteen times on each shoulder and on the loins, i.e. the legal number of 'forty stripes save one'.[1] The face could also be scourged or struck. Roman scourging was far more terrible. Instead of rods, cords or strips of leather were used, each with a pellet of bone or metal at the end, so that the flesh was cut and mangled. It is significant that the job was given to native recruits and not to Italian soldiers. This, for instance, would mean that Christ would have been scourged by Syrian levies, and not by strictly Roman troops.

Other more prolonged punishments consisted of penal labour, usually in mines, or, as we should say, 'concentration camps'. One of these was certainly on the island of Patmos in the Aegean Sea, and the writer of the Apocalypse was evidently confined there (*damnatus in metallum* was the sentence, i.e., 'condemned to quarry ore'). Another camp, for Jews, was in Sardinia.

A punishment less severe but fraught with considerable hardship was that of banishment or *exilium*. The Emperor could forbid anyone who had incurred his displeasure from coming within a certain distance of the capital city, or he might condemn him explicitly to reside in a particular spot. Thus, Nero banished Seneca, his former tutor, to the island of Corsica, and the poet Ovid was banished to a miserable spot on the shores of the Black Sea.

Sometimes punishment involved being put in

[1] This is said to be connected with the threefold recitation of a certain verse of a Psalm containing thirteen words, with a blow for each word (thirty-nine in all).

chains, or condemned to slavery, and for slaves who
offended there were a number of barbarous punishments. They might be obliged to work in chains, they
were frequently beaten with sticks or scourged with
a whip; sometimes they were hung up by their hands
with weights tied to their feet, or suspended so that
their toes only just touched the ground, with the result
that they had to strain their feet painfully in order to
get any support. A very common mode of punishment
was to make them carry a forked structure of wood
around the neck while working. This was rather like
the Chinese board punishment, or the pillory, of which
we hear as late as the time of Charles II. It was called
a *furca*, and slaves were often flogged while bearing it.
Crucifixion was specially an extreme punishment for
slaves. A runaway slave, and also a thief, might be
branded on the forehead with an indelible mark
(known as a *stigma*). Another punishment was to be
sent to grind at the mill, which would be somewhat the
equivalent of the old treadmill in convict prisons.

Chapter VIII

PALESTINIAN HABITS

So far our aim has been to stress the resemblances between the life of the first and that of the twentieth century in Mediterranean lands. The object of this has been to show that the gap between it and ours is not anything like as wide as is often assumed. Much, however, in the habits of dwellers in Palestine is unfamiliar to modern western Europeans, and they, therefore, often miss the significance of the sayings and actions of Jesus of Nazareth. The object of this chapter then will be to try to illustrate some of those words and acts, by describing habits of Syrians which differ very much from our own.

Let us begin with the symbol of the Good Shepherd. To English-speaking boys and girls the word shepherd conjures up the figure of a man *driving* his flock with the aid of a collie or an old English sheep-dog. But the Syrian shepherd *leads*, he does not drive his sheep, and the sheep themselves, instead of being rather apathetic and stupid creatures, respond to his call like dogs, and trot along after him. Travellers in Palestine have reported that shepherds have extraordinary control over their sheep, and are able to move them about by whistling to them or playing the flute. The flute I have sometimes heard in the early morning, whilst in bed, and the sheep come trotting by. Whereas in England a Cumbrian shepherd uses his dog to move the sheep about, and gives the dog his instructions by voice or whistle, the Syrian shepherd will call the sheep to him, or tell them to disperse, or order them to come down to the stream and drink, and even, when they are about to do so, shout to them to stop, and the sheep will instantly obey. One traveller in the year 1754 actually saw a shepherd making his sheep dance by using some musical instrument, the movements being sometimes slow, rather like a musical ride of cavalry horses, and at others quick, so that the sheep actually skipped. Others have seen sheep perform tricks of balancing on the top of artificially made pyramids, again to the notes of the shepherd's pipe. All this throws much light on the metaphor of the Good Shepherd in the gospel. It is intended as a symbol of the relationship between the follower of Jesus and the Leader Himself. The follower, in fact, is not blandly driven, but intelligently led, yet nevertheless renders implicit obedience to the call of his Leader, whom he trusts and knows.

A number of other small items help to make the life of the more conservative people of Palestine more vivid as it was in the first century. The list, of course, cannot be exhaustive, but it may be enough to stimulate the reader to look further for information. Friends go *hand in hand*, not arm in arm. People never sleep in the dark, but always with a lamp burning, presumably to keep demons away. Bread must never be cut with a knife—this is taboo. The loaves are made of such a shape and pattern that they can be broken into small pieces. One of these, when broken, could be made into an *opsarion*, which was in effect a three-cornered spoon, with which the individual could dip into the common central dish, and then pass the contents either to his own mouth or to that of his friend. Ploughs usually had only one handle, so that to put one's hand to the plough would be literally correct. No full-grown dogs are kept domestically, except sometimes as watch-dogs. Most dogs are mongrels and are despised

scavengers. It is only as puppies that they are kept by
children as pets. Hence the retort of the Syrophoe-
nician woman to Christ is correctly rendered 'even the
puppies (not the dogs) eat of the crumbs which fall
from the table', and the story of Lazarus the beggar
gains added point when we read that 'even the dogs',
i.e. the most despised of creatures, were kinder to him
than the rich man and his servants.[1] It was the Gentiles who kept highly bred dogs for hunting and other
purposes.

Many phrases are only properly understood when
we recognise that in Palestinian dialect there is a curious habit of bracketing two words together, both of
them nouns, instead of having an adjective and a
noun. To take such phrases literally as we have so
often done when translating them into English is to
give a slightly distorted meaning. Examples are 'fire
and brimstone' for 'volcanic fire', 'iniquity and the
solemn meeting' meaning 'iniquitous worship', 'a
mouth and wisdom' meaning 'wise speech', 'upon a ten
stringed instrument and upon the lute', meaning
'upon a ten stringed lute', 'grace and truth' meaning
'genuine grace or sincere charm', and finally, 'of Christ
and of God' meaning 'of the Divine Messiah'.

It would be a serious breach of Eastern etiquette for
a man to speak to a woman who is a stranger, except
in an emergency to ask for a drink of water. It was,
therefore, correct enough for Christ to be represented
as asking the woman of Samaria for a drink, but it was
scandalous to be found by his disciples engaging in
a long conversation with the woman afterwards, and
especially so, as she was a Samaritan. The point about
the well is that in the case of old wells in the country

[1] For these and similar items I am indebted to the well-known
work by James Neil.

there was usually no bucket attached, but people on a journey carried their own buckets about with them. Again, the significance of the man carrying a water pot, who was to be followed by the disciples to the place appointed in Jerusalem for the meeting on the eve of the Passover is that it is not usual for men to

78   Shepherd, *leading* his flock, and carrying sick
lamb on his shoulders

carry water pots. That is a menial task usually left to women. Hence a man doing it would be conspicuous. The custom of uncovering the feet on going into a Moslem mosque, is only a particular instance of what has always been the oriental custom, namely that of showing respect to one's superiors by taking off one's shoes or sandals. No Oriental would think of having his head uncovered in the presence of his master, but equally he would not keep his footwear on. To keep on

one's shoes on entering a friend's house was bad manners. The only exception to this rule was the synagogue, where the rabbis allowed people to wear their
shoes in order to indicate that it was not of the same
sanctity as the Temple.

It is possible to increase one's understanding of the
text of the New Testament by travel through out-of-

79   Porter, carrying a 'phortion' on his back

the-way parts of Palestine, especially the Arab districts. One can thus see potters at their wheels (80), old
men in carpenters' shops (29) making yokes and
ploughs just as Joseph may have worked, men ploughing with an ox and a camel yoked side by side, so
illustrating the unequal yoking of believer and unbe-
liever, men using ox-goads, and so on. In the cities one
still sees porters, both boys and men, carrying enor-

mous burdens on their backs, unbelievably heavy. These are the *phortia* of St. Paul's day (see Galatians 6). Transport in the bazaars is in fact still absurdly crude (79). There are no electrically driven trucks. But it is not quite the purpose of this book merely to illustrate the Bible text, since this has so often been done before. What we are here concerned with is rather to stress the likeness and unlikeness in the life of the first century and that of our own day.

80 Potter at his wheel

Finally, it is just as well to recognise the extraordinary difference between first-century Syrian customs as regards marriage, and Christian marriage as we know it today. Neil[1] puts it very clearly under seven headings. First, marriage among Jews was almost universal. There was no such thing as voluntary celibacy, except among the peculiar sect known as Essenes, who were hardly genuine Jews, and perhaps among people like the Nazirites. Second, nobody thought of choosing a partner. Marriages were arranged for young people by their relatives. Thirdly, marriage could be at a very early age, say eleven or twelve, and sometimes even nine. Fourthly, first cousins would be (if possible) chosen for preference. There was obviously no scrupulous feeling against inbreeding. In the fifth place, the wife was *paid for*, just as though she were a chattel. In the sixth place there was no preliminary courtship; and lastly it was said proverbially 'love comes after marriage, not before'.

[1] See p. 210

Many of these items could be paralleled today from India or from New Guinea.

Jewish marriage rules are too complicated to be given here in detail, but a few special points may be noted. (1) Levirate marriage, i.e. marriage with one's brother's widow in order to provide him with a continuance of his stock, should he have died childless. (2) A number of prohibited degrees (given in Leviticus) for the infringement of which there were penalties of varying severity, the most extreme being death by stoning. (3) Fairly easy divorce of the wife by the husband, but not the husband by the wife, except when the influence of Roman law came in in the first century, for the Romans did allow a wife under certain conditions to divorce her husband.

BIRTHS, MARRIAGES AND DEATHS

Among the Hebrews certainly a high value was set upon the possession of children, 'like the olive-branches round about thy table: lo thus shall the man be blessed that feareth Yahweh'. This was also the case among the earlier Romans, with, of course, a preference for sons. The failure of nerve which led to the weakening of the desire for offspring was a sign of world-weariness and fear of the break-up of society, which coincided with the spread of the Christian movement, though it reached its peak later than the first century.

An expectant mother had to keep certain rules. She must not take a hot bath for fear of a miscarriage, and she was told to avoid green vegetables, salt food and fat, as these might affect the constitution of the child adversely, but she must eat salt fish and mustard. At the birth time all the ordinary rules about the keeping of the Sabbath might be broken, especially by the patient, the doctor and the midwife. The doctor was left to decide in the case of twins, which should be first born. To place a new-born infant in a manger or trough was not an out-of-the way proceeding, since the Hebrew word means both trough and cradle, and to this day troughs or mangers are used in the Near East for cradling infants. Congenital diseases such as epilepsy were believed to be due to evil demons or spirits. The words: 'my son is a lunatic' are rendered in the old Syriac, 'my son hath a roof-demon', i.e. a demon who slides down over the eaves of houses into bedrooms and afflicts babies. There were plenty of so-called remedies to ease confinements and prevent miscarriage, barrenness, or too many children. Some of these must have been purely magical. Thus, the wearing of a dead scorpion tied up in crocus-green cloth, and fastened on to the woman's skirt can only be pure magic, but certain herb-remedies may have been found of practical value. Powdered ivory drunk in wine or water was believed to help on an easy birth. On the whole the Christians abandoned most of these beliefs and practices, though as the movement spread, it was difficult to stamp them out among people who had a long pagan tradition behind them.

The newly born Jewish infant was bathed in water, rubbed with salt—to harden it off—and wrapped in swaddling clothes, from the mistaken idea that movement was bad for its limbs, which would not grow straight and strong unless kept as it were in splints. If a boy, it was circumcised on the eighth day and received its name. It was usually breast-fed by the mother, and was not weaned fully for two or three years. Baptism was not invented by Christians. It was a primitive rite of long standing which became adapted by them, or rather by the Jews, from whom the Christians took it over. It is no use pretending that we are certain it was expressly ordained by Christ. The actual command to baptise is probably a late addition and not part of the original sayings, and in the fourth gospel we read 'howbeit Jesus baptised not, but his disciples'; while Paul writes to the Corinthians, 'I thank God I baptised none of you, for God sent me not to baptise, but to preach the Gospel.' These are facts. Nevertheless, the Jews baptised their own proselytes, and John the Baptist practised the rite at his mission, while Jesus himself underwent the ceremony at his hands. It is, therefore, quite reasonable to conclude that the use of baptism as a means of incorporation into the Christian movement must have had the approval of Christ. The early care of children among the Jews we have dealt with in the chapter on education.

Jewish weddings were preceded some time before by the payment of a dowry by the intending bridegroom, and by the betrothal. The latter had to take place before two witnesses, and involved the giving and receiving of a ring, together with a certain formula of question and answer, followed by a benediction. After this the two persons were regarded as being as much bound to one another as if they were already married. The marriage proper followed after an interval of varying length, and consisted chiefly of two items: (1) *The wedding procession,* in which the man fetched his bride to the future home. This procession would be accompanied with shouting, singing and dancing, and the bridegroom would be splendidly attired, and as in India would be adorned with a garland. The story of the foolish virgins does not seem to refer to this, but to a later affair, when the bridegroom, having conducted his wife to the house, had retired to spend the evening with his male friends, and was a long time in rejoining her, so that the women attendants had grown sleepy, and were not all ready to go out and greet the bridegroom on his return. (2) *The marriage supper*. This took place in the house of the husband's family, and was a tremendous affair. Originally the happy pair may have sat under a small tent, but this later on became simply a canopy, under which the bridal couple were enthroned in fine clothing. The meal was lavish to the limit of extravagance, and it was a serious breach of hospitality to run short of anything like wine. The bride would sit crowned and arrayed with her jewels. As time went on, covenant rites would come to be added to this ceremonial feast, which at first, no doubt, was in itself the only ceremony, and involved the solemn eating together of the bridegroom and bride, the only vestige of which now survives to us is the cutting of the cake at the so-called wedding breakfast. Freya Stark says, however, that at a Jewish wedding she attended in Baghdad, the two people drank out of the same cup, which was then solemnly broken, and it is possible that this may have been a very old custom. Roman (Gentile) weddings of the early Empire have been described in the volume in this series on life in Roman Britain, and the reader is referred to this for information.

Some account of Roman burial ceremonies has also been given in the volume of *Everyday Life in Roman Britain*. These, like other Gentile funeral rites, had certain common features, which have survived among European peoples even to this day, and which turn up in areas like Lancashire, Ireland and the Balkans, even in the twentieth century. We may take the Greek ceremonies as an example. At the moment of death it was customary to ensure a number of witnesses, preferably those of the family of the deceased person. The eyes and mouth of the corpse were closed by someone present. A coin was placed in the mouth. The body was then washed, anointed, and clothed in a white garment, with a wreath of flowers on the head. It was then laid out—the *prothesis*—and the near relations of the deceased as well as professional wailers, lamented loudly, tore their hair, and lacerated their cheeks, rending their clothes and casting ashes upon their heads. The funeral procession to the pyre—the *ekphora*—followed, perhaps after a few days' interval, though in a hot climate the funeral might have to take place at once. The Greeks both burned and buried their dead, but on the whole, cremation was the more usual practice, though the Persians before Zoroaster, and (as we shall see) the Jews, both used burial. The Persians as we know, after Zoroaster, practised the exposure of corpses to birds of carrion in their *dakshmas* or towers of silence, but in general the Gentile custom was to cremate. If burial did take place it was usually in a stone or wooden coffin. Immediately after the disposal of the body followed the funeral feast in the house of the nearest relative. Other ceremonies were performed on the third, ninth and thirtieth days after the funeral, and each year on certain days it was the custom to bring offerings of wine, oil, milk or a mixture of honey and either milk or water, and to pour out the offerings upon the grave, which, of course, reminds us greatly of the ancient Chinese ancestor-worship and of the *pitripuja* in India. The period of mourning varied in different localities. At Athens it lasted till thirty days after the funeral. A sort of symbolism was employed to distinguish the causes of death, if unusual. A spear was carried in front of the bier of one who had been murdered. In the case of a suicide, the hand of the person which had done the deed was cut off and buried separately. If after a battle anyone's body was missing, an empty bier was carried in the funeral procession. Special features of Roman funeral rites not perhaps previously mentioned were: (1) the catching of the dying person's breath by someone present, (2) the calling three times of the name, to ensure that death had really taken place, (3) the making of a wax funeral mask or *imago*, which was afterwards hung up in the *atrium* of the house, and subsequently carried in processions at funerals of descendants of the deceased. Roman funerals usually were ordered to take place at night, partly to avoid the inevitable congestion of traffic; but later on, only those of children, and poor persons who could not afford display, took place in this way. Black was generally worn for mourning, except in the case of women, when, under the emperors, white garments came to be worn. The days from the 13th to 21st of February were set apart as *dies parentales* for ceremonies in memory of parents, and sacrifices of black-coloured victims were offered, again a form of ancestor-worship.

Jewish funerals had certain special features. The burial was speedy, either the same day, as in the story of Lazarus, or within twenty-four hours. The corpse was washed, anointed and bound with special grave clothes, and there was the customary lamentation and wailing, especially by professional wailers, but there were no offerings made to the spirit. Ancestor-worship is excluded by the law of Moses (Deut. 26[14]). Coffins were not used for the primary burial among the eastern Jews, nor are they to this day. The body was placed upon a simple bier, and was either buried in the ground or placed in a cave. In the latter case the precaution was taken of closing the cavemouth with a large boulder, to prevent the depredations of such scavengers as jackals.[1] It seems curious that no record exists of actual religious services being conducted at funerals of Jews, and the absence of these is still noticeable among eastern Jews today. Although many Jews believe in a resurrection, there is nothing in their funeral customs to indicate this, and the inference is that the traditional ceremonies date from a time when belief in a future life was practically non-existent among them. We know that at the time of Christ the Pharisees were said to believe in a resurrection, while the Sadducees rejected the very notion of a personal immortality, and equally disbelieved in angels and demons. As early as the time of the Acts there would appear to have been the formation of a kind of guild of devout men who made themselves responsible for laying out corpses and attending to burials, since this would ensure that no one suffered the terrible indignity of remaining unburied. The Jews never cremated their dead. Public provision was made at Jerusalem for the burial of strangers (see Matt. 27[7]), and such a cemetery was where it still is, between the city wall and the valley of the Kidron. The sides of the valley of Jehoshaphat were a favourite burial ground, because of the wide belief that the Messiah would descend on to the Mount of Olives, and pass in procession through the centre of this cemetery in order to enter in glory into Jerusalem. There is one interesting tomb in it known quite wrongly as the tomb of Absalom (97), which is believed to be of the first century, and, if so, shows the style of architecture then prevalent in Jewish

[1] See the illustrations of tombs in Israeli Jerusalem (97, 98), especially the one believed to be that of the family of Herod. Also the picture (67) which shows a tomb similar to the so-called Tomb of Absalom, in the Kidron valley—partly Greek, partly Oriental.

circles, partly Asiatic, partly Graeco-Roman. Other examples of rock-tombs, lately excavated on the Israeli side, are here illustrated, and are also believed to be first century.

When the Jews found that the skeleton of a corpse had crumbled after a long interment, they took it out

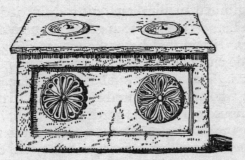

81 Jewish ossuary. At one cemetery of about the first century near Jerusalem, nearly all the inscriptions on Jewish monuments were in Greek, not Hebrew, showing the high percentage of Jews who used Greek as their language

of the tomb, probably to economise in space, and put it into a small, carved, stone box called an ossuary (see illustration). One such ossuary, found a few years ago in Palestine had the inscription: 'Jeshua ben Joseph', but the name was a common one, and the locality where it was found such that any connection with the Great Figure of the Gospels is ruled out. At the same time, the inscription gives some idea as to how Christ might on occasion have signed his name.

Chapter IX

SLAVERY

I F there is one item which is almost wholly absent
from our world but which was universally taken
for granted in the first century A.D. it is that of
slavery. Let us begin by seeing how it operated among
the Jews. If you had been the son or daughter of a
well-to-do citizen of Jerusalem, your father might very
well have had in his establishment one or more
servants who were not hired in the way that we hire
cooks, housemaids and gardeners, but who were
actually the *property* of your father. That is to say he
had bought them somewhere, and they were not free
to leave his service. He owned them as much as you
may own a dog or a pony that has been given you for
a present. There were several ways in which this could
happen. Suppose that a man was destitute. He could,
if he liked, sell himself to somebody, and in that case
he became the bondman of that person. This meant
that except under certain conditions he lost his freedom. He could also, if he had a little girl under the age
of twelve, and whom he was too poor to maintain, sell
her to somebody as a female slave. In this case, however, the child could be bound for no longer than a
maximum of six years, and when she became old
enough to marry, she had either to be taken in marriage by her master or his son, if he had one, or if they
did not want her, she had to be set free. Another way
in which people became slaves was owing to crime or
debt. If someone owed money, he could sell himself to
his creditor, and if he were a thief, and were unable to
make restitution of the stolen goods, the court could

order him to be sold to the person from whom he had stolen them. Prisoners of war could also be bought and sold by the states whose armies had captured them, and so Jews could, if they so wished, buy foreign slaves. Slaves, however, even though they were chattels, had certain privileges, and were under some measure of legal protection. Thus, a foreign slave could be circumcised and become virtually a Jew, being allowed to attend Passover and eat the Passover meal, and if his master were a priest, to share the food of the priest. Also he was not to be allowed to work on a Sabbath. He might be chastised, but he must not be deliberately killed, and he must not suffer mutilation at his master's hands. Indeed, Jews prided themselves that they never treated their slaves with cruelty.[1] That, they said, was only done among the Gentiles. Still the position of slaves was, to our thinking, a degraded one. They could not own property absolutely. Anything which came into their possession belonged to their masters, and they could be bequeathed by will in just the same way as pieces of furniture or livestock on a farm. They could, however, under certain circumstances, be set free, by what was called an act of manumission, or they might be redeemed by their friends or relatives if they had the money to do so. Whenever a slave was freed, he or she was entitled under ordinary conditions to a sum of money as a parting gift or gratuity. This rule did not apply in the case of slaves who had sold themselves into bondage, nor to those who had managed to get redeemed at a lower rate than their original purchase price. And then there was

[1] There was a Roman saying: 'He who buys a Hebrew slave buys a master to himself', because such slaves could demand a special treatment. Juvenal depicts a Roman lady of the smart set as saying haughtily: 'Is a slave really a man?'

always the old Jewish custom of the year of Jubilee, in which slaves could be set free. When freed, they often took the name of their former owner, so that in Rome, many slaves of Jewish origin, when they became freed-men, took good Roman names.[1] Although it was the duty of the master to give decent burial to any slave who died in his service, he was forbidden to make any mourning ceremonies for the deceased.

Let us now turn to the condition of slaves among non-Jewish peoples. Those who admire the Greeks ought to realise how completely Greek civilisation was built upon the existence of a slave class. According to a census made in the state of Attica in 309 B.C., there were then 21,000 male, free citizens of full age against 400,000 slaves and another estimate makes the total population of 500,000 to be made up of 90,000 citizens, 45,000 resident aliens, and 365,000 slaves. Even the poorest citizen in Athens owned at least one slave. The father of Demosthenes owned about fifty, and Nicias had a thousand slaves working for him in the mines. Roman slaves were usually employed in the household or on the farm, and not, as in Greece, for industrial purposes. The conditions of slaves in the Greek mines were disgraceful. Under Greek law all prisoners of war automatically became the property of the conqueror, but a good many were set free on payment of a ransom. Nevertheless, most of the Greek slaves were acquired by purchase, some of them being kidnapped by pirates

[1] The price of Jewish slaves is given in the Talmud as either one to two or five to ten *mnas*, whereas a Gentile slave could fetch as much as 100 *mnas*. This difference was due to the fact that the maximum time for the use of a Jewish slave could only be six years, till the next year of Jubilee, whereas a Gentile slave might remain his master's property all his life and was therefore more valuable.

and sold in the slave markets of Athens and the other
Greek states, and there were also regular slave-traders.
The Greeks, perhaps, on the whole treated their slaves
rather better than neighbouring nations, but that is
not saying much. Slaves in the mines worked in chains,
and the rate of mortality was terribly high, owing to
the lack of ventilation. Slaves generally expected to be
tortured if giving evidence in a law court, but on the
other hand the life of the slave was protected even from
his master, and he could not be put to death without
the sentence of a law court. Slaves in danger of having
their chastity violated could take sanctuary in a
temple, and then claim the privilege of being sold to
a different master. Among the Greeks slavery went on
much in this way up to Christian times, and even then
it persisted for some centuries, and only faded out
gradually.

The status of Roman slaves was in some ways not so
good. The slave was legally a chattel, completely in
the power of his master, and was a 'thing' and not a
'person'. At the same time, unlike an animal, a slave
could change his status, obtain his freedom, and so
become a legal 'person', and slaves were often well
treated, and allowed to eat at the same table as their
owners. Roman slaves, however, could not legally
marry, nor could they actually own any property.
Anything conveyed to them thereby became technically the property of their owner. It was a general rule
that illegitimate children followed the status of the
mother, so that if a female slave had any children, they
became slaves themselves, but the usual way in which
persons became slaves was either by capture, or by
conviction in respect of some crime. Prisoners taken by
the Roman army were usually either kept by the State
as government slaves, or sold by the Treasury to

private purchasers. Very occasionally they were distributed among the troops by lot. Anybody who evaded
military service was also liable to slavery, and some
unfortunate people even sold themselves as slaves.

The two chief ways in which slaves might become
free were either by a legal act on the part of their
owners, or through a remission obtained by various
ways, such as the payment of a ransom, or the quashing
of slave-status by the State; but there were a good
many other ways, such as being turned off by one's
owner on account of ill-health, or as a reward for
detecting crime.

The occupation of slave-dealer was considered dis-
reputable, but a great deal of money was made out of
it. Slaves at Rome were usually sold by auction. They
were put on a rostrum where everybody could see
them, and they were stripped naked and sometimes
medically examined, so as to avoid the concealment of
physical defects by dealers. Slaves newly imported
(being somewhat in demand) had their feet whitened
with chalk, and tied round the neck was a sort of
certificate or written guarantee giving the character of
the slave. Slaves of exceptional beauty were usually
sold by private treaty. A dealer was in theory legally
bound to state all the defects in the slave, and if he
tricked the buyer by falsehood he was liable to have to
take the slave back up to a period of six months from
the time of the sale, or to pay compensation. The
nationality of the slave had also to be declared. It was
a serious criminal offence to harbour runaway slaves,
and was the equivalent of being a receiver of stolen
property.

We must try to picture ourselves what everyday life
both for slaves and free people must have been under
such conditions. Although it was usual to allow slaves

holidays at public festivals, owners might employ their slaves as many hours a day as they pleased, and the punishments inflicted upon them were terrible. Roman ladies barbarously treated female slaves at the slightest error in their toilet. Sometimes slaves had a large forked pole fastened to their necks and their hands tied to it, and were then made to carry it about.

Strange to say, the status of slavery ended with death, so that it was not only the duty of an owner to bury his slave, but slaves were sometimes even given burial along with their owners.

As among the Greeks, so among the Romans and Jews, slavery only gradually declined, but the enhanced status given by Christ to every individual soul, and also the teaching of the Stoic philosophers about the brotherhood of man (which harmonised with it to some extent), made it difficult for the institution of slavery to survive, though it persisted in a measure right on into the Middle Ages, and was unhappily revived in the sixteenth and seventeenth centuries by the white races in their treatment of coloured people, owing to a rather wilful misunderstanding of Scripture.

Salo Wittmayer Baron, in his *Social and Religious History of the Jews* (New York, 1952), says that the rabbis of the first century certainly did much to protect their Gentile slaves. They strongly discouraged concubinage with slaves, as creating a large hereditary class of half-castes. At the same time they also discouraged manumission, since the freeing of slaves created an influx into the Jewish community.

It was said also that the proverbial maxims of slaves were: Love one another. Love robbery. Love licentiousness. Hate your masters, and never tell the truth.

Most of the negresses who control the sale of roast pea-nuts today in the streets of Jerusalem on the

Jordan side, are said to be the descendants of negro slaves, but I doubt whether any of these have a pedigree going back to the first century. Anyhow, they are picturesque figures, wearing the brightest of clothing, with little three-legged stools and charcoal braziers.

Chapter X

EDUCATION

MANY people still seem to think that in the days of Christ there were no schools, and indeed that universal education is something that was brought in during the nineteenth century. Nothing could be farther from the truth. Organised education of children is a most ancient thing. We find it in Mesopotamia perhaps a thousand years before Christ, where the remains of schools with benches for the scholars have been dug up. We find it in Egypt at the same period, and we know, from the papyrus remains, something of what the school books were like. In the age of the New Testament the education of the young was well developed, although the methods differed in different communities. It was, in the opinion of some scholars the age of the widest literacy for about 1800 years to come. Graffiti scrawled on rocks in Trans-jordania show what a very large percentage of the population was in some measure able to read and write.[1]

Let us start with Palestine. It will surprise many to know that there were schools at least in every town, and compulsory education in them for all children above the age of six. But matters went much further than that. From its earliest days every Jewish child was surrounded with a distinct atmosphere. First there was the admission to membership of the community by

---

[1] One of these may be quoted: '—the flute-player went out into the desert and was killed. How vain is life!' (From a rock near the R.A.F. station at Mafrak.)

circumcision. Then, for the very young, there was the simple teachings of the mother, and the child would see all kinds of things being done in the home which had a religious meaning, and were instructive, long before he could read. Thus, there would be all the ceremonies connected with the Sabbath, and with the various festivals, especially the Passover, and each child was taught a text of Scripture which contained the same letters as his Hebrew name, and he would have to memorise some psalms. But at the age of five or six every child had to go to school, and it was said in one of the tractates of the Talmud that it was unlawful to live in a place where there was no school. Although teaching was often carried on in the open air, the schools were held quite generally either in the synagogues themselves or in special school-houses. Seats were not introduced until a later date, and teacher and pupils either stood or sat on the ground in a semicircle. After learning to read and write, the children were exclusively taught up to ten years of age from the text of the Old Testament; between ten and fifteen they went on to study the traditional Law or Mishna; after fifteen the pupil passed on to higher studies involving theological discussion. It is rather curious that the child started the Bible with the Book of Leviticus, and then passed on to the Pentateuch, the Prophets and the other books. The sort of material that was later on put into the Talmud was only taught in the Academies after the pupil had reached the age of fifteen. It must be fairly clear that this was rather a narrow syllabus, and although it could no doubt be made a peg on which to hang a good deal of general knowledge, it was almost entirely a religious syllabus, and contained no mathematics, no science, no physical training, and no general history or geography. It was,

in fact, very much like the syllabus of those Moslem
schools where the principal subject is the memorising
of the Koran.

From the foregoing remarks it must also be pretty
clear that the schooling of a Jewish boy was rather like
that of a Tibetan or Burmese boy in old-fashioned
circles at the present day; that is to say, it was mainly
religious, and the Buddhist monks in both Burma and
Tibet play very much the part that the Rabbis did in
first-century Palestine. (We may note that there is no
word in Tibetan for 'literature' other than a word
which means 'religious literature'.)[1]

When we turn to the countries into which the
Christian movement first spread, the position is somewhat different.

Outside Jewish circles, education in the eastern
Mediterranean and in Rome was carried on on a much
wider basis.[2] It is possible that there was not the same
insistence upon universal attendance, and that the
children in the lower strata of the population escaped
its net, but it was a very real thing, and it had its roots
in ancient Greece. We learn that in the first century
A.D. there were, in the urban centres, not only state
schools and municipal schools, but that these were
for girls as well as boys, while a variety of secular
subjects were taught in them, such, for example, as

[1] In the new republic of Israel the party of Orthodox Jews has
successfully demanded a form of education for its children which
differs from that given in the first century, and these Orthodox
conscientiously object to sending their children to the ordinary
Israeli State schools which they consider encourage habits of
irreligion.

[2] The extent to which even Jews became hellenised, or at any
rate bilingual, may be judged from one recent piece of evidence.
In a Jewish cemetery of our period near Jerusalem, eighty per cent
of the epitaphs were in Greek.

mathematics. In the eastern Mediterranean in Hellenistic circles the school was a very old tradition, and we may say indeed that the education of children outside the home goes back to very early times. We know, for instance, that in ancient Sparta there were what we should call boarding-schools for boys, of a very severe character. In Italy the situation had been somewhat different, and in early times the Roman boy had most of his education at home, beginning with his mother, and passing on to his father, whom he sought in every way to imitate. If his father was a farmer, he would work with him on the farm, and this parental training went on until he was about sixteen or seventeen. Athletics played a large part in his daily life, running, riding, boxing, wrestling, swimming, hunting and the use of weapons. He was expected to rough it a good bit, had only one set of clothes, sandals, but no covering for his legs, rode a horse bareback, and was seldom allowed the luxuries of a bath and a feast. Gradually, however, Greek ideas crept in from the eastern Mediterranean, so that by the beginning of the first century A.D. the Romans had had schools for quite a long time (82), though probably to begin with such schools were very informal, and the schoolmasters were not paid regular fees, but were dependent on whatever the parents of the boys chose to give them, and this system of payment by voluntary contribution went on almost to the Christian era. The status of such schoolmasters was lower in Rome than anywhere in the Greek world. The Greeks respected the teacher, but the Romans thought his job rather a low-grade one, and as often as not teachers were slaves, or men who had been slaves. There was one who started life as a door porter, and who, being a slave, was chained to his master's door, and there is a record that educated slaves who

82 School, with small boy being flogged
(*From a Pompeian wall-painting*)

could teach the young commanded a high price in the
slave market, one of them being sold for 700,000
sesterces, which was a record sum. This situation cannot have been good either for the children or the
teachers, and it seems that under such conditions most
of the teaching was not of a very high order and was
purely utilitarian, merely reading, writing and arithmetic. Bit by bit, however, the standard improved.
When Greek teachers came to Rome, it became
fashionable for those who could afford it to be educated on Greek lines. Thus, by the time of Cicero,
roughly less than a century before Christ, the Romans
were beginning to see the possibilities of what we
should call a liberal education. Cicero, in fact, wrote
a book about it, and from this, and references in Varro
and Vitruvius, we get a good idea of what this 'liberal
education' meant. It is remarkable that the different
branches of it were called *Artes* (plural of *ars*) (the

Greek word for the same thing was Techne). We use the word 'technical education' to mean things like woodwork and engineering, but the Greek idea of 'techne' was an ordered system of human knowledge based on first principles. Cicero, for instance, complains that in his day the study of Roman law was not yet an 'ars', because it had no systematic form, on the basis of which it could be taught. We shall get a better idea of what this new Roman education was, if we see what was happening in the eastern Mediterranean from which it came. In the (practically state) schools of Hellenistic Greece a child's education was graded into elementary and secondary, the secondary beginning, as we should say, at twelve plus. Up to then the elementary schoolmaster taught the child to read, write and count, and perhaps to draw, and there were also classes in music by a special master, and gymnastic classes as well.[1] At the age of twelve, the boy passed on to a higher school, where he was taught literature on the one hand, consisting of Homer and poetry in general, and advanced mathematics on the other, under a special mathematical master who was called a geometres. For these senior scholars there seems to have been as many as seven or even nine 'artes liberales'. Cicero mentions philosophy, mathematics, music, literature and rhetoric, but Varro mentions dialectics, rhetoric, arithmetic, geometry, astronomy, music, medicine and architecture, and Vitruvius gives another list, literature, drawing, geometry, optics, arithmetic, history, philosophy, music, medicine, law and astronomy. We may, perhaps, see what optics and astronomy meant when we come to the chapter on the science of

---

[1] In the Jerusalem museum is a curious pottery lamp shaped in the form of an old schoolmaster, with his mouth open, reading from an open book. This was found at Amka, near Acre.

that day, but it seems odd to us to teach medicine in an
ordinary school, and it would be interesting to know
what the syllabus of it was like. Actually there was
more stress on the literary than on the scientific side,
and this led to the student being taught how to write
elegantly and to make fine, graceful and florid
speeches, but it did not involve teaching the boys to
think much. It will be seen, however, that it was not
really very different from the kind of education that
one could get in a public school in England during the
eighteenth century, and its results were probably
neither better nor worse. Towards the beginning of the
Christian era, Roman society altered a good bit in its
composition. The old aristocratic families declined,
and the Empire bred a new sort of successful civil
servant. Such persons were essentially practical, and
had very little use for a liberal education. Something
of the spirit of this new class seems to be reflected in a
speech which comes in a comedy by the poet Petronius,
where one of the characters airs his views on education
in terms which sound rather like those of some north-
country industrialist in England, and which is so
amusing that I venture to quote it here.

'You think I'm an old chatter box, Agamemnon;
but why don't you answer me, you who've been
taught to make speeches? You're not one of us, and
that's why you laugh at us poor folk, when we open
our mouths. We all know you're mad on books.
But come over to my farm some day, and I'll show
you my little cottage. You'll get something to eat
there: chickens, eggs, something worth eating, even
though the weather has turned everything topsy-
turvy this year. And I've got a young boy who
would make a good pupil for you. He has learnt

simple division already and you may have him as a servant-boy yet, if he lives. For he never has his head out of a book, if you give him a minute to spare. He's clever and a good lad, but he's crazy on birds. I've killed three of his goldfinches already, and told him it was the weasel that ate them. But now he's got a new fad and will do nothing but paint. However, he has begun his Greek at last, and is beginning to like his Latin, though his master is a conceited fellow who is never quiet at any job I give him, but comes and asks for something to copy, and then won't do his own work. I've got another boy too, but he's no scholar. He's anxious to learn, however, and is getting along faster than he thinks. He comes home every holiday and takes whatever you give him. So I've bought the lad some of those red-letter books, for I want him to learn some law and be able to keep himself. That's the job that pays. For he's got education enough for his age. If he comes off, I've made up my mind to teach him a trade. We'll make him a barber or an auctioneer, or at the worst an advocate. Then he's safe for life. So I keep telling him every day: Believe me, my boy, whatever you learn is all for the good. Look at the advocate Phileros. If he hadn't learnt his lessons, he'd go hungry today. It's not so long since he was carrying sacks to the market on his back, and now he's able to hold his own against Norbanus. Education is a gold-mine, my boy, and a trade sticks to you for life.'

Another of the guests at the dinner party represented in the play of Petronius boasts that he has not learnt 'geometry and literature and all the rest of that sort of nonsense', but can read the letters on an inscription, knows his weights and measures, and can add up any sum. Seneca, who was a contemporary of St. Paul, calls such an education only fit for a slave, but it is probable that even many citizens who were free-born did not get any farther, though the important point is that even the slave class was by no means illiterate. In this connection it is rather interesting to see what a man of Seneca's class thought of the different occupations. There seem to have been three grades, first the liberal professions, which were not the same as ours, and were philosophy, law, rhetoric and presumably state administration. Then came medicine, engineering and architecture, which were in a middle position, and then came what Cicero calls 'the sordid trades', such as shopkeeping, cooking, dancing and all forms of manual labour. Cicero thinks that of money-making professions none is better, more fruitful, more pleasant and more worthy of a free man than agriculture. Yet unfortunately at the beginning of the Christian era there was a bitter complaint that scientific agriculture, which would have been of great practical value, was not being taught in the schools, although excellent books on the subject had been written and were in circulation, and that the farms, instead of being worked by Roman citizens who took a personal interest in them, were passing into the hands of rich men who lived in the cities and who rarely, if ever, visited their estates, but left them to be worked by gangs of slaves under the management of a foreman.

As for higher education, it is said that except at Alexandria, little advanced mathematics or science was taught, but there were centres of education of what might be called 'University standard' in many places, such as Carthage, Tarsus and Marseilles, and the common American practice of having distinguished persons as travelling lecturers was already in vogue. These drew large and interested audiences in such places as Smyrna and Pergamum (cities in Asia Minor of which we read in the book of Revelation).

Chapter XI

SCIENCE IN THE FIRST CENTURY—
THEORETICAL AND APPLIED[1]

WE make a great mistake if we think that the
world of the first century was entirely ignorant
of science, whether theoretical or applied. We
have learned that the elements of mathematics and
engineering were in existence in Mesopotamia as far
back as 3500 B.C., and from there they must have
travelled into other countries in the Middle East.
Ancient Babylonian tablets show multiplication tables,
tables of squares and cubes, and a decimal and duo-
decimal system, the latter making it easy to calculate
fractions. In the same way astronomy in Mesopotamia
can be traced back to earlier than 2000 B.C. The rising
and setting of the planet Venus was recorded and
noted down, and by 600 B.C. the periodicity of events
in the heavens had been noted, and men had begun to
calculate in advance the relative positions of the sun
and moon, and by careful records and calculations, to
predict eclipses. It is true that astronomy went wrong,
badly wrong, in assuming that the stars in their courses
had influence over the affairs of men, and 700 years
before Christ a library of clay tablets for divination
and astrological purposes had come to be made, and
was said to have included records 3000 years old.
Astrology reached its height in Babylon about forty
years after the time of Nebuchadnezzar, that is to say
about 540 B.C., and from thence it spread into Greece

[1] I should like to record my indebtedness for part of this chapter
to the fine work of that distinguished member of my college, the
late Sir William Dampier.

and over the whole of the Mediterranean world, only gradually transforming itself into more rational science. In New Testament times astrology was greatly in vogue and was much resorted to. We, who have seen a revival of it in England during the past 40 years can hardly afford to criticise the ancients for their stupidity and wrong-headedness.

Applied mechanics is seen in quite early times in Egypt, where we find various uses of the wheel, accurate weighing by the balance, and weaving of a high order by the loom. In arithmetic and geometry the Egyptians were about on a level with the people of Mesopotamia, but like the latter, they went wrong in astronomy, and thought of the universe as a sort of rectangular box with realms above and below it, and a slightly concave bottom, with Egypt in the middle.

It was Greek free thought after about the year 580 B.C. which made advances in pure science possible. The whole point is that the Milesian philosophers believed that the whole universe was rational, and that it could be explained through knowledge carefully acquired by ordinary means and by research, involving accurate observation. With this began attempts at constructing a theory of the physical universe. The first serious attempt at a map of the world was made by one of these Greeks, and he recognised that bodies in the sky seemed to revolve around the pole star (83). He also saw the visible dome of the sky as only half of what might be visible, and he therefore thought that the sun passed under the earth at night and not around the edge of it, as older astronomers used to think. He still thought of the earth as the centre around which the sun and the stars revolved, but he did make some steps in the right direction. Between two and three hundred years later a very important person, Aris-

tarchus of Samos, put forward the theory that the
earth revolved around the sun on the circumference of
a circle, with the sun lying at the centre of the orbit.
Plutarch, who is roughly contemporary with the
Apostles, mentions this theory, so it was evidently still
well known, although Aristarchus himself had been

83   Astronomer making an observation

dead for over two hundred years. But a great many
people did not accept it, although a little later than
Aristarchus the same idea was put forward by a Babylonian astronomer who argued vigorously in favour of
it. In spite of this, what is called the geocentric theory
took its place, and continued to be the generally
accepted one right up to the time of Galileo. Sir
William Dampier says that we ought not to disparage
it, since it guided the labours of many competent
astronomers, and did for many centuries successfully

interpret the phenomena of the heavens. The worst
thing about it was that it encouraged astrology, since
as long as people thought of the earth as the centre of
the universe, such beliefs seemed inevitable. We find,
therefore, in the first century a great deal of astrology,
and indeed a general feeling of helplessness as a result
of it, since if the stars in their courses really could
determine the fate of human beings, there was nothing
to be done about it, and one was conscious of living
under a tyranny. It has, therefore, to be noted as a
matter of fact that, although the Christian movement
had no direct connection with science, by its teaching
that the whole universe was under the control of one
living super-personal Deity, it did away completely for
the time being with the fear of the *heimarmenē* or fates.
The return of astrology during the last fifty years, in
spite of the immense progress in astronomy, which one
would have thought would have made it impossible,
must therefore, in all probability, be attributed to a
popular weakening in the acceptance of Christian
belief.

About the middle of the third century B.C. a great
institution for research in literature, mathematics,
astronomy and medicine was founded in Alexandria,
and had attached to it the largest library in the
ancient world, containing some four hundred thousand
manuscript books. It is one of the tragedies of history
that part of this library was destroyed in A.D. 390 by
order of a Christian bishop, and the rest of it in 640,
by Moslem invaders. This research institute was
known as the Museum, and it must have had considerable influence on all the inhabitants of Alexandria, and so upon the Hellenistic Jews. It had a very
good school of medicine, which has been referred to in
another chapter, and it is remarkable that its founders

and their pupils worked empirically, and practised human dissections and animal vivisection. The greatest physician was Herophilus, who gave a good account of the brain, nerves, eye, liver, arteries and veins, and maintained that the brain was the seat of conscious intelligence, and not the heart, as Aristotle had said, and as apparently the Jews also believed.

Another important group of great scientists appeared in the third century B.C. Among these was Eratosthenes, who was librarian of the Museum, and the first important authority on physical geography. He taught that the earth was a sphere, and calculated its size, twenty-four thousand miles, which is only eight hundred miles short of the modern estimate. He also calculated that the sun was ninety-two million miles from the earth, as against the modern estimate of ninety-three million miles. He had the right idea about the connection between the Indian and Atlantic Oceans, and was probably the first to conjecture the existence of the American Continent. A little later, great advance was made in mathematics by an expert who collected together all the work done by Euclid and others upon conic sections, and brought the subject much farther on by his own studies. We owe to this man, Apollonius of Perga, the technical names parabola, ellipse and hyperbola. Another astronomer was Claudius Ptolemy, who wrote a book on optics which has been described as the most remarkable experimental research of antiquity. Ptolemy was also a great map-maker, and insisted on correct observation of latitude and longitude as a prelude to doing any surveying or map-drawing. It is a pity that he was hampered by lack of good instruments. Unfortunately, Ptolemy also wrote a book on astrology which had an evil influence after the advent of Christianity.

Chemistry did not emerge at this time as a real science, but was held back by men's obsession with the desire to turn all metals into gold. It is true that these *alchemists*, as we call them, accidentally stumbled upon all kinds of useful facts and processes, such as for instance, making imitation pearls, cheap dyes, and alloys which imitated the appearance of gold and silver, but this happened by the way, and again and again they misunderstood and misinterpreted their chance discoveries.

It is perhaps in mechanics that some of the most useful work was done in antiquity, and especially by a Sicilian Greek, Archimedes, of whom you are sure to have heard, and who was killed by a soldier in the year 212 B.C. after the siege of Syracuse. Archimedes discovered a number of important laws of physics, such as, for example, that any body floating in a liquid is supported by the liquid with a force equal to the weight of liquid of the same volume as itself. He found this out by measuring the amount of water displaced by his own body in the bath, and he went on to study the relative densities of different types of matter, and discovered that for equal weights a lighter alloy would displace more water than a heavier metal like gold.

But Archimedes was more than a physicist. He used the principles which he discovered to make machines, such as compound pulleys and hydraulic screws, as well as military machines, with which he helped his fellow-citizens to keep the Romans from conquering Sicily for three years. We may say, in fact, that he was the first to apply scientific invention to the prosecution of war.

Now it was all this science which was inherited by the men of the first century A.D., to whom the Christian movement came. It is, therefore, an error to assume that the acceptance of Christian belief on the part of the inhabitants of the Mediterranean world was an acceptance by a world which was without science, and without people who made a practice of empirical discovery.

This seems to be the right place in which to say something about Pliny the Elder. He was born in A.D. 23, and lost his life, largely owing to his insatiable curiosity regarding natural phenomena, in the year 79, during the eruption of Vesuvius, when Pompeii was destroyed. We learn much about him from his nephew, who was a great letter-writer, and was for a time Governor of Bithynia, where he had, at the beginning of the second century, to deal with the rapidly growing Christian movement, concerning which he wrote and asked the advice of the Emperor Trajan. Pliny the Elder was also in government service, at one time as a cavalry officer, at another as a high-level civil servant. He was a prolific author, and began by composing a treatise on the use of the javelin by cavalry. Later he wrote a work in twenty volumes on the wars in Germany. By far the most important of his books, however, is his *Natural History*, which is really an encyclopaedia of knowledge divided into thirty-seven volumes, and based partly on personal observation, partly on the authority of other writers, amounting to about 100 or more, nearly all of whose works have now perished. What Pliny records has to be received with caution, because he is not always accurate or consistent, and is often credulous, but used with care, his work is a mine of information on all kinds of subjects. What, perhaps, is most interesting is the trouble he takes to investigate natural phenomena, even if his explanations of them are not always correct. For example, he says that olives and other vegetation grow in the Red Sea, which sounds to us absurd until we realise that he is trying to tell us about the coral beds with their tree-like and shrub formations. His powers of observation are rather like those of Gilbert White of Selborne, and he puts down everything that he can, though he does not always see the true significance of it. But he asks the right questions, even if he gives the wrong answers, and he is thus in line with the original founders of the Royal Society. For instance, he asks, What is the origin of the winds? Why does a corona sometimes spread round the sun? What is the dimension of the earth? Why are the stars of different colours? Why are eclipses sometimes invisible in certain places? How do we know that the earth is a globe? Is the Universe finite, and is there more than one world in it? Are there antipodes? Why is the sea salt? and so on. He has a large section on zoology, and here again he often records peculiar events which are only strange because they are misunderstandings of things that really do happen. Thus, like Virgil, he records that bees breed in the carcases of dead lions, and this is not so very wide of the mark, because there is a certain sort of drone fly, the larvae of which do breed in animal carcases, and these diptera to an untrained eye look very much like bee-drones. Then again he says that there is a river in Arcadia which breeds mice, but this only means that it is inhabited by some sort of small water-vole. He is very much intrigued by the way in which some streams will coat wood and leaves which are put in them with a stony crust. But this again is only the sort of petrifying property which tourists find in the waters of such places as Matlock. He gives a large number of remedies for disease, especially the medicinal properties of various waters. He has accumulated every sort of information about the use of minerals, not least in making pigments for the use of painters. He discusses agriculture and the manufacture of many articles in common use, and finally he turns to an account of gems and precious stones.

Such was the spirit which animated at least one eminent Roman in the time of Christ. In taking, like Bacon, all knowledge as his province, he embarked, perhaps, on too ambitious and extensive a plan: but his industry was most praiseworthy and he wrote in a fine literary style, which is not what scientists always do. There are many faults in the arrangement of his matter, and he is only too ready to repeat tall stories without testing them; but the production and circulation of his work towards the end of the first century must surely have had a profound influence on the minds of educated persons, even though the enormous size of it and the cost of copying it must have meant that it was expensive to buy, and that probably there were not a very large number of copies of it in existence. That it was greatly valued may be judged from the fact that it is the only work of Pliny's which has survived, all his other writings being only known to us by reference to them in contemporary literature.

MEDICINE AND SURGERY

The practice of medicine and surgery is far more ancient than we are apt to imagine, and in order to understand what it was like in the first century A.D. we must go back a good deal farther.

In the legal code of Hammurabi (c. 2100 B.C.) we find that even at that time in Mesopotamia the State fixed the amount of doctors' fees, and imposed penalties upon surgeons who were careless in performing operations. Of course, we have no statistics either of this period or of any later one which would enable us to judge how many physicians and surgeons there were per head for the population, and we must assume that in many communities large masses of people were without any skilled medical aid, and depended mostly upon 'traditional family recipes, partly founded on experience, partly on superstition'. As a Roman writer puts it, 'they were without doctors, yet not without medicine'. From Mesopotamia both surgery and medicine probably passed to the Egyptians, and documents have been discovered which show that the latter, from the point of view of surgery, attained a degree of skill of which few people today have any conception. From Egypt, knowledge of medical and surgical science passed on to the Greeks, who developed it a great deal, but still mixed it up with a certain amount of magic. Nevertheless, it is to the great Greek doctor Hippocrates that we owe the famous oath which still binds the members of the medical profession, and in which the candidates swear to put the life and welfare of the patient above every other consideration, to abstain from all corruption, administration of poison, and immodest action towards woman patients, and not to procure abortion; and finally, to treat as confidential any secret information which happens to be communicated to them.

State doctors were employed in Greece before the Peloponnesian War. They were chosen on the basis of their success in private practice, and after their appointment were paid a salary and their expenses, but took no fees, and had to give free medical service. Anyone who applied to them was bound to receive this, and they were also required to give it to soldiers on active service; but after the war and during a period

of depression this free medical service had to be
discontinued on grounds of economy.

The Romans, to begin with, had hardly any doctors, but depended, as Cato did, on the family manual
of medicine. Cato, in fact, had a strong prejudice

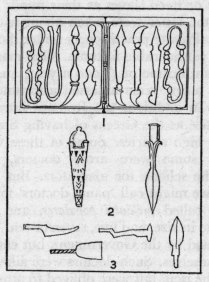

84   Surgical instruments

1. Group of surgical instruments in case
2. Lancet and sheath
3. Various types of razor

against the members of the medical profession, and
warns his son that as a class they are charlatans who
have combined to murder Roman citizens. Gradually,
however, the Romans overcame this prejudice, and
imported a great many Greek doctors. This was
especially done by Julius Caesar, who induced them to
settle in Rome by endowing them with the privilege

of citizenship. Still they were rather looked down
upon, and a great many of the smaller practitioners
were slaves who could be bought up by well-to-do persons and kept for their convenience as household
physicians. Some of these eventually obtained their
freedom, and then set up clinics where they practised
with slaves or freed slaves as their pupils or appren-
tices, and the latter were taken about with them on
their visits. Private practitioners under the early Empire made considerable fortunes. One man is said to
have had an income of £5000 a year, and a famous
surgeon in a few years amassed a fortune of almost
£100,000. In addition, the Romans introduced the
same practice as the Greeks of having State doctors,
with quite high salaries. Some of these were called
physicians, some were army doctors, and some
attended the schools for gladiators. But there were
also what we might call 'panel doctors' for the poor,
who were called *archiatri populares*, and each city,
according to its size, had five, seven or ten. These were
not appointed by the Government, but chosen by the
people themselves. Such doctors were allowed to take
fees from the rich, but were obliged to attend without
fee persons who, on a means test, were shown to have
less than a certain income.

Probably surgery was ahead of medicine (85). We
have records of the operations that could be performed, and by these it appears that from early
Egyptian times amputations were done with instruments which were very similar to those employed today. In Greek times we read of operations on the
skull, cutting for the stone, breaking up a calculus,
using a ligature to prevent haemorrhage from blood
vessels, and incision of the windpipe (commonly called
tracheotomy) to relieve patients suffering from its

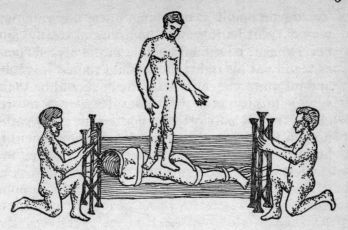

85   Patient being prepared for surgical operation

obstruction. Indeed, the instructions for performing
the latter operation are preserved in detail. Another
interesting case is of a man who was shot through the
lungs by an arrow, and had the arrow extracted, after
which he recovered.

The main difference, of course, in all these operations, between surgeons of the first century and those
of our own day was that they had not the advantage
of either anaesthetics or antiseptics. No doubt in
regard to the latter they learned enough by bitter
experience about the necessity for cleansing ablutions.
Even the Good Samaritan, though not necessarily a
doctor, knew enough to wash the wounds of the man
found at the roadside, who would probably otherwise
have died of tetanus, and in Rabbinical writings we
read about the use of some kind of vinegar for washing
wounds and for gargling; but we have not much more
information than this. The absence of anaesthetics
produced the following description of the necessary
qualifications for a surgeon:

'A surgeon ought to be young, or, at any rate, not very old; his hand should be firm and steady, and never shake; he should be able to use his left hand as readily as his right; his eyesight should be clear, and his mind not easily startled; he should be so far subject to pity as to make him desirous of the recovery of his patient; but not so far as to suffer himself to be moved by his cries; he should neither hurry the operation more than the case requires, nor cut less than is necessary, but do everything just as if the other's screams made no impression upon him.'

There must, of course, have been anodynes extracted from various herbs and probably mixed with wine, with which pain could be to some extent deadened. This happened we know in the case of criminals who were put to death by crucifixion, but it seems hardly credible that something of the same kind was not used to relieve the pain of sick patients.

We know a good deal about the various kinds of surgical instruments which were in use in the first century, and it is said that some of them were so well designed that it has hardly been possible to improve on them even at the present day. Specimens of these are given in the illustration (84), and another collection includes two probes, a cautery, two lancets of different patterns, a knife, possibly used for amputating fingers and toes, and another one for enlarging wounds, a needle for stitching up wounds, an elevator for lifting up depressed portions of the skull (very much like those used at the present day), six sorts of forceps, the last one probably in use for extracting foreign bodies from the throat, two catheters, a pair of scissors for cutting a diseased part of the uvula, two spatulas for examining the throat, and some interesting and rather complicated instruments, worked with a ratchet, for dilating passages in the body, and for internal examination. These again much resemble some used at the present day.

The physicians of the first century, in the matter of drugs, depended very largely upon the remnants of the writings attributed to the great Greek doctor, Hippocrates, but herbalists are of great antiquity, though they used their knowledge very often for magical, if not criminal, purposes, either to render people unconscious or to poison them. Nevertheless, they did discover the use of a good many remedies by observing the instinct which prompts sick animals to seek certain vegetable and mineral substances. It is noticeable that the word 'witch' in one passage in the Old Testament is rendered in the LXX version 'pharmakos', which may mean something like our chemist.

It would seem that there were not only midwives, but also women doctors for attendance on women, and there were also specialists, such as the oculist and the aurist. There were also quite certainly quacks and drug-sellers, and they advertised their nostrums just as they do today. We read of one man who sold a patent cough mixture in the street, and promised immediate relief to all sufferers. Under the Empire, we get more evidence of Government organisation, for it appears to have been prescribed that proper medicines should be sold in accredited shops and labelled with a list of the contents of the mixture, the name of its inventor, the method of taking it and the illnesses which it was intended to cure. Some of these survive in the form of blocks for printing on the labels. As far back as the golden age of Athens, we find it laid down that wills executed by anyone under the influence of drugs are legally invalid. Love potions, then as always, were common.

Such was the general position of health services among Gentiles, at any rate in the time of Christ. We have to consider, however, that in the province of Syria, at any rate, if not in a good many other areas, there were very few qualified practitioners, and the sick were pathetically ready to turn to anyone who seemed able to effect a cure. Moreover, little or nothing was known about the origins and cure of nervous and mental diseases. In this respect the work of Christ may seem to have been of a pioneer nature, and both before and after His time little was done for such sufferers except by persons called exorcists, who spent their time trying to find out the name of the evil spirit who, it was alleged, was afflicting the individual, and then ordering the evil spirit to come out. It would seem that Christ accommodated Himself to this belief, but His methods of exorcism were vastly different from those of the ordinary caster out of devils, who often played off a lesser demon against a greater one; whereas Christ emphasised the supreme power of the One Good God. 'If I by the finger of God cast out demons, assuredly the Rule of God has come in among you.'

The real link between Greek medical science and the Jews may have come through Alexandria, for we know that there was a very definite school of medicine established there, which not only preserved much of the skill and wisdom of the ancient Egyptians, but added to it the discoveries and professional efficiency of the Greeks. In this way the Greek-speaking Jews of Alexandria, many of whom were highly cultured persons, became acquainted with it, and their journeys to Palestine and Jerusalem meant that they introduced into Syria ideas and practices with which they had become familiar in Egypt.

The synthetic drugs on which we pride ourselves today had not, of course, been invented, but this does not mean that there was no scientific use of medicaments at all. It is quite clear that there was plenty of knowledge of herbs, not merely magical, but also quite rational, and extracts were made from them, as well as from minerals. We have special record of ointments, sometimes, for general use, sometimes used by oculists. Thus, a stamp for printing on a box or carton has been found with the inscription 'saffron ointment for scars and discharges prepared by Junius Taurus after the prescription of Paccius'. Another stamp runs 'the anodyne of Q. Junius Taurus for every kind of defective eyesight'. Sometimes there are puff names for the drugs which are described as 'invincible' or 'inimitable'. One piece of stone seems to have been used, from its shape, for the rolling of pills, and we have also a set of Roman lead weights, probably for the weighing of drugs, and marked 1 to 10, with the unit probably 18 grains. From North Africa has come a little bronze box, almost certainly used by a doctor to keep his drugs in. It is divided into several compartments, each with a separate cover, and has a sliding lid. Similar boxes have been found containing surgical instruments.

From the law of Moses it must be quite clear that the Jews in the first century were equipped with a number of regulations which clearly ministered to hygiene. But this was not all. The Rabbis were, we are told, accurate and keen observers of the laws of health, and their regulations were often far in advance at any rate, of mid-nineteenth-century practice. They ordained that every town must have at least either a physician and a surgeon, or at least one physician who was also qualified to practise surgery, and in theory, at any rate, every practitioner was supposed to hold a licence from the Rabbis. Among the temple officials there was always a medical man, whose business it was to attend to the priesthood, since the latter, having to perform their liturgical ministrations barefoot, were no doubt subject to certain occupational diseases. Prescriptions consisted either of 'simples' or of 'compounds', and vegetables were far more in use than minerals. In other words, there was a dependence upon herbal remedies. Goat's milk and barley porridge were recommended in all wasting diseases, and certain forms of diet were indicated in special complaints. The use of cold water compresses was known, and the proper use of baths, sometimes medicated. Jewish surgeons seem to have known how to operate for cataract.

In spite of all this there was a certain cynicism in the attitude of the public towards the medical profession, as may be seen from some of the proverbs. We are familiar with the 'physician heal thyself' of the gospels, but elsewhere we read 'live not in a city whose chief is a medical man, for he will attend to public business and neglect his patients', and again, 'even the best among doctors is deserving of Gehenna'.

DENTISTRY

A remark that you could buy anything in the bazaars of Jerusalem, from a false tooth to a Persian shawl, has led one to verify such a possibility. The facts about dental operations seem to be these. Rough repairs have been observed in a number of early skulls which have been excavated, but more definite information reaches us in the shape of the Ebers papyrus from Egypt, dated 1550 B.C., but containing passages twice as old, and giving methods of dental treatment as far back as approximately 3700 B.C. We learn from this that tooth-stopping was a very ancient practice, and mummies have been found with gold-filled teeth. Herodotus, about 500 B.C., describes the high specialisation which prevailed in his day over the care of teeth, and makes it plain that by then false teeth were already in use. Substitute-teeth were not made of some plastic substance as they are now, but were either the teeth of deceased human beings, or those of some animal. They were, however, by the early Roman period put into groups, and in Etruscan remains have been found teeth fastened together with gold bands, and having the spaces between filled with cement. It must, therefore, have been quite possible for artificial dentures to have been on sale in Jerusalem during the first century A.D.

Powder for polishing the teeth seems also to have been in use during the first century. With what kind of brushes it was applied we do not exactly know, but it was certainly invented by then. Pliny tells us that although powdered pumice might damage the enamel, it was clearly the base of most dentifrices, and there were added to it all sorts of substances, some of them perhaps magical, but others quite recognisable products of scientific observation. Calcined bones were a large ingredient, with the addition of powdered oyster-shells, and all these were mixed with honey, and so converted into a paste. In addition were included myrrh, nitre and hartshorn, clearly not merely for the purpose of making the teeth white, but for strengthening the gums, and so tightening up any loose teeth, and also for soothing possible toothache.

MECHANICAL APPLIANCES

People of the first century, having no steam, electric or atomic power, were rather more limited than people of our own day in their ability to make use of machines, but this does not mean that they had no mechanical devices.

One important change came into operation during our period. This was the introduction of the grain-mill driven by mules or horses (54),[1] which, of course, where water pressure was not available, saved the women a considerable amount of tedious hand-labour (53). It is true that these mills were sometimes worked by hand, usually by slaves (see Punishments). One illustration here given (54) shows that the lower part of the machine consisted of a conical millstone surmounted by a projection with a strong iron pivot, and the upper millstone in place on the top of it. It will be seen that it is somewhat in the form of an hour-glass, and it really consisted of *two* hollow cones, jointed together at the apex, and provided with a socket at this apex by which the upper stone was suspended upon the iron pivot while at the same time the inside of it touched the lower stone all round, so as to grind the corn which was poured in at the top. By adjusting the pivot, the meal could be ground in various consistencies, either coarse, fine or medium. The square slot at the side was for a bar or lever, and it was by this that the mill was turned, either by an animal or by a human being. In the drawing of a horse or mule driving a

---

[1] The horse-mill was an advantage, but only up to a point. When a first-century Emperor requisitioned all the horses of civilians for a large-scale military operation, there was immediately a shortage of flour! This emergency may have actually speeded up the construction of water-driven mills. (See Fig. 86.)

mill (54),[1] the lever is at the top of the upper and inverted cone, instead of half-way down. The flour as it was ground trickled out at the base of the cone into a channel ready to receive it. It must have been, we feel, rather difficult to keep it clean, with the animals so near it.

We have dealt elsewhere with the water-clock, but running water from very ancient times has been used to drive machinery, and the date of the invention of the water-mill is not perhaps ascertainable, though we know that one was used at the palace of a famous king in Asia Minor some centuries before Christ, and water-mills (if we may believe Vitruvius) were employed by the Romans, and probably differed very little from the ones which were in use in England until recent years. It was clearly recognised that they were labour and time-saving devices, and one special and rather unusual type was one which was suspended between two boats moored in the river Tiber about two feet apart, and driven by the force of the current, which, since the boats were anchored and stationary, naturally exerted considerable pressure upon the water-wheel fastened between them. Most water-mills were constructed upon aqueducts and canals, where it was easier to build them, and also to control the flow of the water. Some mills were used for cutting marble and for sawing logs, and we also read of a boxwood mill made for grinding pepper, and of a mill called a *trapetum* for crushing olives to extract the oil. This mill could be driven by water, but it was more commonly

---

[1] I saw in Jerusalem a mill for grinding sesame, exactly of this pattern. It was driven by a mule, and stood inside a shop up a side-turning from the main Suq in the Old City. On examination I found it to be in all essentials the same as the machine of this sort which was used in the first century.

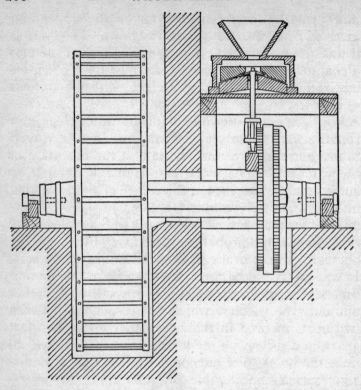

86 Mechanical water-mill (original drawing in Archaeological Museum at Cambridge—a reconstruction from remains of a Roman water-mill discovered near the city)

turned by hand, or possibly, though not certainly, by mules, and the great use of the olive for all kinds of food purposes made it a very important machine. It appears to have consisted of a circular stone basin with a central column. To this were attached two levers which controlled the crushing stone. There were two of these stones placed opposite each other on each side of the column. On the inner side they were flat, and on the outer convex, so as to fit the sides of the basin, and they were fastened apart so as just not to touch the sides of the basin, but to leave room for the olives to be fed into it. The stones were revolved by a lever passing from side to side above the top of the basin, but they also revolved to some degree on their own axis under the pressure of the fruit, so that there was a double motion, but the adjustment had to be sufficiently delicate to avoid crushing the kernels in the olives, as this would have caused the oil to become tainted.

We do not know how far some of the other machines in use among the Greeks and Romans were in use in Palestine, but they were certainly operating in the Mediterranean world, in the course of the first century, and Vitruvius gives many details about them. He refers to a number of different forms of wheels and screws, among them a sort of crane worked by a wheel for raising weights, which was known as a *machina tractoria*.[1] This, of course, involved compound mechanical powers, and the use of pulleys with ropes, and iron grapnels for taking hold of the objects to be lifted. Apart from military engines which have been dealt with elsewhere, there were also hydraulic machines for pumping and conveying water through pipes and channels, including the well-known screw of Archimedes, and certain pumps.[1]

At Pompeii has been found a clothes-press such as may be found in some clothes-repairing shops today. It is really only a larger edition of the trouser-press which so many men keep at home, and the principle of the screw for pressing down the top board is exactly the same as in our machines. A form of mechanical lift had already been invented, but it was chiefly used, so it seems, for elevating wild animals from dens in the

[1] For these see *Everyday Life in Roman Britain*, and especially the illustrations.

basements of arenas where they were kept in reserve, the cages being wound up by a pulley to the level of the amphitheatre, and then the door swung open to discharge the beast into the arena itself.

Simple organs with pipes for making music had been invented, and were already in use. They were hydraulically blown, and the Emperor Nero is said to have been interested in them.

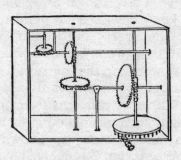

87   Mechanism of a Roman taximeter

The principle of measuring distances traversed in hired vehicles for the purpose of calculating fares (in fact that of the taximeter) was already known, and we possess early examples of such taximeters worked by cogwheels, one for a road carriage, and another for a boat. For each mile a pebble was released into a box, and the pebbles were counted at the end of the journey.

Looms, or machines for weaving textiles are most ancient inventions. There were three main types of loom: (1) the horizontal, (2) the vertical, (3) the treadle loom. Of these three the last was possibly not known in Graeco-Roman times.

Mr. Charlesworth says that Alexandrian scientists in the first century knew enough to utilise air-pressure and even to make a working steam-engine, but they had not got to the stage of using their knowledge for large-scale machinery, only for ingenious toys. He cites as examples a marionette-theatre working mechanically, and an automatic machine for sprinkling holy water!

88   Wheeled (self-propelled) bath-chair for invalid

As for military machines, these have been described and illustrated by Mr. and Mrs. Quennell in *Everyday Life in Roman Britain*. The ballistae and catapultae were elaborate arrangements for propelling missiles, and it is said that the Jews in defending Jerusalem against Titus had 40 ballistae and 300 catapults—no inconsiderable amount of fire-power, as we should term it today. It is also said that catapults could be aimed with considerable precision. Unfortunately, the Jews lacked skilled gunners to use this artillery, so it was of but little help to them.

So skilled and modernistic a builder as Herod the Great can hardly have failed to use the available machinery of his day for shifting his huge blocks of stone, and it must have been very efficient. No doubt, of course, he could command the services of hundreds of *fellahin* as navvies, in spite of what is said about the priests themselves being employed on the work, but they must surely have operated the machines rather than man-handled the blocks; otherwise progress would have been too slow. The stones were no doubt cut and shaped on the spot, just as one can see them being cut today. (For instance as I saw them being prepared at Bethany for the new church of the Franciscans.)

Chapter XII

AMUSEMENTS AND RECREATIONS

PUBLIC GAMES

ONE of the splendid sights of Jerusalem in the days of Christ must have been the great stadium or *xystus*. It would seem that this was an enlargement by Herod of an earlier one built by one of the corrupt High Priests, a man called Joshua, who changed his name to the Greek one of Jason, and who built a hippodrome and also a gymnasium, in his attempts to impose Greek customs upon the young Jews. (See 2 Maccabees 4 [11-15].) As developed by Herod, this building was decorated with gold, silver and precious stones, and had trophies in honour of the victories of Augustus. It was essentially a heathen institution, and its nearness to the Temple must have been a constant source of annoyance to orthodox Jews, who, of course, would never go near it. In addition, Herod, who, on one occasion, was actually the president of the Olympic Games, also built a huge amphitheatre, probably to the north-west of the city, outside the second wall.[1] The existence of such places of amusement raises the question, what went on in them, and how did the authorities conduct them? It is certain that most large centres of population had these *stadia*, and in Rome in particular, the spectacles exhibited in them were immense and very costly. Of course, actual athletic contests formed part of the programme, and there were also exercises, and practice

[1] Though some hold that it was down in the Jordan valley, near Jericho.

for the games. But we have to face the fact that a good deal of the entertainment consisted in actual combats between human beings, or between human beings and beasts, and not always armed human beings in the latter case, so that the chance of seeing a man or woman killed in public was very considerable.

GLADIATORIAL SHOWS

Dangerous sports have appealed to men all the world over, but these shows were something more than an exhibition of dangerous sport. They were frankly an exhibition of people being killed by one another or by animals for the entertainment of the audience, and they took place not only in Rome, but in other large centres of population. Paul plainly knew about them when he speaks of the Apostles being set forth as 'a spectacle'. Such a show might even have taken place in the stadium at Jerusalem during Christ's ministry. Women attended these shows as well as men, and boys were allotted seats, provided they were accompanied by an adult, probably a household slave (this reminds us of the modern cinema). The shows took their origin in a very ancient custom connected with funerals, and were devised by the Etruscans (who were in many ways a cruel race) as a development of the practice of killing slaves and captives at public funerals to accompany the deceased out of the world if he were a king or a nobleman. (Similar practices are known to have existed in pre-Christian Uganda, and in old Japan.) Latterly, the show became detached from funeral occasions, and was exhibited by nobles and public men as an entertainment for their guests and dependants or retainers. It was then called a *munus* or 'free show'. Finally, it became a municipal or State affair. It was under the Empire that the custom reached its height of popularity, and the number of gladiators fighting on some occasions was incredibly large. The combatants consisted of captives taken in war, slaves and condemned criminals, and they were, thus, given a (perhaps rather slender) chance for their life. A few freemen of low origin also took up the calling, but it was regarded as rather a degrading one, as indeed it was, though it had attractions for those who were good at it. Later on, people of higher rank fought in the arena, and even women, until a decree forbade them to do so.

Gladiators were trained in schools called *ludi*, and their trainers were called *lanistae*. Sometimes the latter owned a troupe of them, and let them out for hire. On other occasions they might be the property of some citizen, who engaged a *lanista* to train them. They were given a special diet, and trained with dummy weapons. Notices of shows were placarded several days before, and one of these bills has been found at Pompeii. When the day for the spectacle arrived, the troupe were led in procession round the arena, and then paired off. They began as we might say 'loosening up' with dummy wooden swords, and then on the sound of a trumpet, they exchanged these for real weapons, and a series of hand-to-hand battles began. When a combatant was wounded, the people in the audience called out '*habet*', and the wounded person had to lower his arms. If the audience turned up their thumbs, his assailant was permitted to kill him. In one picture which has been preserved, a woman is holding up her thumbs in this way, thus giving leave for a defeated gladiator to be slaughtered. If the audience were desirous of sparing the life of the vanquished they did so by waving handkerchiefs. Criminals were enrolled as gladiators in two classes. The first, condemned '*ad gladium*', were obliged to be killed at least within a year. Others, if they managed to avoid being killed, might obtain their discharge at the end of three years. Officially these shows were abolished by the Emperor Constantine after A.D. 313, as incompatible with Christianity, but it appears that they went on unofficially for some years after that, and the old story used to be that they were only ended by the public protest of a monk. Palms were given to victorious gladiators, and sometimes the public formally requested the presiding official or *editor* to discharge the combatant, especially if he were an elderly gladiator.

There were a great number of different types of gladiators, and they all wore different costumes (89). Thus, there were some who fought blindfold, usually on horseback, others who fought in pairs, others again who fought with two swords, some who fought in chariots, some who carried a noose with which they tried to catch their opponents, some who fought in complete suits of armour, some who carried a trident and a net with which to entangle their opponents, others who were called *Samnites*, and who wore a helmet with a high crest, others again called *myrmillones*,

89 Gladiators

who had a helmet with a fish for a crest, and who usually fought with the net-carriers or *retiarii*. Gladiators were favourite subjects for painting and sculpture.

We may see in some of these combats nothing very different from the tournaments of the Middle Ages, but in the latter there was no deliberate intention of killing one's opponent any more than there is in a prize-fight. One thinks also of the Mediterranean bull-fight, which is often informal, and takes place, in some Spanish towns, actually in the streets, where bulls are let loose for the young men to practise on, and where there is no actual intention of killing the bull or even of being killed by the animal one's self. But the gladiatorial show was one in which it was definitely expected that somebody would be killed, and be killed before the audience, and so it was a revolting and thoroughly brutalising sport, at least as much as the practice of going to see a man hanged in public. We do well to remember that there is a strain of cruelty in human nature which will burst out again and again if it is not kept in check, and that although Christianity did set itself to get rid of such horrors, it only partially succeeded, and has had to struggle against their revival even at the present day. But in the first century A.D. such shows were taken for granted, even by women and children.

Besides fights between human beings there were at these shows combats between animals and men, and also between animals themselves. Such a contest was called a *venatio*. The Romans liked these *venationes* quite as much as the exhibitions of gladiators, and Julius Caesar was the first to build a special sort of amphitheatre for them, in which the spectators were protected from attacks of the wild beasts by a sort of trench or moat. There was a shocking waste of life on these occasions, and splendid animals were slaughtered ruthlessly and without regard for the consequences, so that the diminution in the numbers of some of them may well have been due to the senseless destruction which went on for the amusement of a brutal public. On one occasion three hundred lions were killed in the course of a single show, while at the opening ceremony of the great amphitheatre of Titus, as many as five thousand wild beasts and four thousand tame ones were slaughtered. A favourite spectacle introduced by Julius Caesar and repeated by Claudius and Nero was the bull-fight, which seems to have been very much on the Spanish lines. The bulls were let loose and chased by horsemen around the arena, and when they grew weary, were seized by the horns and put to death. Other animals exhibited in the amphitheatre were elephants, tigers and panthers, which were allowed to fight, and also rhinoceri, hippopotami, snakes, and in a show under the patronage of the emperor Augustus, thirty-six crocodiles. One genial pantomime, said to have been rather a favourite, represented the crucifixion of a criminal, followed up by the dismembering of his body by wild beasts.

So much has already been written about the chariot-races of the Romans, and so many attempts have been made to depict them on the stage and in films, that the subject has become somewhat stale, and needs little more to be said about it. The main point is that apart from the gladiatorial shows, the principal amusement of the populace would seem to have been then, as now, racing displays. The race-meetings, especially speedway contests, motor-cycle scrambles and high-speed motor-car races on road or track with which we are familiar, had their equivalents in the spectacles of the various *stadia*. Up till the time of

Augustus there were apparently no reserved seats. After that the emperors ordained that senators were to have special places allotted them, and seats were also reserved for soldiers, married plebeians, children accompanied by an adult attendant, women, etc. A plan of one of the circuses shows a royal box for the Imperial family, a box for the judges and another set of reserved seats for the giver of the games and his own friends. The chariots were light vehicles of wood bound with bronze, and the drivers were usually slaves or persons of low social rank. A winning driver received a money prize,[1] and a slave sometimes won his freedom. The life was a dangerous one, and fatal accidents were frequent, yet skilful drivers sometimes lived long and won a great many races. One in particular is said to have retired at the age of 42 after winning 3000 races with two horses, and 1462 with a team of more than two.

Where did the Romans procure their fine horses, whether for chariot-races or for their army transport?

Sir William Ridgeway, a good many years ago, worked out that the best horses in those days came from Libya, and he maintained that the Libyan horse was the distinct breed which had existed in North Africa before the second millenium B.C. and that this Libyan breed was already distinguished by its bay colour (with a star in the forehead), which is the feature of the Libyan stock and its posterity to this very day. From Libya came the horses of Egypt and in all probability the Arab horses. Ridgeway thinks that this Libyan horse is really a native African stock sprung

---

[1] Juvenal says ruefully that a driver often received a hundred times the fee of an advocate in the law-courts. Prizes won by such often amounted to 30,000 to 60,000 sesterces. Drivers in fact were paid like Hollywood stars.

from wild horses which in the beginning were striped like the quagga, and he points out that vestiges of this striping are to be found in the foals of thoroughbred horses right up to the present day. The swiftest horse in Homeric days was a bay with a star in his forehead, and in Greek classical times these same Libyan horses were by far the swiftest known, and later won all the races in the Roman circus in the first century. Ridgeway observes that exactly the same type of horse is successful today, and that in the thirty years preceding 1866 the Derby was won sixteen times by such horses. It would seem, therefore, that most of the modern British thoroughbreds are descendants of the same stock which achieved success in the first century.

In 1903, some fragments of a long Latin inscription were found at Rome built into the wall to the north of the castle of St. Angelo. They turned out to be part of an inscription in memory of a famous jockey or charioteer of the second half of the first century, and they give not only a record of his racing career, but also a list of the names of all the winners which he rode, and the breeds to which each belonged. Of these, thirty-eight out of forty-two are actual North African horses, and strange to say there is no mention of any Arabs, a clear proof that the racing men of that day did not look to Arabia, or indeed, as it happens, to any other part of Asia, for horses of exceptional swiftness. A hundred years later a writer on hunting enumerates fifteen breeds of horses, but of these not one is Arab, and the majority are known to be derivatives from the Libyan breed. At the same time the best heavy warhorses do seem to have been Asiatic, and one of the difficulties that the Romans had to face for some time was the inferiority of their heavy cavalry to that of the Eastern armies opposed to them.

No expense was spared in training race-horses, and the Romans were careful not to spoil them by using them too soon. They were not broken in until the age of three, and not allowed to run in a race till they were five. As a result, some of them were extraordinarily successful. One horse called Tuscus, mentioned in an inscription, is said to have won 426 races. Geldings were not used in the races, and very seldom mares. The initial or badge of the owner was branded on the horse's flank.

The size of the *stadia* must have increased as time went on, since at first only four chariots ran in a heat, but later on eight or even ten chariots were run at one time. The starter was the presiding magistrate. The usual length of a race was seven laps, but Domitian reduced the number on one occasion to five laps, in order to get 100 events into one day. Under Julius Caesar it was customary to run only ten or twelve races in a day, but as time went on the number greatly increased. In between each race the time was filled up with a sort of variety show, including tumbling, rope-dancing, etc. Betting was as common as it is now. Large sums of money were lost and won. Race-cards were on sale with the list of horses and the names of the drivers and riders. The actual provision of the horses and chariots was in the hands of contractors who were in the pay of those who provided the games. Each group of contractors was called a *factio*, and was distinguished in the arena by its colour, and the heavy betting and the keen competition between the different *factiones* led to fights rather like those between different race-gangs, involving scenes of riot and bloodshed.

Theatres were common, and not only to be found in cities like Jerusalem, Athens and Antioch, but in small places (one quite obscure spot, Brough-on-Humber,

near Hull, had one). There were also touring com-
panies, and travelling variety artistes. Moralists often
objected to the latter, just as people do today to certain
types of film. A kind of organ, consisting of a series of
flutes bound together in rows, and blown with a bellows (in fact a mechanised syrinx) was used in some
stadia, to accompany displays.

CHILDREN'S GAMES

It is no easy matter to find out what kind of games
were played by children in Palestine during the first
century. To assume that they were the same as the
games which children play there today is risky, since
Arab influence and the Turkish occupation, not to
mention the periods of Greek and Roman dominance,
may have introduced quite new factors. We do, however, know something of games played by Gentile
children in various parts of the Mediterranean during
the first century, and it is not at all unlikely that some
of these were played in Palestine. The following games
and toys were certainly known in Asia Minor in the
first century and some of them are found to have been
in use in the country around Pompeii. The list includes dice, knuckle-bones, balls, draughts (or at least
a game resembling either draughts or backgammon).
Some of the pieces in one of these games are oblong,
with a handle at the end, rather like the label that we
see tied on exhibits in botanical gardens, and on these
pieces, which are made of ivory, are words on the one
side and numbers on the other. The highest numbers
have pleasant words such as 'happy' and 'kindly',
while the lower numbers have terms of an abusive
character inscribed on the back such as 'thief', 'trifler'
or 'bad tempered fellow'. In the British Museum is an
oblong marble board which was evidently used for

some sort of game, though we do not know how. It is inscribed with words, which in themselves throw light upon the kind of advertisements that may have appeared outside amphitheatres, for they read:

CIRCUS PLENUS
CLAMOR INGENS
IANUAE TE[NSAE]

We may translate the foregoing:

House full
Tremendous applause
Doors bursting

It is said that many similar stones have been found, always with six words of six letters each, but what the game was and how it was played we do not know.

Toys are often of much the same sort as toys today. That is to say dolls are a recognised item, and some of these have not only jointed limbs, but holes pierced through the top of their heads to connect up with strings manipulating the arms and legs. Such dolls were known as far back in Greece as the fourth century B.C., and Xenophon mentions a travelling showman who used them to run a puppet show. A good many of these dolls were made of terra-cotta, and with them we may group small reproductions of furniture and tools, somewhat like the contents of a modern doll's house. Coming from about the first century A.D. are to be found a wooden horse, and a rag doll, both from Egypt. The whipping top was a plaything certainly as far back as ancient Greece and probably earlier, and it is curious to think that a toy with such a very long history should, like the hoop, which was also well known as a toy in antiquity, only seem to have gone out of fashion during the last forty or fifty years.

Among the Greeks and Romans we have record of a large number of games, but we do not know how many of these were also known in Palestine, though the movement of Jews and the influx of Greeks and Romans may have introduced some of them. There are plenty of ball games, but, curiously enough, there is no trace of the use of any racquet or bat. Only the hand seems to have been used for striking, as in the case of our game of fives, which may on that account be a very old one. We find also the following: Swings, hide and seek, spillikins, gambling on odds and evens, a guessing game with the fingers which is apparently still played in Italy and is now called *morra*, a game played with a board rather like our backgammon board in appearance, and known as *duodecim scripta*, and *cottabē*, a game which was played with wine, and in which sometimes the players threw the wine on to saucers floating in a basin, he, who, in this way, sank one of them being accounted a winner. Another form of *cottabē* was much more elaborate, and involved the use of a special sort of apparatus, a stand with a little bowl, and a small figure beside it. Then there was blind man's buff, and I am afraid this was probably a rather cruel game, because it seems from its name (*myinda*) to have been the same game which is still played by naughty boys in Crete. In this a cockchafer has a piece of lighted material tied to it and is chased as it flies about. But the real blind man's buff was also played, in which the blindfolded person chases the rest of the players. We know that fights between birds, whether cocks or quails, certainly went on in the Mediterranean world, but again we have no evidence as to whether they were native to Palestine or whether they came to be introduced there by soldiers from legions quartered in the country, but recruited from outside. One picture we have seen shows two boys with their cocks under their arms. There were also plenty of children's pets, and stories of their affection for their little owners are recounted. Thus, a goose is recorded by Pliny to have had a great love for a female flute-player of one of the Ptolemies who were kings of Egypt, and he also tells the tale of a pet eagle or hawk which burnt itself to death on the funeral pyre of its young mistress. This may be a rather tall story, but it is at any rate a pretty one. The rattle for little children is a most natural development, and it is doubtful whether there was ever a time when some such noise-making instrument was not in use for infants, even if it was only a bunch of rustling leaves. The solitaire board, which we now so rarely see, but which was certainly in use among people in the earlier nineteenth century, is found in the first century A.D. Hopscotch is said to be found all over the Orient, and the only variation appears to have been in the number of lines drawn on the ground, and in the number of counters used. One writer on oriental games says that it was often called the Triodium, because of the three routes by which the player could travel.

Plutarch says that soldiers in camp, when off duty, always played dice or draughts. Dice we can understand, and we know that the soldiers occupied themselves in this way when on duty at the foot of the Cross, but one is tempted to speculate as to whether 'draughts' really means such a very mild game, for soldiers are said to have been so infatuated with it that they played impromptu on table tops placed upside down on the ground. This suggests to us that the word used really means a gambling game with a board similar to our 'Crown and Anchor', and I think it is very likely that this is what it was, no doubt in a

modified form. Chess was not known, and came in
from the East much later. There was a game called
Latruncula which some have thought to have been the
same as chess, but the evidence on the whole suggests
that although it was a board game, and played with
pieces made of wax or glass, it was not chess, but a
game somewhat similar to the Greek game called City
(*Polis*), which was also called *Plinthion*. It is said to
have needed a large number of pieces, and these seem
to have been little cylindrical objects with a dog's head
carved on the top. As far as we can judge from the very
scrappy evidence, it was more like draughts than
chess, though, perhaps, the best thing we can say is
that *Latruncula* was a more highly elaborated and
perfected form of *Plinthion*.

The Romans are said to have used five different
sorts of balls, but we never seem to read of an organised
game like our football or netball. Balls, sometimes
multi-coloured, were thrown about and caught very
much as they are by bathers on the beach after a swim.
There was also a game played with a large number of
smaller balls. The players stood in a circle and swiftly

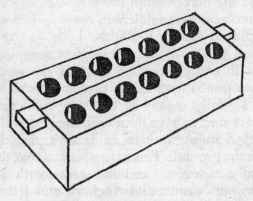

90   Diagram of a *mangala* board

threw these balls to one another, and if anyone dropped his or her catch it counted against the offender. A slave stood on each side of the diameter of the circle. One held a silver bowl to receive any balls that were dropped. The other had a bag with a supply of spare balls, so that as soon as one was dropped another was ready to take its place. The game no doubt ended when the balls were used up, and the winner was the player who had dropped fewest catches.

There were games with pebbles, in one of which a small trench or pocket was dug in the ground, and the object was, from a prescribed distance, to throw small pellets of stone or bone into it. This was not the same as the game called *Mancala*[1] among the Orientals,

[1] *Mancala* or *mangala* is certainly a very old Palestinian game, and survives in the villages of Transjordania quite unmodified. A game was specially played for me by two peasants on one of my visits, and proved to be a complicated affair. The board was an oblong one with two rows of seven holes each, and in each hole were placed seven counters (90).

The game began with one player removing the contents of a single compartment and distributing these round the board in seven consecutive holes. His opponent was then allowed to make a move in which he could transfer only a prescribed number of counters at once, but the object was to get somewhere on his side a compartment containing only two or three pieces, in which case he was allowed to take them up and hold them in his hand. Then the other man had his turn, and they went on, turn and turn about, until the whole board was cleared in this way. The number of pieces held by each player was then counted, and the one who had succeeded in lifting the majority of them was declared the winner. There were all sorts of small rules about distribution and removal of counters, and it seemed to me that the same might, if properly learned, become as popular in Europe as Canasta or Mah-Jong, but from all I could ascertain, it was a game much older than the Moslem invasions, and might very well have been played in Palestine in the first century A.D.

in which pellets or counters are transferred from one pigeon-hole to another according to certain rules. The poet Ovid gives an account of several children's games played with nuts, and we know that *nuces* was a kind of slang for triviality, just as 'nuts' is, even today. Another rather coarse game was to try to pick something out of a basin of scum or wine dregs while at the same time having one's hands folded behind one's back.

Undergraduates are much the same in every generation, and we read that in the first century the students at Athens ragged every newcomer when he entered the baths for the first time. There were also a number of jokes and pleasantries such as one associates with carnivals.

It would seem that Roman soldiers knew very well how to toss recruits in a blanket, though what they used was more likely to have been a large cloak.

At home there were word competitions, charades and guessing games.

Chapter XIII

JERUSALEM

THE CITY IN GENERAL

THE circumference of Jerusalem is not more than two and three-quarter miles. Although it lies between 2000 and 2500 feet above sea level, it is in a basin, and three ridges of higher hills shut it off from the surrounding country. There is one break, to the south-east, where there is a view towards the desert, and it is from the desert that the hot wind or *sharqiyya* blows in during the summer.[1] After intensely hot days, the summer evenings are suddenly cool. In the winter the rains sweep in from the sea lying to the west. There has been, perhaps, no great climatic change since the first century, except in the amount of rain. (See Chapter I.)

The general appearance of the city has been described as the colour of an old lionskin. This only applies to the older buildings. But it is fair to suppose that the Jerusalem of Christ's day, except for its more recent marble buildings, which would have been white, was constructed of the local golden limestone, not unlike that which is to be seen in the eastern villages of the Cotswolds. It needed then no great stretch of imagination to picture the new Jerusalem, coming down out of Heaven, as golden in colour.

The old city lies between two valleys, both running north and south, and was originally divided down the middle by a third valley, now almost silted up, which

---

[1] *Khamsin*, the term often used by Europeans, is a misnomer, and really applies to a wind which blows in Egypt.

thus separated the two hills on which the old city is built. In Herod's day a viaduct ran across this middle valley, joining the west side, where he had a palace, to the Temple precincts on the east side. In the days of Nehemiah it must have had a small brook running down it, but there is now no more sign of this than there is of the Walbrook near the London Stock Exchange. In the first century this old city was smaller even than it is now, and the present sites of Calvary and the Holy Sepulchre were probably not as they are at present *within* the walls, but *outside*, as will be seen from the map. There is now almost nothing of the original masonry to be seen, apart from a few huge blocks of the Herodian period in the lower course of the city fortifications, and some of the pavement in the Temple area.

TRADE AND THE COST OF LIVING

Dr. Edersheim has given us a vivid picture of the trading quarter of Jeusalem in the time of Christ. The whole city was not, according to our ideas, a very large one, but it was closely packed on to about 300 acres. Because of the hilly nature of the ground most of the streets went up and down and were narrow, and therefore unsuited for wheeled traffic; camels, mules, horses and donkeys being the chief means of transport, except where people were carried in litters or went on foot. It was a busy place. Beside the business quarter, there were bazaars and shops, and not far from them were fine houses of wealthy merchants and palaces of persons of rank. The Eastern shop, as we know from the bazaars of India, was (and is) very much open to the street, so that as you went along you were able to see the shoemaker busy with sandals, and the tailor with a needle stuck in his clothes sewing away cross-legged;

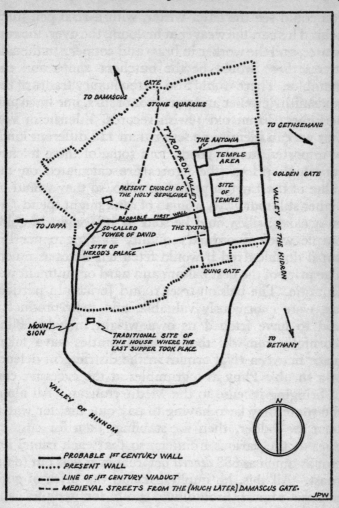

91 Sketch-plan of Jerusalem in first century A.D.

you could see the letter-writer, with a reed pen stuck behind his ear, the weaver at his loom, the dyer, the carpenter, and the worker in brass and copper. In the side streets there would be the butchers' shops and the shambles. There would also be the luxury trades of the goldsmith, jeweller and purveyor of silks, fine linen and perfumes. From old Jewish records, Edersheim says that we can identify no fewer than 118 different kinds of imported luxury goods, and some of these fetched very high prices (the figures are calculated on the value of the English pound in 1880, so they would be higher still today). A woman of rank might spend £36 on a cloak; silk would be sold by its weight in gold; purple wool of ordinary quality at £3.25p per lb., but if double-dyed it would fetch ten times as much. The price of the best balsam and nard or ointment was fantastic. The balsam trees round Jericho in particular, were enormously valuable, and their product is said to have fetched its own weight in gold. Pliny scornfully remarks that pitched battles have taken place between rival armies in the district, 'in defence of a shrub'. Pliny also grumbles at the excessive cost of bringing incense to the Mediterranean. 'All along the route they keep having to pay out, first for water, then for fodder, then for stabling, then for customs dues at the various frontiers, so that each camel has cost as much as 688 *denarii* before it ever gets out to the coast.' All this, he implies, makes the price of good incense almost prohibitive, both for temples and individuals.

On the other hand, the cost of ordinary living, about which we hear so much today, was at that time very low. Edersheim says that bazaar prices were something like this: a complete suit for your slave, £1.30p or £1.35p, and a reasonable outfit for yourself, £3 to £6.

The same sum would buy an ass, an ox or a cow, and a little more would buy a horse. A calf might fetch less than 75p, and a goat 25p or 30p. Sheep were dearer, and ranged from 20p to 75p or 80p, but a lamb might sometimes be had for 1p. (One wonders whether price went up much at Passover time.) Meat was about ½p. per lb., and corn, fruit, wine and oil also cost very little. Lodgings for a single man, if small and unfurnished, could be had for about 2½p a week. Wages were, in consequence, very low. Though skilled labour commanded a higher rate, the ordinary day labourer seems to have been paid about 3p a day, and it is said that property to the extent of about £6 excluded you on a means-test from the right to charity, such, for example, as the right to glean in the corn-fields.

The population of Jerusalem has been estimated at this time as about a quarter of a million, but how many of these were pilgrims, and how many permanent residents it is not easy to say. The Temple called priests by the thousand into the city, together with their families, but they would not all have been in residence at once, and there were also educational centres or academies with hundreds of scholars, but these again must have sometimes gone away for vacation. The nearest harbour was at Joppa (the modern Jaffa), but there must have been many warehouses to which goods were brought up from the port, and there were also at least seven different markets for cattle, wool, ironware, clothes, wood, bread, fruit and vegetables. Market days were Monday and Thursday, and later Monday and Friday. Outside Jerusalem there were large fairs from time to time, at Gaza, Tyre, Acco, and in Transjordania, at Botnah, the latter perhaps being the largest, but in Jerusalem the markets were held every week, and perishable goods such as greengrocery and meat were on sale every day. It seems that, in addition, every caravanserai or inn tended to have a sort of small market attached to it, especially for cattle. Besides the fixed shops, there were also, as in parts of England, movable stalls in the streets. As in Rome, so in the provinces and at Jerusalem, there were municipal officials who controlled the markets, and they had the business of fixing market prices, which it is said were supposed to leave to the producer a profit of one-sixth on the cost of production. To Jerusalem would be sent not only the local products of Judaea, but the provisions and manufactures of Galilee. As we have seen already, there was a considerable business in salting fish on the shores of the Sea of Galilee, but fresh fish and fruit were also sent in to market, besides oil, grape syrup and wine. There were many restaurants and wine shops in Jerusalem, and here you might be served with fresh or salt fish, fried locusts, a vegetable dish, soup, pastry, sweetmeats or fruit-cake, and for drink, wine of the country or foreign beer. It must not be supposed that the lower city was entirely given over to commerce, for we have record that in it, besides the houses of the rich bourgeois, were the palaces of Graptē and Queen Helena of Adiabene. If, however, you had gone for a walk into the upper city, the contrast would have been rather like that between the cathedral precincts at an old English city like Lincoln on the top of the hill, and modern commercial and industrial Lincoln at the foot of it. None of the buildings then to be seen can be found there today, but you would have passed first the High Priest's palace on the slope of the hill, with the principal apartments on the first floor, and the servants' quarters below, with a porch in front. Here it was that Peter stood and warmed himself with the servants on the night of the betrayal. Then you would come to the palace of the Maccabees, which at this time was in the possession of Herod Antipas, and, near by, the Temple and the Theatre. Of the Theatre we have already spoken, when dealing with the matter of public games and amusements, but the Temple will need a section to itself.

THE TEMPLE: AN EVERYDAY SIGHT

If you had lived in Jerusalem at the time of Christ you could not fail to have seen, as you went to school or to shop, a very remarkable building. It stood on the east side of the city in the midst of a great quadrilateral courtyard of irregular proportions, measuring about twice the length of St. Paul's Cathedral each way, and surrounded by a high wall surmounted by spikes. On the inside of this wall and running all round the courtyard were rows of columns, forming a sort of cloister with double porticoes. The roofs of these cloisters were of carved cedarwood. On the south side were what were called the royal porticoes, with two extra rows of columns having Corinthian Greek capitals. To the east of the court was a double portico known as Solomon's Porch, because part of the structure was believed, probably in error, to belong to a building erected by King Solomon. This double portico, according to the measurements given by Josephus, covered an area greater than that occupied by Westminster Abbey. Rather towards the northern part of this great courtyard stood a vast sanctuary which was divided into an outer and an inner court, the latter with three subdivisions, for women, male Jewish laymen and priests respectively. In the centre

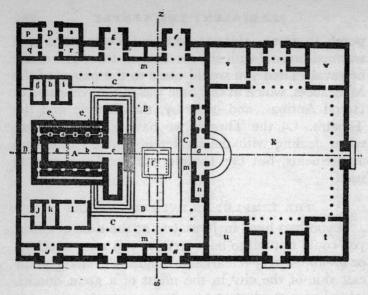

92   Ground-plan of Herod's Temple

A. *The Temple*
  a. The Holy of Holies
  b. The Holy Place
  c. The Porch
  d. The Little Chambers
  e. The Ascent to the Upper
    Chamber

B. *The Court of the Priests*
  f. The Altar of Sacrifice
  g. The Chamber of Salt
  h. The Chamber of Parvah
  i. The Chamber of the Washing
  j. The Chamber of Wood or
    Palhedrin
  k. The Chamber of the Draw
    Well
  l. The Chamber of Gazith, or
    of the Sanhedrin

C. *The Court of Israel*
  m. The Inner Cloisters
  n. The Chambers of the Vest-
    ments.
  o. The Chamber of the Pancake
    Maker

The Gates of the Inner Court
D. The House Moked, or House
    of the Hearth
  p. The Chamber Moked and
    Descent to the Bath-room
  q. The Chamber of the Lambs
  r. The Chamber of the Shew
    Bread
  s. The Chamber of the Stones of
    the Altar or Chamber of
    Seals
E. The Gate and House Abtinas
F. The Gate and House Nitsus
    (storehouse for salt)
G. The Gate Nicanor
H. The Water Gate
I. The Gate of the First born
J. The Gate of Kindling

K. *The Court of the Women*
  t. The Chamber of the Nazirites
  u. The Chamber of Oil
  v. The Chamber of the Lepers
  w. The Chamber of Wood

of this court stood a T-shaped inner sanctum with another great porch. To the east of this porch was a large altar for animal sacrifices, and to the north of this altar a series of rings in the floor to which animals were tethered while being slaughtered. There were also eight marble tables on which the carcases were flayed, washed and prepared for the altar. At the south-west corner of the altar (which rose in three tiers) were holes for draining away the blood of the victims, and to the south of the steps which led up from the altar to the inner sanctum were places where the priests could wash their hands and feet, which must certainly have been necessary, considering that the vicinity of the altar was rather like the floor of a butcher's slaughterhouse. Entering the sanctum, one came first into a porch or vestibule, and then into the *hekal* or holy place, which contained certain special sacred objects such as the altar of incense and the seven-branched candlestick. Opening off this *hekal* was the Holy of Holies, or *debir*, to which there was no door, but only an open space screened by two veils or curtains. No natural light came into this sanctum. It depended entirely upon the artificial light from the seven-branched lamp-stand, which came to assume a kind of symbolical value, so that it is constantly represented in synagogue sculpture, and is still copied in small models, which are on sale in Jerusalem at the present day.

On the outside of the great central porch was carved a golden grape-vine, which misled some Romans into thinking that the Jews worshipped Dionysus, the god of wine.

We must not suppose that a good deal of this elaborate arrangement would have been unfamiliar to any visitor from some other part of the Mediterranean if he had been privileged to see inside it (which is most unlikely, since even lay Jews could not enter the *hekal* and *debir*). Sanctuaries something like it were to be found built in honour of divine beings all over the world at this time, from Europe to the Pacific, and some of the finest and most ancient were to be seen in Egypt, while Greece had many, and Rome had also some, built in imitation of the Greek ones. In nearly all these there were daily offerings of food and incense, and the food was as often as not animal flesh, though in some cases it consisted of that of birds, and in others of fruit, cereals and wine.

There was, however, one striking difference between the Jerusalem sanctuary and all these other temples. The *debir* at Jerusalem contained no image, nothing at all, except, on the ground, a piece of rock which was believed to cover the mouth of the abyss, and on which the world was thought to be founded. 'It was a matter of common knowledge that there were no representations of the gods in the temple, but that the place was empty, and contained nothing.' So wrote a Roman writer in the second half of the first century, possibly during Paul's lifetime. This was a great contrast to the other temples of the Mediterranean world, in which the innermost sanctuary almost always contained some statue representing the image of the divine being in whose honour the sacred house had been built, and only in rare cases a monolith or menhir.

In other respects the Temple more or less conformed to the pattern well known in the Graeco-Roman world. It had its animal sacrifices, its treasury, in which were preserved not only the sacred vessels, but the votive offerings of the faithful, its multitude of priests serving on a rota, its incense and its music, no doubt of the plainsong order. It was a very costly affair, and most expensive to maintain. It is estimated that about seven per cent of the population of the Roman Empire at this time were Jews, and as every adult male was expected to contribute a half-shekel annually to the upkeep of the national sanctuary, the Temple revenues must have been immense. About fifty years before Christ, a Roman governor of the province of Asia got into trouble for taking a step which to some of us would seem laudable. He found that the export of currency to Jerusalem from his province was interfering with its economic stability, and so he stopped it. But Jews were difficult people to offend, and they complained against him to the central government. The man was impeached, and a well-known barrister, no less a person than Cicero himself, was briefed to defend him. Cicero succeeded in getting him acquitted on a point of law. Marcus Agrippa, however, the viceroy of the Emperor Augustus, then had the Temple placed under the same law as all other sanctuaries within the Empire, which meant severe penalties against anyone who robbed it, and so overrode any prohibition of currency export.

There was great strictness in the exclusion of Gentiles from the Temple precincts. It is true that there was an area called the Court of the Gentiles, but it was hardly part of the Temple proper, which was surrounded by a wall called the Soreg. Herod had a notice in Greek, Latin and Hebrew put up, forbidding Gentiles to pass beyond it. A fragment of the Greek version was found as recently as 1935 built into part of the Haram es Sherif, and with some of the original red paint still showing, after nineteen hundred and fifty years. A picture of this is given (73), with a free translation of the original:

'No non-Jew is permitted to pass beyond this
boundary-point. Anyone who does, does so at his
own risk, and will be liable to the death-
penalty.'

There were two very different opinions held by the
Gentiles about the Jewish people. Some thought that
their belief in an invisible God who presided over their
sanctuary was all bogus, and that although their
solidarity in helping each other when in distress com-
pelled one's admiration, they were really rather per-
verse and tiresome folk: 'Regarding as profane all that
we hold sacred, and permitting all that we abhor.'
They were considered eccentric in their feeding
habits, and insulted their neighbours by declining to
eat with them, and by saying that their deity, called
Yahweh, was not the same as Zeus or Jupiter under
another name, but the Living God of the whole
universe, which so many outsiders seemed rather pre-
posterous. Other Gentiles who visited their synagogues
out of curiosity formed a better opinion, and some of
them went on attending, and perhaps even became
proselytes, while we read of one centurion who
actually built (or at least provided) a synagogue for
Jews at his own expense. Indeed, in one Gentile
writer we find them referred to as 'a nation of philosophers'. The fact was that while on the one side they
held a form of worship which seemed very much the
same as that prevailing in other temples, on the other
they held open a way, as we shall see, to a totally
different view of what religion ought to be, both in
belief and practice, and in this way performed a great
service to mankind, and to a high degree justified their
exclusiveness.

Now how did this great temple at Jerusalem come

into being? There had been a sanctuary of some sort on the site for hundreds of years, very likely long before the days of Solomon; but it was he who had the first great edifice put up. Later it was reduced to ruins by the Babylonian sack of the city. It was rebuilt by a Jew called Zerubbabel, who brought back some of his displaced countrymen from Babylonia. Then a succession of invaders, Greek, Roman and Edomite, plundered and damaged it. Finally, the Edomite king, Herod the Great, set about clearing the site and putting up a magnificent new building. This was about twenty years before the birth of Christ. It was, curiously enough, a great time throughout the whole Mediterranean area for repairing public buildings, probably because during the wars at the end of the Roman Republic, very little maintenance work could be done. We ourselves know how easy it is for buildings to get into disrepair during a war, when labour and capital are turned to other uses, and although there were no atom bombs, an army with incendiary torches could soon reduce a whole city to ashes, including its temples. So when Augustus brought in a long period of peace and the reorganisation of society under a strong government (almost a dictatorship), it was not surprising that people hailed him as a saviour, and set about large building programmes, with some assurance that there would not be another war for an indefinite period. This Jerusalem project, therefore, was only one among many others. But the more earnest Jews did not like it, partly because they suspected Herod's motive to be self-aggrandisement[1]

[1] Herod's building activity was extraordinary. Besides his various palaces and the Temple, he engaged in large building schemes at Beryta (Beirut), Tyre, Sidon, Damascus, Sebaste (Samaria), Caesarea, Byblus, Ptolemais, Tripoli and the island of Rhodes.

rather than piety (as indeed it was), partly because they disliked foreign patronage, and partly because Herod was himself not a true Jew, and outraged their feelings by putting the sign of the Roman eagle on the outside of the building. Nevertheless, it was a splendid piece of architecture. The style is held by Tissot to have been mixed. In part there were undoubtedly features drawn from Greek styles of building, but he thinks that other elements were probably more like those of some richly designed Arab mosque of today, with bands of pattern in different coloured bricks or stone. More recent archaeologists disagree with him, and think that Herod built his Temple entirely in the style of late Greek architecture—of the so-called Hellenistic period. The principal material was snowy white marble, and large areas of the walls of the actual sanctuary were covered with plates of gold, which must have shone brilliantly in the sun. It was, in fact, a spectacle of dazzling splendour, and the only building in the modern world with which we can fitly compare it is the Arya Dharma temple built in 1938 at New Delhi by Seth Baldeolas Birla, for the attempted unification of all the different varieties of Indian religion. Anyhow, for weal or woe, there was the Temple at Jerusalem, and children must have thought it a very wonderful place, especially when their elders took them to see it as far as they were allowed to go, for it is said that it was in its day the largest religious sanctuary in the world. Whether it was larger than the Temple of Heaven at Peking is uncertain; but the latter was, and still is, merely a sacred enclosure, and its central sanctuary, reached by a series of steps, is open to the sky.

THE PASSOVER AND THE DAILY SACRIFICE

In spite of all that the Hebrew prophets had spoken, there were some features of temple ritual that must seem to us as we read about them not unlike the ceremonies at the Kali Ghat in Calcutta during the nineteenth century. To explain this it is necessary to describe a little of what happened at the great annual Jewish festival of the Passover (or Pesach). To this great national festival came pilgrims from all over the Mediterranean world. When possible, they walked. Longer journeys were made by camel, donkey or ship. On land they went in large caravans to avoid attacks by brigands. The good roads between the Eurphrates and the Jordan made transport easier. Exemption was given to the sick and to minors. Women voluntarily participated. Pilgrims travelled with song and merrymaking.

About the middle of the month before Passover workmen were to be seen repairing bridges, mending roads, whitewashing tombs (so that people could see and avoid contamination by touching them),[1] and at home cleaning down and scouring all the domestic utensils. On the evening of the thirteenth of the month the father of the family went round the whole house with a lighted candle searching out all cakes made from ordinary cereals with the addition of leaven. After that until the end of the festival no leaven was allowed to be used. The next morning all work

[1] There is nothing today in the world which so well compares with this as the Mecca pilgrimage of Moslems. I saw 6000 aged male pilgrims on the eve of being conveyed by the U.S.A. Air Force from Beirut to Mecca, and I also saw the return of the Mecca train to Amman, with streets and taxis decorated with garlands, hooters blowing and flags waving.

stopped except that of tailors, barbers and washer-women. Then in the evening the regulation was observed that all male Jews within a radius of fifteen miles were to appear at the Temple bringing an offering, to consist of a lamb not less than eight days and not more than a year old. These lambs were brought by groups of men containing ten to twenty persons, and to avoid crowding, they were admitted by relays into the Temple court where the altar stood. There each man killed his lamb, and the priests, standing in two rows with bowls of gold and silver respectively, caught the blood as it flowed, and dashed it at the foot of the altar, where the drain conveyed it away quickly. Each lamb was then hung on a nail or peg, flayed and dressed, and its fat offered on the altar. During this ceremony the choir of Levites chanted Psalms 113 to 118, and repeated the chanting until the whole sacrifice was over. The lambs were afterwards taken home, and roasted on spits of pomegranate wood. No bone was allowed to be broken. After the roasting came the *seder* meal, with the usual questioning of the father by the eldest child, 'Why do we have this service?' With the usual answer as prescribed. Everyone wore best clothes, and had to be provided with at least four cups of red wine, even if the head of the household had to pawn his garments to buy it.[1]

As will be seen, the whole ceremony was very highly organised, and this would apply to everything that went on in the Temple and around it. There was a daily offering of ritual sacrifice, and everyone knew the time when this took place, because it was heralded by the blowing of silver trumpets, the signal for which was

[1] It has been estimated that the average number of pilgrims attending Passover each year was about 125,000. Others, however, have estimated it at about a million.

93   The looting of the Temple by the Romans. Note the seven-branched candlestick and the silver trumpets being carried away

given by a priest standing on the highest pinnacle of
the Temple, and watching for the first sign of dawn.
These musical instruments are interesting. There are
said to have been seven of them, and they were blown
not only at the sacrifice, but also at three pauses in the
daily chanting of the psalms, on each occasion three
times, to summon the congregation to prostrate themselves in worship. The sound would echo all over the
city, and must have thrilled all who heard it.[1] We can
see a picture of one of these trumpets on the arch of
Titus, where the loot taken from the Temple at its
destruction by the Romans is depicted in relief. There
would seem to have been about fifty priests on duty
each day, together with Levites and representative
laity. When the priests assembled in a special place
called the Hall of Hewn Polished Stones, they were
chosen for their duties by lot, so as to avoid jealousy,
and then they went on to prepare the sacrifice of the

[1] It has been estimated that the total number of priests was
about 7200, and of Levites about 12,000.

lamb. Meanwhile, the lot was cast again for the duty
of making the solemn offering of incense, and whoever
was chosen was only allowed this privilege once in his
lifetime. But besides these ritual and symbolical acts
there were also held in the Temple prayers similar to,
though, of course, not exactly the same, as the ones
prescribed in the English Book of Common Prayer,
with confession, reading of the Hebrew Scriptures (two
lessons), and sermon, the reciting of the Ten Commandments and the singing of psalms. Devotions of
this sort were customary in the meeting-houses or
synagogues of Jews throughout the world of that day,
and there is no doubt that parts of them passed on into
the usage of the Christian Church, such, for instance,
as the Holy, Holy, Holy, in the Communion service,
with its linking up of the earthly congregation with the
worship of the heavenly multitude. Any Jewish boy,
after he had passed a certain age, and had been in-
vested with the *tallith* or special vestment, would
become quite familiar with these synagogue services,
and they were timed to coincide with those of the
Temple, so that Jews right away in Rome or even
farther west could feel that when they were saying
their prayers their brothers in Jerusalem were praying
with them.

Besides Pesach there were, of course, other religious
occasions of special moment, such as the New Year
Festival, or Rosh Hashannah (with the blowing of the
ram's horn), the Feast of Succoth or Tabernacles (the
conclusion of the harvest), and Yom Kippur, or The
Day of Atonement, a fast for sin, with a special
sacrificial rite attached to it.

The wealth of the Temple must have been very
great. (When Crassus, that very vulgar Roman,
sacked Jerusalem, he is said to have carried away the

equivalent of eighteen million U.S. dollars' worth of
Temple revenue—in gold!) It was controlled by a
staff of officials, whose functions corresponded to those
of the treasurer or chancellor of an English cathedral,
and this department defrayed all the expenses of the
services of the sanctuary, from the purchases of bread
and incense to the fees of rabbis and the renewals of
curtains. But there was an immense surplus which was
enough to pay for the repairs of the city walls and the
maintenance of the roads and public buildings about
Jerusalem.

There was also the Temple music to be provided
for. The references in the Book of Revelation to great
choirs, and to 'harpers harping with their harps', is
probably a reminiscence of temple-worship as seen and
heard in Jerusalem. The first music to be recorded is
that of the silver trumpets blown by the priests. There
were two forms of this, the short sound called the

94   Music of the silver trumpets

Thekiah and the long blasts of many notes called the Theruah. (See Music score.) On ordinary days the priests blew seven times, and each time three blasts, a Thekiah and Theruah and Thekiah again (94). The first three were blown when the great gates of the Temple were opened for the day, and other blasts were

95 Jew announcing Sabbath by blowing ram's horn

blown on the evening of the Sabbath (95), to inaugurate it, and at various times during Temple worship.

In addition to the trumpets, thirty-six different instruments are mentioned, including the harp, lute (of which latter it was provided that there should be not less than two and not more than six in the Temple orchestra) and a flute or reed pipe. It appears that a kind of organ called a *magraphah* was also in use, but for what purpose cannot be exactly determined.

Finally there was the Shophar or ram's horn,[1] which was blown especially at the Feast of the New Year. The choir in the Temple of Herod was supplied by Levite boys. It is not clear that there was any congregational singing or chanting, as in the synagogues, but the congregation seems only to have joined in the Amens.

All these elaborate and dignified temple services came to a sad end after the first rebellion of the Jews in A.D. 70, when their temple was destroyed (93). After that only the synagogues inside and outside the Holy City carried on with their prayers. Yet even before that, many educated Jews had begun to question whether animal sacrifices were necessary, and whether the prophets had not been right in laying stress on the sacrifice of personal life. One famous Jew, indeed, after the destruction of the Temple by fire said: 'We still have an altar—deeds of mercy and pity', and others taught that although sacrifice in the ritual sense was now ended, almsgiving and a good life were adequate substitutes. But this teaching seemed to suggest too much self-sufficiency on the part of mankind, so many earnest Jews reacted against it. Although the Day of Atonement, Yom Kippur, thus went on being observed in the synagogues after the destruction of the Temple without the killing of any animal, popular feeling was not satisfied, and came to demand some substitute for the old scape-goat, and so gradually and unofficially there came in the so-called Hahnen Kappara or sacrifice of a white fowl. This goes on even today, and some rabbis actually perform

[1] I have been listening, as I write this note, to the blowing of the Shophar at the Rosh Hashannah, but it is not an impressive sound, and seemed, as I heard it, rather like a child's toy trumpet. Its associations, however, make it a ceremony very dear to Jews.

it themselves. But it is done privately at home, not
even in the synagogue, and the widespread prevalence
of it is said to be attested by the large masses of white
chicken feathers to be seen floating about in the
Orthodox quarters of Jerusalem after Yom Kippur.
You can see the sort of protest which the older ritual
practices aroused in Christians during the first century,
if you look at a work like the anonymous Epistle to
Hebrews in the New Testament.

The social life of Palestine after the first century falls
outside the scope of this book, but it may be fitly
mentioned that the losses of the Jews in their two
wars against the Romans must on any estimate have
been crippling and disastrous, between 600,000 and
2,000,000 in the battles against Titus, and half a
million in the second Jewish war. Such defeat to
military arms not unnaturally left the Christian movement the residuary legatee of whatever spiritual force
Israel had to bequeath.

Chapter XIV

RELIGIOUS WORSHIP AND
EVERYDAY THOUGHT

So far we have spoken mainly about the Jews' religion. Although we have not finished with it, we must now turn for a little to that of the other inhabitants of the Empire, and then come back to it again.

We must try to imagine ourselves in a society, the larger part of which did not have what we are accustomed to know as 'weekly church-going'. That is to say, it did not divide its life into Sundays and week-days, but into sacred days and secular days, which might or might not occur in intervals of seven. The smaller part of society, consisting of the Jews, did have a week, but as we know it ran from Saturday to Saturday, and the seventh day was the Jews' Sabbath or rest-day, ordained for them by the fourth commandment in the Decalogue. But this was not the only difference between the first century and our own, before the beginning of the Christian movement. Most people, if they did go to some public building for religious worship, went to what we commonly call a temple, and the temples of that day were in many respects, though not in all, similar to the temples which may be seen today in India, that is to say, they had an outer court, and an inner sanctuary which contained something sacred, either a statue, or a large block of stone. In the case of the latter, it was a natural object, generally of very great antiquity, and was a sign or sacrament of some divine presence. In the case of a statue, however, it was a man-made object, usually

of a beautiful human being (102), though sometimes of
an animal or bird or reptile, or even a composite
figure, half human, half animal, or perhaps a human
being with some organ of the body multiplied many
times to signify intense power—a custom which is
quite common in India even today. People did not
usually come to a temple in a body for what we call
'congregational worship'. They might come in a
crowd, but still as individuals, and they would make
their offerings as individuals. They would also be
more like spectators than like people joining in a service, because practically everything that happened
when they sat there was done on their behalf by the
staff of the temple, its priests and their attendants. The
temples would be open every day, so that there could
be a continual stream of worshippers bringing their
offerings, but there would also be special holy days
when more people than usual would attend, and when
perhaps a special sacred ritual, often in dramatic form,
would take place, to commemorate an event in the
activities or career of the deity to whom that particular
temple belonged. These festivals would most likely
coincide with something in the world of nature, such
as a new moon, spring-time, harvest, or first-fruits, the
vintage, or the winter solstice. The offerings of the
people would be material. They would be sacrifices of
living things, such as oxen, pigs, sheep, fowls, pigeons
or goats. Sometimes there might be offerings of
cereals, either in grain or in the form of cakes or
loaves, and sometimes offerings of wine and incense.
Even in the Jews' Temple in Jerusalem offerings of
this kind were made.

The kinds of divine being worshipped in these
temples would be numerous, and they were believed
to preside over different aspects of life, sometimes

nature and its seasons, sometimes human occupations and trades, sometimes the after-life.[1] Some were able to bestow gifts of healing, and people would come and sleep in their temples in the hope of getting cured of some ailment. Other gods claimed to have Oracles (celestial 'citizens' bureaux'!) where you could go and get answers to your problems: Shall I divorce my wife? Have I been poisoned by somebody? What's my chance of election to the Senate? and so on. The Romans had a great number of these departmental divinities, such as Pales, who presided over cowsheds, and Pomona, who was the goddess of orchards, and they had even a goddess whom they called Cloacina who presided over the drainage, and a god called Stercutius who was the patron of manure-heaps! Many of the greater gods and goddesses were personifications of some celestial or earthly object, such as the sun or sky on the one hand, or a sacred mountain or river on the other, but sometimes they would seem to have been heroic or famous human beings who had gradually come to be thought of as manifestations of a Divine Spirit, and who had, therefore, ceased in popular thought to be merely human. This was quite as much the case with someone like the Greek general Demetrius, as with the Roman emperor Augustus, who is spoken of by a Roman poet as the incarnation of the god Mercury (in Greek Hermes). It was not normal to worship an Emperor during his lifetime, and since

---

[1] One of the favourite female divinities worshipped in Palestine during the first century was the goddess Korē, or as she is sometimes known, Persephone. There was a sanctuary to her at Samaria in the Graeco-Roman Sesbaste, and a statue from this place, with an inscription, is preserved in the Museum at Jerusalem. At Caesarea Philippi, the very scene of Peter's confession, there was also an important shrine to the god Pan.

there is no evidence of petitionary prayer to any deified emperors, it seems that they must always have been rather minor divinities.

The idea of divine beings becoming visible in human form is quite common almost all over the world, and it is perhaps one of the chief ways in which people have accounted for the emergence from time to time of great kings or leaders, great warriors or men of genius, and even great philosophers and poets, and especially of persons possessing what we commonly call 'the prophetic gift', i.e. men and women who have the gift of eloquence, who can inspire others with impassioned speeches, or who have more than normal insight and can interpret the course of history, and even predict future events.

At the back of all this lay the ordinary everyday belief that the supernatural powers which controlled the affairs of the world were plural and not singular. We are so used to thinking of Deity as One, that it does not come easily to us to imagine a state of society in which almost everybody took the opposite view for granted. At the same time, we must recognise that not only Jews but Gentiles as well were beginning to give up what is called polytheism. Like people in India, they were beginning to say that the different deities of the temples were only aspects of one Reality, and the cleverer men among them said that the curious stories about the Greek and Roman gods and goddesses which we call myths were not to be taken at their face value, but were allegories, and they tried to explain them in a more edifying manner. This didn't work very well beyond a certain point, because when the Christians came along with the gospel story which they said was fact and not allegory, people not unnaturally came to prefer it to something which they felt did not mean what it said, and which they had to twist about in order to get at the idea behind it. At the same time, like a great many thoughtful people in India, the Gentiles had little idea of the importance of historical events, or of purpose in history, and this actually set them against the gospel story. In the end history won through, but at some sacrifice, since a number of myths became attached to the plain story of the New Testament, and these have been an embarrassment to it ever since.[1]

Probably for most of us the really interesting development at this period is that of a type of public worship which, for want of a better phrase, we may have to call 'Protestant'. Of course, this is to use a word entirely out of its time and context, but we will try to explain what is meant. As the leading thinkers in various countries came to discount the value of ritual sacrifices, new forms of prayer began to grow up. In India, people began to retire into the forests and hills, and to meditate, with the use of a certain technique. In China they turned to sages who taught them the art of good conduct, and some of them also resorted to meditation. In Iran they listened to a prophet who apparently said that it was more just and religious to use the dung of the ox to grow more crops, than to kill the beast in an offering of bloody sacrifice. In Israel, the prophets such as Micah, taught: 'He (God) hath shewed thee O man what is good, and what doth the Lord require of thee but to do justly and to love mercy and to walk humbly with thy God?'

[1] We now hear a good deal about the necessity for what is called 'de-mythologising' the New Testament literature, and this from ardent believers; not from people who want to destroy Christianity, but from those who wish to interpret it for the world of today, without depriving it of its essential meaning.

All this went on some time before the first century
A.D., but the result was that the Jews, after they were
cut off from their temple by exile, in Babylonia, and
still more after its destruction in A.D. 70, developed
meetings, at first in one another's houses, but later in
buildings specially set apart for the purpose, in which
there was worship not at all unlike that of an English,
Scotch or American chapel. Such a meeting was
called a *kinneseth*,[1] or *knishta*, in the Aramaic dialect
spoken by Jesus and his disciples, and in Greek a
'synagogue', i.e. a 'gathering together', and even after
the Jews recovered Palestine and rebuilt their temple,
they went on using synagogues. In fact, there were
said to have been as many as 480 of them in Jerusalem
at the time of its downfall (not many more than it is
estimated exist in Israeli Jerusalem today), and in all
the cities of the Roman Empire, wherever there were
at least ten Jews, there would be a synagogue, and a
special building would be erected for the purpose, if
there was a large enough congregation to be able to
afford to pay for one (101). Such a building was
always put in a conspicuous place, either on high
ground, or at a street corner, so as to be prominent.
It was usually circular or rectangular, with a single or
double colonnade, and ornamented with carvings, not
usually, perhaps, such as would be judged idolatrous,
but sometimes symbolical, e.g. representations of the
seven-branched candlestick, or the pot of manna, and
at one synagogue on the Sea of Galilee, at Chorazin,
most rich and elaborate carving of all descriptions.
Off the coast of North Africa lies the small island of
Djerba, where still stands what is believed to be the

[1] The very word now used by the Republic of Israel for its
Chamber of Deputies.

oldest known synagogue building in the world.[1] This, if it is any indication of what the earlier synagogues were like, is in three parts, so that although not planned at all for sacrificial worship, it still represents the three main divisions of the Jerusalem Temple. In all synagogues the sexes were separated and the women put behind a screen. Kohl and Watzinger have excavated in the ruins of a number of the oldest Palestinian synagogues, and have tried to reconstruct what they were like. In general, they have found that Galilean synagogues were almost all directed towards the south, trans-Jordanian towards the west, and western synagogues towards the east, the intention being to enable the worshippers to face towards Jerusalem. The shrines for the scrolls of the sacred books were, at Capernaum and Chorazin, of stone, and probably so in most other local synagogues, and not, as they usually are today, of wood. In the middle of the floor rose the platform or *bima*. On the *bima* stood a wooden pulpit, or *migdal ez*, together with a chair or *churseja*. The *bima* must have been of wood (as it still is) because there are no traces of *bimas* in the ruins—they have evidently all perished. We can, therefore, only reconstruct these platforms and pulpits from surviving ones in the Near East (e.g. Damascus and Tiberias) which may very well have preserved the old patter (99). Yet pulpits of this sort would have looked out of place in a Greek-built synagogue such as the one at Capernaum. At Chorazin has been found what was apparently a stone seat for the ruler of the synagogue, or perhaps for the preacher.

The reader stood up, but the preacher sat down. Prayer was offered standing. Behind the *migdal*, and at

[1] The original was burnt down, but the present building is said to be a copy of it, incorporating old fragments.

99 Interior of a Jerusalem synagogue (from Tissot)

the back you would have seen the ark or tabernacle containing the scrolls of the Hebrew Scriptures. This was made movable in later times so as to be able to be carried in procession, on the festive occasion known as 'the rejoicing in the Law'[1] (as in our picture of Djerba) (96), but at Capernaum and Chorazin it was of stone. Sometimes there were two arks, one for the Law or Torah, and a second one for the prophets or Nebiim. In front of the ark or *aron* you would see a veil, and above it a lamp which was always kept burning, together with a many-branched candlestick, for use on special occasions. The congregation would have been seen facing the ark, and the ruler of the synagogue and other leading persons would be in the chief seats with their backs to it, and so facing the

[1] The Sem Hattorah, or 'the rejoicing in the Law', comes in the autumn, at the end of the Feast of Succoth or Tabernacles. The scrolls are taken in procession, and there is a solemn dance in the synagogue, in which the Rabbis join.

congregation. The worship would have been found to be rather like that in some Anglican Churches. That is to say it would not have been extempore, but following a set form not unlike Morning or Evening Prayer—in effect a 'word of God service' with psalms, prayers and readings of scripture, but with everybody sitting down most of the time. The first part of the prayers would be said at the lectern, the second in front of the ark and facing it. The music would be unaccompanied, and would be not unlike the plainsong which is heard in Roman or Anglo-Catholic churches. As the readers chanted, they would rock slowly to and fro over their book or scroll. The sermon would have followed the reading of a lesson from the prophets, and would have been either a *darash* or 'inquiry' or a *meamar* or 'talk'. The person who read from the Prophets was also expected to say the sentence known as the Shema (Hear O Israel, the Lord our God, the Lord is One), and certain accompanying benedictions from the lectern. The celebrated Eighteen benedictions, or Shemoneh 'Esreh, which, together with other prayers constituted the *tephillah* or supplications, were said in front of the ark. Besides a number of services on the Sabbath itself, you would have found people frequenting the building on the second and fifth days of the week, and in large centres of population you might even have found daily services. In addition to this, you would have found the synagogue being used as a school, and sometimes as a law-court, and on occasion you might have found the local Jewish community having a meal in it. Memorial services for the departed were also held there in communities of Jews where the belief in personal survival had developed.

These synagogue buildings of the first century, as will be evident, belonged to an entirely different type of religious activity from anything connected with a temple. To begin with, they included a certain amount of definitely congregational worship.[1] That is to say, people recited prayers *together*, and joined in responses. But more than that, in a synagogue, there was no altar and there were no material sacrifices. There was nothing but a rostrum from which readings and sermons and the recital of prayers took place, and a small recess with a curtain in front of it containing the press or cupboard in which were preserved some of the holy books of the Jews.

If, therefore, children had gone with their father to a synagogue, this is all they would have seen, but if their father had taken them to a temple, there would have been a great deal more to see, and it might have been a good deal more exciting, and of varied interest. And yet, if we are to understand the social life of the first century, we have to try to grasp the importance of what was happening at this time all over the world. Practically everywhere for many centuries there had been temples with sacrifices and ceremonial. But it seems that, for three or four hundred years, there had been growing, not only among the Hebrews, but also in India, in China and in Greece, as well as for a time in Persia, a grave doubt in the minds of thoughtful persons, as to whether these material sacrifices were either necessary, or even useful. Indeed, not many years before the birth of Christ, a famous Roman writer had declared (or rather had made one of the characters in a dialogue written by him to declare) that the best sacrifice anyone could offer was that of a good life, while a Greek preacher who was alive at the same time as Jesus of Nazareth had said that it was

[1] For some further notes on synagogue worship see the end of this chapter.

wrong to keep killing animals and birds in sacrifices
because it was cruel and wasteful, and also unnecessary, and that the true sacrifice was the sacrifice of the
mind and spirit. We can find sayings like this a good
deal earlier among sages in India and China, and it is
impossible to discover whether the idea grew up more
or less simultaneously in different countries, or whether
it began somewhere and then travelled to a number of
different areas.

In addition to this change in the attitude to sacrifice,
there was also, during this first century, a marked
decline in interest in the old beliefs connected with
Gentile religion. It became possible for things which
had previously been held in reverence to become a
matter for schoolboys' jokes, which is not a very
healthy sign where any religion is concerned, and a
writer just after the end of the first century comments
on the decline in attendance at the temples, and the
difficulty in finding people who were ready to provide
animals for the sacrifices, which shows that the system
was decaying, although some of the Roman emperors
tried to revive it, and to put new life into the old
religious institutions. It will be seen that the worship
of the Jews and that of the early Christians which
developed out of it was thus a real advance in the
expression of religious devotional life.

It is difficult to be sure how many people at this
time disbelieved in any kind of spiritual life at all.
They were certainly in a good many cases very vague
about it, and a dialogue composed by Cicero shows
that the kind of attitude represented by one speaker
must have been common enough to be thought worth
reproducing, in which the latter doubts whether
the gods have any interest in or influence over the
affairs of humanity, and suggests that a humane

kind of pleasure is or ought to be the chief end of life.

If, therefore, you had been a boy or girl in the first century, you might have found that your parents did not go to temple, and that they even made fun of its ceremonies, but that if your father was a serious-minded and educated man, he might, perhaps, like similar persons in both India and China, have had a working theory as to the nature of the good life based upon some philosophy or other, probably in his case that of the school of thought called Stoic,[1] which was the commonest one, and which taught that the universe was held together and guided by a central Principle called the Logos (Reason or Word) which was the self-expression of a single rather vaguely conceived Supreme Being, scarcely describable by our word 'God', although one of the Stoics wrote a hymn to this Being in which he addressed It in terms not differing very much from those in some of the psalms and hymns which we sing in church. The Logos was believed to appear in visible form in a number of personages, some of them mythical, but others more or less historical. Some said Hermes or the god Mercury (the chief speaker of the gods) was one of these appearances, and since from the times of the Greeks onwards into Roman times, little statues of Hermes or Mercury were to be found in shops and houses and streets, it became easy for people in saluting these shrines of Hermes (100) to believe that they were making an act of worship to the Power or Logos behind the world.

One thing is certain. In a society which had, as Paul said, 'gods many and lords many', there was no question of false gods. People were quite tolerant of one

---

[1] From the Greek word *stoa*, a porch. The teachers of this philosophy used to frequent a famous painted porch in Athens.

another's divinities, and thought them all equally useful and beneficial, and if they found a goddess in
different countries worshipped by different names,
they would say that it was all the same goddess, and
that she was simply known by various epithets. In this
respect, as in many others, the Mediterranean world
was very much like the India that we have come to

100 Worship at a street-shrine of the god Hermes

know. Both were very ready to see in famous persons
an incarnation of the Logos (India had, of course, a
different word for saying this), and both had a philosophy for the enlightened, and a popular and sometimes rather childish religion for the uneducated,
which the cultured folk were careful not to disturb by
too much inquiry, because they secretly felt that it
would not stand the test, while they recognised that it
had a strong emotional appeal, so that if it was
destroyed the masses would be left without any
anchorage.

Another type of religious activity which had a good

many adherents was that which offered a haven of safety from the perishing world. This was found in certain sanctuaries to which people went for a cere-mony which was a cross between being confirmed and being admitted to one of the degrees of Freemasonry. You had to pay a fee for this to the priests of the sanctuary and go through certain ritual acts which were said to be secret, but in them you believed that you were granted a vision of some supernatural beings, and guaranteed against eternal extinction at death.

Finally, we must say something about the men among the Gentiles who set up to teach virtue and wisdom to the people of the first century. Of these we will take three, Seneca, Epictetus and Plutarch, though there were plenty of lesser individuals.

Seneca was a court philosopher. He was banished by the Emperor Claudius, but eventually became the tutor of Nero, and it is said that he sought to dis-courage the major vices of the latter by tolerating the minor ones. One of his leading ideas was that anybody could be good if he wanted to. 'Nature', he said, 'hath given us sufficient strength, if we would exert ourselves in the use of it. . . . We pretend we cannot, when the truth is, we will not. We defend our vices because we love them. I have a better opinion of people than they have of themselves. I think they can do what is re-quired but they will not.' Many of his sayings are noble enough to sound like echoes of Christ's teaching, and since Seneca was certainly a contemporary of St. Paul, some have thought that he may have been influenced by him. This, however, cannot be proved. What is likely is that both Paul and Seneca knew and quoted Stoic maxims. But Paul the Jew never agreed that people could be virtuous if they wanted to. In-deed, he said exactly the opposite (Romans 7^{15-22}).

Epictetus was the slave of a private owner who treated him brutally, breaking his leg so that he became a cripple. He was born about A.D. 60, and acquired his position from the custom among Roman parvenus of having philosophers among their attendants, so as to appear cultured. Somehow or other Epictetus gained his freedom and set up as an independent teacher. He was always poor, and never married, but adopted a child which had been abandoned to die of exposure. He is a much nobler figure than Seneca, and would seem to have been wholly sincere. While accepting the ordinary standards and customs of his age, such as prostitution, and the resort to fortune tellers, he lays down certain principles of detachment and disinterestedness which at times bring him very near to the Christian view of life. Among his most famous and characteristic sayings are the following:

1. 'If you kiss your child or your wife, tell yourself that you kiss a being subject to the accidents of humanity; and thus you will not be disturbed if either of them dies.'

2. 'Lameness is an impediment to the leg, but not to the faculty of choice, say this to yourself in regard to everything that happens.'

3. 'Remember that you are an actor in a drama, of such a kind as the author pleases to make of it. If short, of a short one: if long, of a long one. If it be his pleasure you should act a poor man, a cripple, a governor, or a private person, see that you act it naturally. For this is your business, to act well the character assigned you; to choose it is another's business.'

4. 'If you have an earnest desire of attaining to

philosophy, prepare yourself from the very first to be laughed at, to be sneered at by the multitude, to hear them say he is returned to us a philosopher all at once, and whence this supercilious look? Now for your part, do not have a supercilious look indeed; but keep steadily to those things which appear best to you as one appointed to Deity to this station. For remember that if you adhere to the same point, those very persons who at first ridiculed you will afterwards admire you. But if you are conquered by them, you will incur a double ridicule.'

5. 'First acquire a distinct knowledge that every event is indifferent and nothing to you, of whatever sort it may be, for it will be in your power to make a right use of it, and this no one can hinder.'

6. 'In parties of conversation avoid a frequent and excessive mention of your own actions and dangers. For however agreeable it may be to yourself, to mention the risks you have run, it is not equally agreeable to others to hear your adventures. Avoid likewise an endeavour to excite laughter, for this is a slippery point, which may throw you into vulgar manners, and besides may be apt to lessen you in the esteem of your acquaintance.'

7. 'What do I desire? To understand Nature and to follow her.'

Like all Stoics, Epictetus aimed at being a proficient or perfect man (the Greek work is *teleios* or *sophos*) and of the latter he says that the proficient person censures no one and praises no one, suppresses all desire in himself, and if he outwardly appears stupid or ignorant, does not care. His ideally perfect person seems to have been Socrates.

Anybody who reads even these few extracts cannot help seeing how deeply the Stoic teaching of the first century has sunk into our European life. No. 3 seems to have inspired one of Shakespeare's most famous speeches, and equally one of Charles Wesley's best hymns. Substitute, in No. 4, 'ordination' for 'philosophy', and it is the sort of thing that is said to budding curates at theological colleges. No. 6 sounds exactly like the training in manners administered to an English public-school boy.

Plutarch's dates again overlap the age of the New Testament. We think of him chiefly as a biographer whose lives of great contemporaries furnished material for Shakespeare and others. But he was also something of a religious teacher, and wrote essays to explain the spiritual and allegorical meanings of the myths about the gods. Had he been successful, he might have held back the world of his day from accepting Christianity, but in spite of his tolerant persuasiveness, he and his colleagues somehow failed to seem convincing to the public, and the latter gradually drifted away into indifference, or into some measure of Christian belief.

With all this relatively high moral and spiritual teaching there was a good deal of uncertainty as to the worth of life. Most grave inscriptions are of the pattern: 'O Claudia, freed from sorrow, farewell,' or 'Be of good courage, Marcus, no one is going to live for ever.' No non-Christian inscription breathes any hope for the future. The good pagan, as has been said, was in his way an admirable person, but he had two grave defects. First, he had hardly any faith, he had almost no hope, and he did not cultivate loving-kindness towards mankind as a whole. Second, he might be moral and chaste himself, but he tolerated the most appalling vices among those around him, and, like Gandhi, preserved a gentle indifference towards the unpleasant side of pagan religion. He was, in fact, very much like the best sort of Hindu today, and, I am afraid, like some of our own nominal Christians.

I have no doubt that the synagogues which I was privileged to attend on the Sabbath during my stay in Jerusalem conducted their worship in some respects differently from those of the first century, but I am inclined to believe that in principle they preserved their original form of divine service. Essentially it was one of words rather than of actions. Most of the time the congregation remained seated, although they stood at certain moments, especially at the opening of the *aron*. But the proceedings consisted mainly of reading, carefully followed in books by everyone present. (In the old days, when printed books were not available, and manuscripts scarce, this could hardly have happened.) The reading was intoned nasally, and a number of different persons were called up to the *bima* to take part in it, and were coached a little by their seniors, if they failed to do it quite correctly. I am informed that in some synagogues the cantors chant very musically, and with a good deal of *coloratura*. At intervals there were responses from the seated congregation. The members present rocked themselves to and fro in a curious rhythm while reciting. One synagogue I visited was in an upper room, approached by an outside staircase, and the congregation was peculiarly fervent (Chasidic is the title of the sect or group). The shouting of the responses was deafening, and the rocking of the body intense and exaggerated, so that some bent almost double. Here and there a man clenched his fist and struck the board in front of him, and in other cases smote his head or his breast or lifted his hand in the air, while his face was convulsed as he almost shrieked out his responses. Although the whole service was controlled by the use of a set form of words, the recitation of these words was filled with such intensity and accompanied by such movements of the body that the whole scene became one of frenzied ecstasy. There was certainly life in this synagogue, although to a Western European it might have appeared rather barbaric. At the same time one seemed to detect signs of a temper which must have been traditional, and which may well have led to scenes in the synagogues of the first century such as may be read about in the New Testament. It was easy to imagine Jesus of Nazareth swept out by a turbulent crowd of Orthodox Jews in his own village, and threatened with stoning. I could also well picture this Chasidic congregation interrupting St. Paul with angry contradictions. Their faces and costume, as well as their excitability, seemed to belong to the Jerusalem of the first rather than of the twentieth century. The long beards, skull-caps and immense striped prayer-shawls of most of the men present gave a strange far-away aspect to the whole gathering. It was also easy to understand how the Apostles, coming out of their meeting on the first Whitsunday, might have been mistaken by unsympathetic bystanders for people under the influence of strong drink. The early Jewish Christians, who were told by St. Paul: 'Be filled with the Spirit, speaking to yourselves in psalms and hymns and spiritual songs' may not have been at all unlike these Chasidic Jews, and like the early Christians. These Chasids did not keep unison in their devotions, but tended to speak irregularly and out of order, just as the Spirit moved them. It was easy to believe that the fervour of such gatherings might at times get a bit out of hand and need the restraining rule of an Apostolic leader to tell the congregation to do things 'decently and in order'. Some of the Chasids I saw were clearly on the edge of 'speaking with tongues', and there was an undisciplined but very sincere spontaneity in their devotions which almost exactly reproduced the conditions described in 1 Corinthians 14, especially verses 23 to 29. (Readers must please look these up.) The women in these synagogues were, as usual, either behind a lattice or curtain on one side of the building, following the service silently and unseen, or they were outside in the courtyard, reading devoutly from their service-books. (See again 1 Corinthians 14[34-5].) The last thing I want to do is to belittle or deride the devotions of these good people, whose earnestness would put the congregations in some other synagogues to shame, and from whom Christians themselves could also learn. All I wish to do is to make clear that this conservative revival of Hebrew piety effectively reproduces the conditions of zealous Judaism in the time of Christ, and makes it much easier to understand some of the scenes and passages in the New Testament.

EPILOGUE

You who have read this book may well ask: 'What does it all add up to? Have the facts as presented any more meaning than the contents of one of those fascinating junk shops that we so often find in the side streets of our older towns, where the exhibits are set out all in a jumble, with perhaps a Persian rug draped over an Elizabethan court cupboard, or an eastern water-pipe perched on the top of a walnut bureau of the reign of Queen Anne?' Such a shop is a good place of refuge, if one wishes to forget the world outside, and to dream about the past.

But this is not meant to be an escapist book. It is intended to give information, and also among other things, to set you asking some straight questions. Therefore, if you now ask the particular questions which head this page, you are doing just what the author wants you to do, and he is going to try to suggest one possible answer.

You must notice that a good bit of our survey has shown us people doing much the same thing that we do today, and doing them almost as effectively. We have seen them rationing and controlling the supply of food, cooking and serving elaborate meals, full of delicacies, organising transport by land and water, building blocks of flats, employing an inter-provincial banking system, instituting State schools and colleges, and even a State medical and surgical service, maintaining a vast army and continually improving its technique, engaging in scientific research, and learning how to lighten labour by mechanical devices.

If their world had gone on without any break in the direction in which it was going, they might well have got to the point we ourselves have reached, some centuries sooner than has actually been the case. As we know this did not occur. The clock was put back, and the everyday life of the first century, after two or three more centuries, gave way to the everyday life of the Dark Ages. Once again wars and invasions, and the submergence of a relatively civilised area by the influx of people with a much lower standard of living, retarded what might otherwise have been continuous progress. Yet the educated people who lived in Rome and Athens in the days of Christ and St. Paul did not themselves really think that progress was going to keep on indefinitely in an upward path. The gods they once believed in seemed no longer to influence the course of events, and it was indeed doubtful whether such beings existed, or, if they did exist, whether they took any interest in the struggles of humanity. And further, these educated folk usually held not what we call a *linear*, but a *cyclic* idea of history, or if they did hold a linear one, it was that of a fortuitous stream of atoms falling vertically downwards to a dead level of inertia. Perhaps, being nearer than we are to the civilisations of Mesopotamia and Egypt, it was easier for them to realise that the latter had ended in utter decay, and to suspect that the same fate might befall theirs also. Their wise men certainly taught that if there had been a golden age it was now past, and that the civilisation they knew was 'perishing and running down to its last end' (even though it might perhaps be wound up again), and they tried to steel themselves to face such an immediate prospect. In any case, they saw that they were confronted with it in their own lives, when each came to the end of his earthly pilgrimage, and they said: 'Nothing can happen to you but what is part of the constitution and course of nature. Therefore do not worry, but be brave and dignified, and avoid showing too much enthusiasm over anything, since all around you will soon vanish away.' Some sought by a process partly ritual, partly psychological, to gain a sense of escaping out of the perishable world, and of being, as they put it, 'reborn into eternity'. They did this without much evidence that it could really happen, but perhaps with the intuition that it ought to be possible.

Right up against this busy and ingenious, but half-hearted world, came something from the Middle East which was entirely different. It collided with it like an arrow striking the edge of a revolving wheel—the wheel of history—jerking that wheel from its course and upsetting its cyclic motion—forever.

This something was the belief of the Jews. Their rather strange exclusiveness made them attract attention, and they certainly believed that the Divine Being they called Yahweh (see below for the meaning of the word)[1] was not only their God, but the morally holy Lord of the whole world, and the Director of its history, with a special purpose which was being worked out. Much of the teaching contained in their sacred

[1] It may very well be that the word which, without vowel points, in Hebrew letters is something like YHVH or YHH, becomes, with the vowels put in, either YAHOH or YAHWEH. The Arabic word for 'to blow' is *hawah*, so it may very likely be that the original deity known by such a name was a wind-god, though in India the same sort of idea is connected with the air that a person breathes in or out, and the divine name is connected with 'breath'. What ever the original meaning, there can be no doubt that by the time the book of Exodus was written, YHVH had come to mean: 'He who is or will be', i.e. 'the Self-Existent Being who determines His own destiny and that of the world'.

literature was very fine and noble, and even today compels our admiration.

Dispersed as they were throughout the Roman Empire, they formed a kind of religious fifth column in its various provinces, but their ceremonial bigotry and nationalist egoism spoilt their influence, and rendered them less effective than they might otherwise have been in spreading this kind of prophetic teaching. Although they did try to make converts, and indeed not without some success, it is doubtful whether they could ever have captured the whole of their world, because they insisted on their disciples adopting specifically Jewish customs, to wit circumcision, and the eating of *kōsher* food, and their claim to be physically God's chosen people seemed arrogant and fantastic. It was rather as though modern Europeans might be invited to become Hindus on condition that they took over some special Indian ceremonial observances, and recognised the hereditary superiority of the Brahmin caste.

One Jew, however, apparently of royal Davidic ancestry,[1] followed by a small band of adherents, adopted a new line, and with unique vision stripped Judaism of its national and ceremonial exclusiveness, and proclaimed it as the common world religion. He was judicially murdered in the midst of his revolutionary efforts, but it was immediately seen that some special valuation of his person and authority was inevitably bound up with his teaching. (See, for example, the prologue to our Fourth Gospel.) It was this movement (subsequently known as 'Christian' or 'Messianist')

[1] Recent discoveries of ancient manuscripts have made us aware that there were a number of these reforming movements, but the one which we associate with Jesus of Nazareth stands out as unique in the quality of its message and in its dynamic force.

which impinged upon the society of the first century,
and which that society accepted with increasing readi-
ness. The message of the movement was simple, and
was religious and moral rather than intellectual, and
it must be recognised in fairness that it was Asiatic
rather than European in its origin. The remarkable
thing is that, whatever may be thought of its value, it
has since ceased to be purely Asiatic or purely European, and has ended by becoming a world-wide affair.
Clearly it is a solution of life's problems which a considerable section of humanity has tended to find
acceptable.

But, in fairness again, we cannot see the meaning of
what happened unless we also see it as a particular
instance (some would say the most considerable
instance) of a thing that has happened a good many
times in the history of the planet. Europe and its
western developments across the Atlantic have not
been greatly interested in ultimate questions which for
their answer require in the widest sense the *religious*
interpretation of life. They have not, therefore, *created*
any religion, though they have accepted many, or at
least have studied many with tolerance. The religious
impulse (so far as what we may call 'high religion' is
concerned) has always come from east of the Aegean
Sea, and although it may have flowed back again into
Asia, it is from Asia that it has always proceeded.

Thus, we have the influence of India upon Greece,
shown, for example, in Pythagoras. We have the westward dispersion of the Jews. We have the Christian
movement. A little before the advent of Christianity
we have also the eastward and westward spread of
ideas, possibly from Iran, about special discontinuous
invasions of the world of time and space by a Divine
Being or Beings from the supernatural plane for the

purpose of bringing liberation, rescue or healing to a world which was losing heart, or losing its nerve or falling under the domination of wickedness. Again, we have the entry of Stoic teaching into the world of Greece and Rome, and this, too, may perhaps be counted as Asian, since Zeno,[1] its founder, was of Phoenician descent, and it has affinities with teaching which occur much farther east (in China especially). Greek philosophy, more particularly that of Plato, might not have developed as it did if the thought of the Ionian Greeks on the Asian side of the Aegean had not been fertilised from India. And then, a little later than the earliest Christianity, we have the westward migration of ideas which had arisen earlier in India, which led to the formation of world-renouncing and ascetic communities modelled upon those of the Jains and Buddhists in that country, and from which issued not only orthodox Christian monasticism, but also Manichaeism and kindred movements. We ought, however, to note that the flow from Sumeria and India equally went eastward to Malaya, China and Japan, though it is not impossible that there may also have been a flow of ideas westward from China in the age of the hundred philosophies. Then, six hundred years after the rise of Christianity, we have the westward transit of Islam, a genuinely Semitic faith, cradled in Arabia, though indebted both to Judaism and Christianity. This faith, had it not been for the military defeat of the Arabs near Poitiers in A.D. 732, might have conquered the whole of Europe, and in any case, under the Arabs it put new intellectual life into the medieval Latin Church, while in the hands of the Turks it subjugated the Byzantine Church. Later we have the reaction of Chinese thought upon eighteenth-

[1] Actually born in Cyprus.

century Europe, as the result of the work of the Jesuit missionaries in China, who translated some of its classics into Latin, and made them accessible to such persons as Leibnitz and Voltaire. Then at the beginning of the nineteenth century we have the commencement of the influence upon Europe of philosophic Hinduism, beginning with the translation of the Upanishads into European versions, and ending in our own day with the propaganda of Radakrishnan and Aldous Huxley. More recently we have seen the westward trend of Buddhism, beginning with the work of Count Hermann Keyserling in establishing his school of wisdom at Darmstadt, and ending with that of Mr. Christmas Humphreys. It is also significant that Marxism is the creation of a Jew, and is really Messianic Judaism standing on its head, and that its chief apostles have come from the most Asiatic of European countries, Russia, where they seem to be trying to establish a sort of infallible Marxist Church. It may not unjustly be said that without the successive world-affirmations of Judaism, Christianity and Islam, western science might not have developed as it did. World-negation does not encourage the study of nature, and although the practical Chinese might have taken to it, no such impulse has hitherto come from the land which produced Hinduism and Buddhism.

We can, I admit, make too much of the regularity of these attacks upon the West by Asia,[1] and, of course, they have taken place at different levels, sometimes religious, sometimes philosophical, sometimes literary, but there is no denying that they certainly occurred, and in the first century their impact was recognised by

[1] I feel bound to make it clear that this Epilogue had reached its final form some months before the delivery of Professor Toynbee's Reith Lectures.

a Roman writer who in a picturesque phrase spoke of
the Orontes (the Syrian river on which stood the huge
half-Oriental city of Antioch) 'flowing into the Tiber'.
In spite of their apparent successiveness they have
really arrived almost concurrently. If, therefore, we
take into account the immense age of the earth
and the vast antiquity of the human race, we are
able to see them, so to speak, as *timeless* alternatives,
proposed for the consideration of the inhabitants of the
earth, who are chiefly concerned with the business of
living. The answers put forward by these alternatives
vary to the extent of contradicting one another. Either
they suggest that it is best to abandon the visible
world, and to take refuge from its suffering and vanity
in a role of dreamy meditation, or they advocate the
transformation of the world we know into a better one,
though they sometimes seem to overlook the fact that
even such an improved world may be no more
permanent than its predecessor. Or again, although
they may advocate the transformation of our world of
time and space, they may regard it as avowedly no
more than an interim preparation for a new world
which is bounded neither by time nor space, and
which is actually beyond our definition.

There is one special feature about the world of the
first century, both in the Middle East and in India,
namely that instead of thinking that mankind was able
to achieve progress and regeneration from within itself, it developed the belief that this must inevitably
come as a gift from Divine intervention, either once for
all, as in the case of the Messiah, or at spaced intervals,
as in the case of the Indian *avatars*. India, however, did
not believe enough in the reality of history to take these
avatars seriously. The Messiah, on the other hand, both
to Jews and Christians, is of the real stuff of history,

just as truly as if his record came out of the pages of the best sort of newspaper, and he is certainly no mere edifying fiction.

There is, as we have seen, a good deal of similarity between the first century and ours in the matter of material adjustments to life. A line of culture, albeit with some bad breaks, runs from it to us. But whether we trot from Ostia to Rome in a *cisium* behind a fast horse, or drive to the theatre in a taxi, or fly to Beirut in a Constellation, there is still a question-mark in front of our life. Is it any good? What is it all for? And how are we to explain the sense of strain and incompleteness, of frustration and sadness, which at times almost seems to paralyse all our efforts? Even if our weather, owing to the movement of the earth, comes mainly 'spreading from the west to all districts', the proffered answers to these momentous questions arrive from the East.

We may, of course, take them as: (1) no more than the theories of explorers, or we may see in them (2) the partial unveilings of a Supreme Reality which, in its fullness, is still hid from us. Or we may believe—as I do myself (3) that we can detect in the centre of what a Swiss philosopher has lately christened for us: 'The Axial Age'—which extends from about 800 B.C. to A.D. 300—such a close drawing together of two dimensions or planes of existence as to bring about a situation in which a more complete and normative unveiling was possible, and in which, indeed, it was actually achieved, once and for all.

A modern poet has given us one picture of this in unforgettable words:

I dimly guess what Time in mists confounds
Yet ever and anon a trumpet sounds

From the hid battlements of Eternity;
Those shaken mists a space unsettle, then
Round the half-glimpsed turrets slowly wash again.
  But not ere Him who summoneth
  I first have seen, enwound
With glooming robes purpureal, cypress-crowned;
His name I know, and what his trumpet saith.

Whichever solution we choose to accept, the first, the second or the third, there is matter here which calls for sober reflection.

INDEX

The numerals in **heavy type** refer to the *figure numbers* of the illustrations

EVERYDAY LIFE IN OLD TESTAMENT TIMES
by E. W. HEATON   35p

552 54045 5   Carousel Non-Fiction

The phrase 'Old Testament Times' covers no less than eighteen
centuries from 1950 B.C. to 165 B.C. and Canon Heaton takes an
authoritative look at the middle of this long period from 1250
B.C. to 586 B.C. It brings the age and the Jewish way of life alive
for the reader, and also provides the essential detail and fact for
the script teacher of scripture.

HEROES AND SAINTS *by* R. J UNSTEAD   25p
552 54050 1   Carousel Non-Fiction

What kind of men and women became Heroes and Saints? What
dangers and hardships did they have to overcome? R. J. Unstead
has chosen some of the most courageous heroes and saints—
Julius Caesar and the Emperor Hadrian are among them—and
tells their stories.

ROYAL ADVENTURERS *by* R. J. UNSTEAD   25p
552 54018 8

R. J. Unstead, the top children's historian, writes in ROYAL
ADVENTURERS that kings and queens are 'more powerful,
more generous, foolish or cruel than the rest of mankind.' He
then delves into both the careers and personalities of a variety
of regal figures, from Julius Caesar and Genghis Khan to Charle-
magne and Marie Antoinette.

THE STORY OF JODRELL BANK *by* ROGER PIPER 30p
552 54028 5

We now live in the space age, and Jodrell Bank stands as one of
the greatest achievements of stellar technology. Here is the whole
story of the 'Big Dish', including its history, how it works, and
some of the amazing facts discovered by this modern wonder of
the world. Also included are eight pages of photographs.

TOMORROW'S WORLD—
  Vol. 1: THE LAST FRONTIER
by JAMES BURKE *and* RAYMOND BAXTER   30p
552 99582 7   Carousel/Corgi

TOMORROW'S WORLD—
  Vol 2: THE TOOLS OF CHANGE
by JAMES BURKE *and* RAYMOND BAXTER   30p
552 99583 5   Carousel/Corgi

Based on the BBC T.V. programme, TOMORROW'S WORLD,
this book takes a look at some of the latest developments in
science and technology. Readers of all ages will find it a fascinating and stimulating book, profusely illustrated with photographs.

EVERYDAY LIFE IN ROMAN TIMES
by MARJORIE *and* C. H. B. QUENNELL   25p
552 54014 5   Carousel Non-Fiction

What changes did the Roman Occupation of Britain bring about
and how did the European civilisation with its science, art and
wealth of ideas affect the turbulent tribesmen of Britain? These
points are dealt with in detail by the author as well as the intri-
cacies and rituals of their social lives.

HOW AND WHY WONDER BOOK OF FOSSILS   30p
552 86564 8

This is a comprehensive study of fossils, expertly illustrated and
easy to follow. The author is an ardent naturalist and conserva-
tionist.

All these books are available at your bookshop or can be ordered
direct from Transworld Publishers Ltd., Cash Sales Dept., P.O.
Box 11, Falmouth, Cornwall.

Please send full name and address together with cheque or postal
order—no currency and allow 10p per book to cover the cost of
postage and packing (plus 5p each for additional copies).

If you would like to receive a newsletter telling you about our
new children's books, send your name and address to Gillian
Osband, Transworld Publishers Ltd., 57/59 Uxbridge Road,
Ealing, London, W5, and mention 'CHILDREN'S NEWSLETTER'.